The State and Community Action

Terry Robson

Pluto Press

LONDON • STERLING, VIRGINIA

First published 2000 by Pluto Press
345 Archway Road, London N6 5AA
and 22883 Quicksilver Drive,
Sterling, VA 21066–2012, USA

British Library Cataloguing in Publication Data
A catalogue record for this book is available from
the British Library

ISBN 0 7453 1479 1 hbk

Library of Congress Cataloging in Publication Data
Robson, Terry.
    The state and community action / Terry Robson.
        p.   cm.
    Includes bibliographical references.
    ISBN 0–7453–1479–1 (hbk)
    1. Civil society. 2. Civil society Case studies. 3. Gramsci,
    Antonio, 1891–1937—Contributions in political science. I. Title.
    JC337.R63   2000
    361.8—dc21   99–38284
                                                                       CIP

Designed and produced for Pluto Press by
Chase Production Services, Chadlington OX7 3LN
Typeset from disk by Stanford DTP Services, Northampton
Printed in the EC by T.J. International, Padstow

Contents

Introduction

Our lives are controlled and organised nowadays, not only because we live in a fast-food society, but by the exigencies of a fast-moving and fast-reaction society in which our lives are influenced by the philosophy of the short-cut to decision making. We rhyme off ideas, concepts and abstractions as if we were nurtured by them. The idea of community, with which most identify, becomes something quite different as we instantaneously draw from it meanings and understandings and provide it with additional significance and a new dynamic. We are encouraged to accept that civil society is something to which we should all aspire and, thanks in part to German sociologist Ferdinand Tonnies (1855–1936), community emerges, not just as a word to describe our understanding of connected human relationships, but of power, of control and of change.

Any study of what has turned out to be a widespread development in human progress must necessarily become a focused and limited one. Therefore, any attempt to provide a definitive account of the impact of community action on our lives would require much more than is capable of being produced in a single volume. But whilst the volume of work on community-related issues is beginning to grow, in the form of reports, journals and issue-focused magazines, the range of contributions which take account of a theoretical critique of community action is still pitifully small.

What draws this work together is a recognition of an unsteady and occasionally fractious relationship between the state and the community and voluntary sector, which makes for considerable unease amongst many of its participants. This is reinforced by the popular view that the need for independent community action is constantly compromised by the dominating needs of the state.

Consequently, this work takes as its baseline the view that the state is omnipotent and all embracing. Furthermore, in examining the existence of a conjunction between the community 'movement' and the state, it discusses whether within this civil society, such a relationship can be a stable one, based on an equal partnership or whether, instead, it is imbalanced, with one in a position to dominate the other through a process of ideological hegemony.

In examining these issues this book makes use of the Gramscian, theoretical ideas of hegemony and civil society as a method of placing the question of the independence of community action and the state into a more precise conceptual framework. In doing this, it discusses a number of changes in the area of community development which have taken place in Britain and Ireland and examines by way of contrast, three case examples which include the United States, Romania and Northern Ireland.

In what became popularly known as the *Prison Notebooks*, the Italian Marxist Antonio Gramsci outlined a number of areas which he thought were appropriate for an analysis of society in general, as well as providing the basis for developing a strategy for change in modern Western capitalist societies in particular. Suggesting that civil society, containing a balance of both consent and coercion, was a means of resolving the problems of class conflict which were deep-rooted in society, he argued that it requires a new form of control which takes account, not only of the economic development of that society, but of its cultural one as well. This hegemonic monopoly which he referred to, within a civil society, is problematic, not least of all because of the differing degrees of hegemony which exist within some societies but also because it is difficult to clearly identify especially within multicultural societies. The consequence arising from such a difficulty is the problem of building what Gramsci identified as a political alternative to the dominant ideological hegemony, in other words a 'counter-hegemony'.

It is important to state clearly, at this point, that the matter of Gramsci's lucidity is significant. There are certain drawbacks to an understanding of Gramsci's theories which have raised questions in the past about the value of his ideas because of the methods he adopted to ensure the security of his writings and the permanence of his ideas. It is often argued that Gramsci was forced, because of the determination of his fascist gaolers and censors to stop his political writings seeing the light of day, to adopt a series of codes and disguises to ensure that his writings emerged from prison. So, civil society and hegemony became, according to the sceptics, euphemisms for the orthodox Marxist concepts of the state and control. Political society and counter-hegemony replaced the state, alienation, the revolutionary party and class consciousness. Radical intellectual and organic intellectual became synonyms for cadre and proletarian. The sceptics, therefore, argue that his writings must be seen in the more traditional light of classical Marxism, rather than as an attempt to develop a new and radical theoretical departure from more conventionally Marxist views of the nature of the state and the strategies to be employed for its demise. However, there is little strong evidence for this and his references throughout the *Prison Notebooks* to leading personalities within the Communist International, such as Lenin and Trotsky, suggest that either his censors were not aware of who they were, which is unlikely, or that it did not really matter, which is improbable. However, there are those who remain dubious and who prefer to consider his ideas in the context of the several interpretations which exist. But for the purposes of this work his ideas are taken at face value.

The State and Community Action emerges not just as an attempt to draw together two seemingly contrasting sets of conceptual ideas, but to make some sense of their respective dynamics. Often the literature responds to both, as separate and distinct ideas in which there is little real impact by one on the other.

There are many who view the emergence of a community action dynamic as one which has the constituency and the power to affect the pace of local development. Several years ago, many who were disenchanted by the failure of those political parties with a 'left' or 'liberal' agenda to respond effectively to the widening gulf between rich and poor, turned to 'community' politics as a new alternative. This 'new' concept of intervention, located at the very heart of an impoverished working class, allowed for the widening of the political agenda and a more inclusive approach to social issues such as those involving gender, race and the rights of the individual which were traditionally marginalised by the official trade union movement. A new political correctness appeared in which community rather than class became the motor for change and in which energy emanated from the 'new' community worker rather than from the 'old', 'class-conscious' socialist.

Arising from this development was a growing belief in the power of the community to initiate change. Right across the globe the community worker presents a new doctrine that the community has an innate authority to make fundamental adjustments to its social condition. Three contrasting examples are presented in this book as evidence of these changes. One represents the post-colonial political development of a European nation in transition, another the social convulsions of a major power constantly engaged in the process of structural and cultural transformation. The third depicts a nation delicately poised between Europe and Asia, disturbed by the incompetence of the response to post-Stalinist economic orthodoxy. In Ireland, the growth of widespread opposition to the British presence amongst the nationalist working class crystallised into a tangible movement which became the motor of the civil rights movement, afterwards forming the base of support for the Republican Movement. In the United States, in spite of the early optimism of a strong labour movement emerging out of the Industrial Workers of the World (IWW), working-class Americans remained divided into ethnic and racial groups as they became involved in the great wars and confronted each other in the great debates of the civil rights and anti-Vietnam war movements. In Romania, the notion of community was tied up in the belief that the guidance and leadership of the Communist Party would prevail and that the class war was a thing of distant and fading memory. Poverty became equated with the inefficiency of the bureaucratic machine rather than with the nature of the class system itself.

This book is separated into two parts. The first discusses a number of theoretical perspectives involving the community movement today, in which some consideration is given to the main questions which the community worker faces as he or she deals with the dilemma of the involvement of the state.

The expression 'community action' is used as a generic term to describe the process of activity which takes place within the community. There are those who prefer instead to refer to it as 'community development', thus emphasising the positive aspects of such activity as distinct from what some, such as the members of the Community Development Review Group in Northern Ireland and an increasing band of supporters within government, feel the notion of 'action' suggests. Any form of action, positive or negative, can be more usefully described in that way, thus allowing advocates of the less generic terms such as 'organisation' and 'development' to interpret their form of 'activity' within those enclosures.

The state's monopolisation of ideas and social initiative which hinder the development of an independent 'civil society' are discussed in Chapter One. The relations between the state and society assume paternalistic forms which have difficulty in accommodating political demands and initiatives which are not prompted or controlled from above. The concept of civil society emerges as an ambiguous one which is appropriated and its implications diluted by the state and its representatives. The chapter examines some of the origins of 'civil society', particularly those from the Marxist tradition, especially Antonio Gramsci who pointed to its properties of both consent and coercion. The chapter contains a broad sweep of socialist historiography focusing, to a large extent, on the debates within the second International on the nature of the state. Given Gramsci's experience of struggle in Italy, it explores the relevance of the concepts of hegemony and counter-hegemony and the significance and implications for the community development and democratic process of the philosophy of praxis.

Chapter Two examines the issue of civil society much more closely by placing it in a more conventional sociological framework: that of socialisation and of social control. Against that background, the chapter examines the theoretical and historical setting in which social control is seen as the 'coercive' arm of the 'civil society' and within which the ideas of Brigadier Frank Kitson and other leading 'securocrats' such as Anderton and Newman find a common currency. Such ideas are developed within the debate on the existence of an ideological hegemony and set against the general understanding of the concept of social control being regarded as a 'blunt' instrument in the armoury of the state.

The range of views on the value and potential for political as well as social and economic change of involvement in community-related action are explored in Chapter Three. There was a growing belief amongst many sections of the radical 'community' that labour was in the process of abandoning its traditional constituency. The successful struggle by Neil Kinnock against the Militant tendency was symptomatic of the frustration felt by many in the right wing of the Labour Party that the sentimental attachment to what were regarded as ideological dinosaurs such as Clause Four were losing them the opportunity to form a government. Such frustration manifested itself in the Labour Party tearing itself apart, with the right wing attempting to exorcise the ghosts of its past, and those remaining on the left either being forced into an increasingly more entrenched position or moving out of the Labour Party entirely. Meanwhile another revolution in attitudes was taking place. The poor were increasingly being referred to as the 'disadvantaged', the 'marginalised' and the 'socially excluded'. Just as the word 'poverty' was being replaced by other synonyms, so traditional solutions for a resolution of poverty were also being replaced by new solutions which placed the responsibility for both the origin as well as the solution of the problem on the individual most affected by it. It was no longer identified as a class dilemma, but a community one in which the neighbourhood, the village and the municipality could play decisive roles in the search for a resolution. The poor were being told to pay for their own poverty.

In Chapter Four, the problems emerging from the frustrations of the left in Britain, particularly, are traced to the point in which the Home Office decided to adopt the US models of tackling poverty which were implemented during the Kennedy and Johnson administrations. The establishment of community development projects as a means not just of addressing inner-city poverty were also used to counter the growing disruption to the major cities in Britain arising from black frustration with widespread unemployment, racism and discrimination. The chapter continues with an exploration of the origins and ideology of the advocates of community as a motor for change by tracing its origins to the British Colonial Office experiments in Africa and the counter-insurgency strategies adopted by the US government in South-east Asia, particularly during the war in Vietnam. It examines the problems which emerged from those earlier Home Office experiments, particularly the disillusionment felt by many community workers who saw the development as merely another conspiracy by the state to control disaffected working-class communities. It examines the prospects for change emerging out of these new development strategies by sketching the parallel developments in the United States through the *laissez faire* period of President Dwight D. Eisenhower into the Grey Area and Poverty Programmes associated with Presidents John F. Kennedy and Lyndon Baines Johnson.

The fifth and final chapter in Part I continues with an analysis of some more recent developments, particularly the communitarian movement and the impact of the Roman Catholic Church and its social teaching on the influence of the community movement. It is particularly concerned with the influences on certain tendencies within the labour movement in Britain and especially amongst a number of its leading members, including government ministers, who regard the emergence of communitarianism as providing the ideological foundation for a new political alliance with community forming the basis for a new social movement. The chapter concerns itself with the Catholic origins of communitarian thought, in which the family is revived as a fundamental tenet of social structure and in which individual rights are supplanted by an emphasis on the responsibilities of the individual as a part of the wider community. It opens up to scrutiny the 'debate' which continues between advocates of a 'liberal' perspective of human development and that of the 'communitarian' position, and which illustrates the inconsistency of the authenticity of the debate.

Part II examines some of the issues of state and community action in three separate parts of the world – Romania, Northern Ireland and the United States – and draws some conclusions regarding the relationship between developments in all three.

Chapter Six examines a number of issues in community development within Northern Ireland by looking at some examples of community action as working-class communities attempt to cope with the many and varied problems associated with poverty and inequality. Against this background, the struggle of such communities to redress some of the imbalances of Northern Ireland society is complicated by the nature of the politics of the state; its relationship to Britain and the Republic of Ireland as well as the hegemonic authority of the Unionist Party and the attendant problems of sectarianism and discrimination. It considers some of those processes within the context of more recent developments, particularly those which emerge from contemporary events surrounding and following from the demands of one section of the community for equality of opportunity. In this context, therefore, the development of a Catholic middle class and the emergence of the civil rights struggles act as a watershed in the evolution of community action suggesting, perhaps, the embryo of a counter-hegemonic force. The creation of the Race Relations Commission in Britain and the Community Relations Commission in Northern Ireland is central to an understanding of the focus of government's attention in considering solutions to the problem of inter-community strife, suggesting a recognition by government, in the absence of a consensus in Northern Ireland, of the need to address the problems of inequality by extending their hegemonic control through quasi-governmental agencies based on a notion of the easing of community relations. Arising from that the attempt by government, in line with policy already in place in Britain to pilot a community development approach to the problems of poverty in the inner cities, initiates community development and community workers' projects which engage in strategies based on the experiences gained from a greater understanding of community education and community relations problems. Many of these developments are set against the view that a hegemonic relationship exists throughout Northern Ireland between those who have, and those who do not. Such a view tends to ignore both the existence of two quite separate hegemonic relationships within Northern Ireland and the historical development which allowed this to take place. It is this area which offers the most productive ground for an examination of community action as a foundation for a new counter-hegemonic bloc.

Chapter Seven assesses the impact of community development work in the United States and focuses specifically on the work of one project in Baltimore, Maryland, known as Viva House. It considers the impact of the Catholic Worker movement on such developments and explores some of the reasons why the labour movement no longer enjoys any form of political base even in areas which have a record of working-class struggle and achievement. The development of radical community action in the United States has its roots, not just in the more recent events surrounding the struggle for black civil rights and the anti-war protests, but much further back in the populist and agrarian protests of the latter end of the nineteenth century. The Catholic Worker movement emerges as a strand, albeit an unusual one, in that historical development. The influence of its late founder, Dorothy Day, with her background in post-First World War socialist and labour politics, is still considerable. Present-day members, who still continue to call their premises 'soup kitchens', are reminiscent of a period in American life which hearkens back to the days when the labour movement was indistinguishable from the growing network of religiously based, charitable institutions. The chapter examines its record of activity particularly in the overwhelmingly black ghettos of cities such as New York and Baltimore and assesses the problem of political isolationism, of which the Catholic Worker movement is a typical example, and in which they attempt to remain aloof from the problems of the dichotomy of street and state.

The final chapter concentrates on the history and development of community action in a former Eastern bloc country which has moved away from the bureaucratic stranglehold of Stalinism and attempted to embrace the seemingly anarchic free market philosophy. Romania entered world consciousness after the fall and eventual execution of

Nicolae and Elena Ceausescu and the full effect of the high levels of poverty and deprivation became for many a symptom of the problem of post-war communism. The chapter examines a number of initiatives taken by Irish-based charitable organisations and assesses both their impact on the people of Fagaras, a town in the centre of Romania, as well as their contribution to what is described as the 'export of charity' and the objectively dependent effect of such work on the people of the area. More importantly, perhaps, it also examines the motivations of the principal actors in the operation and questions the value of engaging in the export of charity, not just in the material transportation of goods, but in its philosophical value to the people of Romania as a part of the process of socialisation, of reinforcing dependency and of isolating initiative and independence. The chapter argues that such work both reinforces the problem of dependency on people who are involved in community-based work in the area, as well as allowing the state to avoid the central problems of poverty and alienation. In those circumstances, it is argued, charitable organisations contribute to a situation in which independent voluntary, community-based work is unlikely to originate and develop.

Finally, the book concludes with a recognition of the value, to the dominant class, of the community process as a means of drawing local communities under the influence of the prevailing hegemony. The radicalism of the community worker, acting as organic intellectual, dissipates under the weight of state supervision. In those circumstances, therefore, the emergence of a counter-hegemony proves unlikely and the community 'movement' emerges as a principal agent of the dominant ideological hegemony.

Part I
The Theoretical Context

1
The State and Hegemony

Gramsci and the emergence of the ideology of civil society

It is often argued by revisionist historians that the divisions and arguments which took place within the communist Internationals have little relevance to the developments, social and technological, which have occurred throughout the course of the twentieth century. The issues raised at those affairs must seem so remote in the human cultural and political consciousness that they now form a part of a dim and distant, even irrelevant, historical memory. And yet the language and rhetoric of those gatherings of socialist practitioners and theoreticians persist to this day. Since the great social experiment that was Marxism crystallised into the more tangible October revolution with its radical reforms made redundant by the barbarous convulsion of the world at war, the vocabulary of communism entered the mass human consciousness.

Some of the language co-opted by those arguing for more moderate approaches to social and political change, such as commune, community and communitarianism, suggested not so much an acceptance of a new and revolutionary ideology as much as a desire to draw such ideas closer to the breast of the dominant democratic order. So, for example, Frank Field's recent conversion to communitarianism has more to do with a desire to recreate a society dominated by oppressive Victorian values than with an urge to advocate a communisation of human relations.[1] The subsequent effect of this confusing appropriation of language reduced communism to the status of being an impossible ideal, enhanced community as an instrument of social change, whilst socialism was rendered incompatible within the new, inclusive society. Meanwhile, we were all declared to be 'stakeholders' in a rediscovered, repackaged 'civil society'.

Rediscovering civil society

It is the rediscovery of 'civil society' which is at issue and which forms the basis of speculation in this chapter. What do those within government who constantly refer to 'civil society' actually mean? For example, John Hall had some difficulty in finding a clear and precise definition which satisfied his own understanding in *Search for Civil Society*. In the opening statement of his work he argued that 'civil society was placed at the forefront of public attention by attempts to establish decency in societies where it had most conspicuously been absent.'[2] Such a suggestion, that the advocates of civil society were only engaged in a form of moral crusade against the enemies of 'decency' and righteousness, leaves open the door to considerable cynicism and suspicion.

What is interesting about much of the literature on civil society is the almost total neglect of Gramsci as an authority. Except for an infrequent genuflection to his contribution on the 'debate' on civil society, little is made of his vast original contribution. Perhaps with good reason. Gramsci's view of civil society as one consisting of equal measures of consent and coercion is sanitised by many, including Hall, as 'a complex balance of consensus and conflict'.[3] Clearly this is not the same, nor even a similar correlation; the attempt to introduce 'conflict' suggests a reluctance to introduce the idea of coercion as a fundamental assumption of the nature of civil society. Undoubtedly, this is either a total rejection of the Gramscian analysis, or a clear attempt to appropriate an idea and translate its critical meaning into something more in keeping with the prevailing ideological mood.

As we enter the third millennium the tendency towards the appropriation of the ideas of others multiplies. The emergence of a 'new' Labour with its eyes firmly set on the re-creation of a 'new' Britain in which 'old' ideas are measured, at least in part, by one's association with socialist ideas raises serious questions about the *raison d'être* of the Blairite agenda. The fact that the concept of 'civil society' is one with roots firmly located within a Marxist tradition is of no apparent importance. 'New' Labour appropriates what it deems to be useful. We now have the British Prime Minister, his Deputy, Chancellor and other supporters applauding the virtues of this new abstraction as if the society over which they preside was born on 1 May 1997, the date of their landslide sweep to victory. Civil society, for New Labour, did not exist before then.

But of course it is not just to 'new' Labour that the finger of accusation should be pointed. The rump of the former revolutionaries, who identified new battlefields and alternative means with which to wage war on the state and who discarded 'class' for the new battalions of 'communities', drew heavily on the rhetoric of their past, translating it into a form of politically acceptable 'community speak' as they in turn sought justification for the new relationship with the state.[4] Civil society became the basis of social transformation, and 'social partnership' – a vague alliance of those at the base and those who manage the superstructure – as the means of acquiring that civil society.

The fact that the concept of a 'civil society' had passed through Hegel to Marx and thereon to Lenin and the Italian Gramsci, probably never occurred to any of those who cheered the success in 1997 of the 'new' party of the working class. Nor does it really matter for those supporters except to suggest that its past meaning bears no relation to its present usage. However, if we accept the view of Gramsci that civil society, as we understand it to mean the complex relationships within advanced capitalist societies, becomes at some point monopolised by the state, then its meaning is not only clearer, but a matter of some concern for all of us. It should focus our mind on the reasoning behind the Blairite enthusiasm for the concept. Indeed in those circumstances it would be fitting to examine fully Gramsci's ideas on the nature of 'civil society' before we draw any conclusions about the correctness of other approaches.

Gramsci died on 27 April 1937, his death brought on by years of ill treatment in fascist prisons. But in some ways, he has suffered more misfortune since his death from the distortion of his ideas by many who have nothing in common with his revolutionary principles.

Born at Ales in Sardinia, Gramsci was the fourth son of a minor public official who was imprisoned as a result of a minor discrepancy in his accounts. The family suffered badly during this period, but Antonio was awarded a scholarship to the University of Turin, specialising in linguistics. It could be said that he was a professional revolutionary from 1914 until his death, but he began by contributing articles to the socialist newspaper *Il Grido del Popolo* and afterwards to the Socialist Party newspaper, *Avanti*, which at one time had been edited by Mussolini. He became the co-founder and first editor of *L'Ordine Nuovo*. Throughout this period of journalistic activity he was insistent on the need for a revolutionary transformation of society through the overthrow of the capitalist state.

It was this that put him as a journalist in the front rank of those demanding revolutionary action from the Italian Socialist Party in the fight against capitalism and war in the years 1916–18. It was this that led him to the centre of the Turin Factory Councils' movement in 1919 and 1920 and spurred him to take part in the split from the reformist Socialist Party in 1921 to set up the Italian Communist Party. He took charge of that party in the years 1924–26 and was ultimately incarcerated in Mussolini's gaols where, through the *Prison Notebooks*, he developed many of his ideas about the nature of Italian society, the strategy and tactics of the struggle for state power, and the building of a revolutionary party. He was sentenced in 1928 to 20 years' imprisonment and transferred to a clinic in Rome in 1935 suffering from ill health. He died two years later of a brain haemorrhage. He was only 46 years old.

Salamini claimed that Gramsci was very much influenced in his early life by the Italian Marxist Antonio Labriola. He vehemently opposed the empiricist interpretations of Marxism by Kautsky, denounced by Lenin as a 'renegade', and by Plekhanov and Bukharin.[5] Gramsci argued that Marxism, 'originated as a philosophical system and matured through the imperatives of historical research and political struggle'.[6]

Many of the theorists of the Second International argued the principle that the 'historical process obeys specific laws of regularity and necessity – hence the belief that the growing numerical strength of the working classes would eventually result in the automatic transition from capitalism to socialism.'[7] Much of this emerged, in the first instance, from a belief that capitalism was in a high state of development and that the working classes were incapable of 'accelerating' or hastening the process of transition from a capitalist society to a socialist one.

Such views allowed for the emergence of a revision of the Marxist doctrine of the irreconcilability of the classes and the need for class struggle. The alternative, described as a more democratic approach, argued that only a legal and parliamentary strategy could result in a socialist transformation of power. Bernstein, the main advocate of this formula, based his view on the argument that industrialisation and capitalist economic development did not result in the separation or 'polarisation' of the classes into a bourgeoisie and proletariat in the way envisaged by Marx. Salamini claimed that Kautsky persisted in a belief in a set of 'iron laws' – a reaffirmation of basic Marxist principles, that the proletarian revolution was inevitable given the concentration of economic power amongst an increasingly smaller group of capitalists.

The polemics developing between these two quite opposite groups of theoreticians resulted in the 'death of critical Marxism' in so far as it 'generated political passivity among the masses. Thus Marxism, divorced from revolutionary praxis – the infusion of political practice and political theory – became increasingly abstract and ineffectual in inspiring concrete political strategies for the attainment of political hegemony.'[8]

Gramsci considered this 'automatism' in the light of Marx's position in his *XI Thesis on Feuerbach*: 'The philosophers have only interpreted the world, in various ways; the point is to change it.' What he was arguing was that the historical process is nothing less than the concentration of 'individual' wills into a 'collective will'. Marx was convinced that capitalism was doomed because of the contradictions contained within it but that such a transformation could not take place automatically without the realisation of a politically conscious working class.

After Marx, this human element became subordinated to the more inevitabilist and mechanistic arguments of Kautsky and Bukharin, on the grounds that scientific laws, which exclude the subjective nature of human will, are more reliable scientific determinants of the historical process contained in the transformation from a capitalist society to a socialist one.

It was this fundamental flaw in the programme of the Second International which resulted in Gramsci in Italy, Rosa Luxemburg in Germany and Lenin in Russia independently adopting diametrically opposite positions to Bukharin and the other leaders of the International about the nature of the state and the revolutionary party. Although, for many, the reformist position of the leadership of the Second International was related to the 'political and organisational immaturity of the masses', others, such as Luxemburg, in spite of their opposition to the leadership of the International, nevertheless adopted similarly mechanistic analyses which drew conclusions about the potential for revolutionary struggle which were related to the level of organisation of the capitalist system.[9] In other words, the failure of the revolutionary party was not related at all to the political consciousness of the working class but to the state of capitalism at any given point in time. It was in this context that Lenin developed the thesis that capitalism did not automatically crash at a point in its development but, instead moved to a new, higher, stage as it sought new markets and new areas of expansion. Imperialism, as the highest stage of capitalism, became a new theory which allowed for a recognition that capitalism was capable of absorbing new ideas and new pressures and had the capacity to eliminate many of the class antagonisms which were manifest during the earlier stages of its development.

Such a view had implications for the ideas being developed by Gramsci and exposed to criticism those theories being advanced by Bernstein and Kautsky that the 'iron laws' were absolute and that the organisation of the proletariat was almost incidental to the development of capital. Lenin was insistent that a party of the organised working class was capable of accelerating the process of the destruction of capitalism. The examples of the Russian revolutions of 1917 were a case in point in which Gramsci described the October revolution as a great 'metaphysical event' which reflected the 'theorisation and realisation of hegemony, carried out by Illich [Lenin]'.[10]

But Lenin's concept of revolutionary transformation differed in some significant circumstances from Gramsci's. Lenin's reliance on the 'classical model' of revolutionary action, which emphasised both the need for military as well as political activity in conjunction with the development of a mass party capable of taking state power, was in direct contrast, programatically, to Gramsci's emphasis on ideological hegemony.

'At the core of these crucial differences is Gramsci's "dual perspective", rooted in the dichotomy between force and consent in politics, which he conceptualised in terms of "organic" and "conjunctural" dimensions of change. By "conjunctural" Gramsci meant the passing and momentary period of crisis in which the contesting political forces struggle for state power – a stage roughly equivalent to his strategic concept "war of movement" or "war of manoeuvre". This was the realm of historical contingency, unpredictability (fortuna in Machiavelli's language), tactical decision-making, and of course military confrontation. It was for this arena of political activity and combat that Lenin's highly-centralised party of professional revolutionaries was primarily designed.'[11]

However, it is the contrast between Lenin and Gramsci on the issue of the subjective and relative maturity of the working classes and their relationship to the state which suggests the difference in their approach and which marks the unique contribution of Gramsci to the development of Marxism in western Europe in the twentieth century.

The State

The quintessential Marxist view of the state expounded by Lenin is that it is the 'product and manifestation of the irreconcilability of class antagonisms'.[12] Gramsci argued that Western society is markedly different from the 'traditional' Marxist definition which was based on Lenin's analysis of conditions in Tsarist Russia during the latter half of the nineteenth century. What Gramsci meant was that the power of the ruling class in the West rests not on the physical manifestations of the police-state apparatus, but on its ideological domination which is exercised through a network of voluntary institutions that dominate everyday life (civil society) – the political parties, trade unions, churches, media and the repressive state apparatus are merely part of a series of defensive measures available to capitalist society. Gramsci departed from the conventional view of the state by reinforcing the Leninist view that

> The concept of revolutionary and of internationalist, in the modern sense of the word, is correlative with the precise concept of state and class. State means little class consciousness (an understanding of the state exists not only when one defends it, but also when one attacks it in order to overthrow it).[13]

What follows is that the starting point to an understanding of the concepts contained in the *Prison Notebooks* is a proper understanding of the concept of the state. Following from this the key struggle for socialists is not a direct assault on state power, but the struggle for ideological dominance, for what Gramsci described as hegemony: 'the acceptance by the subordinate classes of the culture of the ruling class, without either rulers or ruled necessarily being aware of the political consequences or functions of this acceptance.' Hegemony, therefore, is won by a long and protracted process that takes many years and demands infinite patience to achieve. In particular, the working class can only achieve a 'counter-hegemony', in other words one which replaces the other, by winning over the main sections of the intellectuals and classes they represent, because of the crucial role they play in facilitating the apparatus of ideological domination. Gramsci was arguing for a revolution before the revolution. In those circumstances, the workers must sacrifice their own short-term economic goals in order to achieve this. Consequently, until it has achieved this task, until it becomes the 'hegemonic' class, attempts to win power can only end in disaster. The prerequisite for all of this must depend on an understanding of a precise concept of the state.

This is the starting point. Gramsci's concepts of hegemony, civil and political society and the historical bloc are dependent on his understanding of the concept of the state. Consequently, the economist view of the state, that it is merely an extension of the power of the prevailing ruling class, has been under attack for some considerable time. Often described as 'vulgar materialism', this view has been associated with those who advocate a more economically determinist position in relation to the needs of the revolutionary party at the point of transition, that is, the point during which the proletariat are in the process of seizing power.

It is now being suggested that the state is not and never has been a partisan manifestation but is, instead, independent of any specific class interest. The state is omnipotent in that it monopolises the legitimate use of force yet subservient in that it responds to whatever pressures are exerted upon it. Both Marx and Engels recognised that government, regardless of class, was obliged to address the interests of society as a whole: As the state arose from the need to hold class antagonisms in check ... it is as a rule the state of the most powerful, economically dominant class.'[14] This suggestion, that the state operates both to contain class conflict and at the same time, to act in the specific interest of one class appears ambiguous. In other words, the state is not the caretaker of any specific class, but of all classes and, more specifically, of a dominant class.

This question weighed heavily on the deliberations of the nineteenth-century Marxists, not least of all because they saw it as the 'epiphenomenon' of the struggle between the classes. The state was crucial to an understanding of the nature and development of capitalism. Marx believed that the state was fundamental to the continuing dominance of a ruling class and recognised that even in the circumstances in which the state began the transitional process of withering from its capitalist to its socialist or communist stage, it would not be entirely free of the structures associated with the state.

Gramsci's view that there are two distinguishing features of the state and the social forces within it – that determined by civil needs and that governed by political considerations – must be seen against a background of growing totalitarianism in Europe. Divisions within his own country and the failure of the Italian Socialist Party to capitalise on the successes of the Factory Council movement and the occupation of the land in the south by the peasantry tended to confirm this view. A politically and economically divided Italy, with an industrially developed north and an underdeveloped south, added force to his thesis that there was no uniform 'iron law' which could be applied in this context.

The growing influence of the Fascist Party was to provide, for most in the Italian Communist Party, the single most important issue facing the revolutionary left. They were to find that the task of maintaining some degree of party organisation in the face of intimidation and threat was increasingly vital. Gramsci believed that the failure to build a party organisation during the period of the Factory Council movement resulted finally in its collapse. He set about attempting to develop ideas about the transformation of the party into a highly disciplined, centrally organised party structure in his deliberations on the potential of the Leninist concept of democratic centralism.

By contrast, the Socialist Party leader, Serrati, explained his own view of revolutionary struggle as 'the sum of varied and diverse circumstances, of multiplex elements that together add up and lead to the solution in a given historical moment of a crisis that has stubborn and economic causes'.[15] Such arguments would probably have been acceptable to Gramsci as a satisfactory explanation of the eclectic influences within a revolutionary situation if it had not been for the peculiar circumstances of the period 1920–21 and the divisions between the leaders of the Italian Socialist Party at that time. However, it is the specific development of those ideas which mark the point of departure, both practically and theoretically, between those who continued to support Serrati and the founders, including Gramsci, of the new Communist Party of Italy.

Hegemony and counter-hegemony

It is probably true to say that Gramsci's greatest and most profound contribution to Marxist philosophy is his recognition of the significance of the theory of hegemony. He believed that because the structures of society were so different and diverse, a single strategy

designed to counter such structures would be inadequate and insufficient. There was a need, he argued, for a variety of differing strategies.
Justification for this fundamental theoretical departure rested on the
distinction Gramsci makes in his *Prison Notebooks* between two quite
separate types of war.

The War of Manoeuvre, which involves rapid movement by the
rival armies, with thrusts forwards and backwards as each tries to
outflank the other and its cities. This was only possible in societies
which had a 'civil society' which was relatively weak, such as Russia
in 1917. However, in those societies which have an advanced and
developed 'civil society', such as those advanced industrial nations
in the West, frontal assaults on capitalism are doomed to failure. In
such circumstances different strategies are required.

The War of Position, a long drawn out struggle in which the two
armies are deadlocked in battle, each hardly able to move forward,
like the trench warfare of 1914–18. Such a situation requires a
different approach. In those circumstances the class struggle is
reinforced by the introduction of additional tactics which draw on
other political, cultural and social issues as opposed to the more
direct, confrontational one, more appropriate to that advanced in
the former. The aim of such a strategy is to struggle against the
hegemony of the ruling class by developing a counter-hegemony –
one which will strengthen the working-class and provide for the
eventual transition to a socialist society:

> Military experts ... maintain that in wars among the more indus-
> trially and socially advanced states the war of manoeuvre must be
> considered as reduced to more of a tactical than a strategic function
> ... the same reduction must take place in the art and science of
> politics, at least in the case of the most advanced states, where
> 'civil society' has become a very complex structure and one which
> is resistant to the catastrophic 'incursions' of the immediate
> economic elements (crises, depressions, etc.).[16]

The last example of the war of manoeuvre, in other words, a frontal
assault on the state – was the October revolution of 1917: 'It seems
to me that Illich [Lenin] understood that change was necessary from
the war of manoeuvre applied victoriously in the East in 1917, to a
war of position that was the only form possible in the West.'[17] The
basis for this switch in strategy lay in the different social structures
of Tsarist Russia and western Europe: 'In Russia the state was

everything, civil society was primordial and gelatinous; in the West ... when the state trembled a sturdy structure of civil society was at once revealed. The state was only an outer ditch, behind which there stood a powerful system of fortresses and earthworks.'[18]

It is in this situation that the new strategy – that of developing counter-hegemonic structures – begins to come into play. There is a basic assumption: that hegemony is rule through consent. Such a rule is organised primarily in civil society where the organs of power are maintained often by the employment of discrete measures of coercion and set in place as a result of consent and agreement. Naturally, this operates in direct contrast to that situation when state power is seized, either during a *coup d'état* or as a result of a revolution.

Whilst hegemony is claimed by Gramsci as a fundamental tenet of Marxist theory, it is almost certainly true that Marx never at any time made any specific reference to it. There is some evidence, however, that a brief reference was made to it, according to Stuart Hall when he points to the existence, in both *The Class Struggles in France* and *The 18th Brumaire of Louis Bonaparte,* of evidence suggesting that Marx had considered the concept.[19] Equally the formula of Permanent Revolution, normally regarded as the property of Lev Davidovitch Bronstein (Trotsky), has a basis in conventional Marxist thought, although Gramsci argued in the *Prison Notebooks* that it:

> ... belongs to a historical period in which the great mass political parties and the great economic trade unions did not yet exist, and society was still, so to speak, in a state of fluidity from many points of view ... In the period after 1870 ... the internal and international organisational relations of the State became more complex and massive, and the Forty Eightist formula of the 'Permanent Revolution' [Marx adopted this slogan after the 1848 revolution] is expanded and transcended in political science by the formula of 'civil hegemony'.[20]

The use of the term 'civil hegemony' is especially interesting because he draws together two fundamental concepts – that of civil society and of hegemony. The idea that the two can collide at any given point is interesting in that it implies that hegemony exists within civil society. The only question that remains is in whose interest does the hegemony function? But first of all when is hegemony achieved? When:

... one's own corporate interests, in their present and future development, transcend the corporate limits of the purely economic class, and can and must become the interests of the subordinate groups too. This is the most purely political phase and marks the decisive passage from the structure to the sphere of complex superstructures; it is the phase in which previously germinated ideologies become 'party', come into confrontation and conflict, until one of them, or at least a single combination of them, tends to prevail, to gain the upper hand, to propagate itself through society – bringing about not only a unison of economic and political aims, but also intellectual and moral unity, posing all the questions around which struggle rages not on a corporate but on a 'universal' plane and thus creating the hegemony of a fundamental social group over a series of subordinate groups.[21]

For those classes in society who struggle, either to assert their position in society, or alternatively, to change it, they would first of all need to win state power. That seems clear. Gramsci argued that in those circumstances they would need to construct a new hegemony. The counter-hegemony, therefore, suggests the creation of a new, distinct and separate historic bloc. In these circumstances, the mass of ordinary people would assume an entirely different role as they move from a passive position to a new, more active, one. Again, this raises a number of questions regarding the interests of the working class and whether or not in those circumstances they can draw on other influences, political, social or cultural as distinct from the purely economic, to achieve those objectives. Gramsci's arguments against the economists of the Second International provided the force for this. That is not to say that he ignored the significance of economic questions. He uses pre-revolutionary France to make the point that the suggestion that the French economy was healthy and that other reasons were the cause of the revolution, was not borne out by the facts:

> It should be observed that the State was in the throes of a mortal financial crisis and considering which of the privileged social orders would have to bear the sacrifices and burdens necessary for the State and Royal finances to be put back in order ... if the economic position of the bourgeoisie was flourishing, the situation of the popular classes was certainly not good either in the towns or, especially, on the land – where they suffered from endemic poverty.[22]

Hegemony and political and civil society

Rule by force – coercion – is exercised by a political society, whilst rule by consent, or hegemony, is more often applied in civil society. The suggestion is that the hegemony of any class is its success in convincing other classes of the need to accept its cultural, moral and, ultimately, its political values. If such a class is successful in achieving such hegemony, as occurred in the liberal reforms of the nineteenth century, it will involve a minimum use of force to achieve such aims. In the case of Ireland during the same period such hegemony did not succeed and force was the means to establish control and order. In socialist terms, Gramsci's ideas are seen as controversial especially when the concept of hegemony, regarded as one set of 'iron rules' against the 'rigidity' of another set of 'iron rules' – economic determinism – is presented as a revolutionary method. Although he reacted against the prevailing tendency to consider only the materialist, economic side of Marxism as the motor for revolutionary change, it is clear that he continued to have an open mind on it.

Does Gramsci's view of the significance of the hegemonic approach to the establishment of a ruling elite through a varied use of diverse influences, operate at all levels and in all situations? Can such an analysis dictate a response which is based on an entirely different set of political, social, cultural and historic conditions? Such questions raise the problem of the 'transportability' of concepts from one historic period to another and from one country to another.

Clearly, developments within the revolutionary left in Europe militated against the dominant viewpoint that orthodox Marxism or 'simplistic materialism – an epistemology that reduced the sphere of ideas and consciousness to epiphenomena, mere reflections of objective historical forces' would lead, ultimately, to a series of defeats, 'political quietism and passivity'. Gramsci was convinced of this view because of the failure of the Left to deal effectively with the growing social movements in Italy after the First World War.

There are some limited parallels between the social and economic conditions of Italy and other parts of Europe including Ireland during the early part of the century, but the social and cultural conditions and the political responses to such conditions must, by their very nature, be substantially different. As there are no iron laws for Gramsci in the case of the materialist approach to history, so therefore, there can be no iron laws in the case of nations whose history is formed by their separate developments, with some founded on the development of an imperialist agenda whereas others, particularly Ireland were based on a colonised one. Italy, Britain, Germany and others on the one hand, Ireland on the other.

A philosophy of praxis

And so it is precisely the relationship between theory and practice, the union or infusion of both, in Marxist terms – a philosophy of praxis – which marks Gramsci's concepts as significant in political and sociological terms and allows us to understand his method. The suggestion that such an infusion – the informing of political theory with political practice and political practice with political theory – has widespread implications for activities which operate at the base. Furthermore, it is the understanding of the central role of the human consciousness in history which becomes the emissary between structure and superstructure:

> Structures and superstructures form an 'historical bloc' that is to say the complex, contradictory and discordant ensemble of the superstructure is the reflection of the ensemble of the social relations of production ... This reasoning is based on the necessary reciprocity between structure and superstructure, a reciprocity which is nothing other than the real dialectical process.[23]

It is precisely the 'dialectical' nature of the relationship between theory and practice, between structure and superstructure, which gives the philosophy of praxis its specifically Marxist character. The debates and arguments dominating intellectual life in early twentieth-century Italy – specifically, the arguments raging between Gramsci and Croce – became the focus for the debate on the 'mechanistic and deterministic orientation of Marxism'.[24] It was to result in Croce rejecting Marxism and becoming its most forceful opponent in arguments which were based substantially on the controversies arising from the disagreement over the 'transposing' of 'concrete realities of social conflicts to the level of ideas' and the failure to solve the 'conflict between theory and praxis'.[25] Gramsci eventually parted company with the Italian philosopher on the function of man in the process of history and his role in it.

Even though Croce was the principal protagonist within the Italian socialist tradition, Salamini suggests that Lenin, also, was generally complacent with the view that Marxism was more than mere 'mechanical materialism'. He emphasised the idea that materialism recognises beyond phenomena a reality existing independently from the human spirit. Materialism therefore, became, *a priori*, more significant than 'nature over spirit, matter over mind, body over consciousness'.[26] These ideas became fused with orthodox Marxist theory because of the influences and successes of the scientific achievements of natural science, and orthodox Marxism pronounced itself for the objectivity of the external world. This new realism, Gramsci believed, would render truth and objectivity extra-historical and extra-human. Such realism would result in a continuing regression into passivity.

Gramsci suggested that the tendency to isolate single factors or elements of human existence whether it be the philosophical ('idealist') or the economic ('materialist') merely resulted in the conversion of theory into 'empty metaphysics'.[27] He considered these issues in the context of the arguments raging at the time between supporters of Bukharin's theory of the system of causal laws on the one side and Croce, whom he dismissed and described as the 'high priest of contemporary historicist religion', on the other.[28]

If Croce was described in Italy as the high priest of historicism, then Gramsci became identified as the high priest of the theory of the superstructures. The arguments about civil and political society and hegemony can be identified as having a resonance within some of the main theoretical concepts of Marxist ideology, particularly those questions related to structure (base) and superstructure.

In spite of their significance, Gramsci's new formulations should not be accepted uncritically. Regardless of his own criticisms of some of the orthodox Marxists, most notably those associated with the Second International, he acknowledged the primary role of the mode of production in shaping historical development.[29] Where he differed, of course, was that he believed that such a framework was an unsatisfactory means of explaining those 'transformative' times when, as a result of revolutionary struggles, conflict and social upheaval, change could result. As a consequence, revolutionary theory must take into account the interplay of the wide range of forces and influences during those periods of transformation, in addition to the specific relationships of those opposing forces engaged in production. More specifically, Boggs argued that, 'any conceptual schema based upon the strict and unwavering determination of economic conditions would inevitably be undialectical and mechanical – devoid of historical and political content.'[30] Gramsci goes a little further, of course, by demonstrating that Marx went beyond issues of a purely materialist nature: 'another proposition of Marx is that a popular conviction often has the same energy as a material force or something of the kind.'[31] The suggestion that there were issues, perhaps metaphysical, certainly cultural, which had as much influence on the course of human history and the development of social relations as did the modes of production, ran contrary to all the arguments about the primacy of economic forces. However, he qualified his statement by pointing to a dependent relationship between the 'material' and the 'ideological' forces, a suggestion that there was an empirical element to his arguments which did not lend itself solely and exclusively to what has been described as a metaphysical one:

> The analysis of these propositions tends, I think, to reinforce the conception of historical bloc in which precisely material forces are the content and ideologies are the form, though this distinction between form and content has purely didactic value, since the material forces would be inconceivable historically without form and the ideologies would be individual fancies without the material forces.[32]

But just as Gramsci was the theorist of the superstructures, so also, was he conscious of the relationship between those superstructures and the base. Indeed it is that relationship which forms the core of the debate within the Marxist tradition. In rejecting the arguments of the economism of the Second International, Gramsci embraced the concept of the superstructure and the base as the 'totality of a social formation'.[33] Indeed this view is supported by Engels in his rejection of the economic element as the only determining one in that relationship. Furthermore, it is this argument – that there are 'various elements' in the superstructure – which provides the sharpest focus of support for the view that within the social formation there are other elements which must be considered.

It is in this area of the debate on the primacy of the role of economic determinism in the context of the ideological superstructures that Gramsci departs significantly from the economism of the Second International. Indeed, he looked to the view of Engels that there are other 'various elements' which should be considered. Gramsci understood in the influences of the common-sense ideas, values and culture of the subaltern classes contributory factors in the development of the superstructure. Indeed the relationship between base and superstructure is reciprocal. The superstructure in turn influences the consciousness of humankind, affecting their creativity, ideas and development. For Gramsci this was a historical process: 'The passage from a phase of necessity to a phase of freedom, from common sense to weltanschauung, from economic corporatism to hegemony, from passivity to consciousness, from quantity to quality, from force to consensus, from objectivity to "collective subjectivity"'.[34]

But not only is this development a historical process, it synthesises the base–superstructure dichotomy into an inseparable totality – the foundation for the concept of hegemony, that is, the 'dialectical unity of civil and political society of structure and superstructure'.[35] For Gramsci it is the reciprocal nature, within the superstructure, of the relationship of civil society to political society in which 'the state is born in the civil society, and acts back on it', which is crucial.[36] It is precisely this notion of the state acting back on civil society which focuses attention on the dominance of the ruling class in civil society and the diffusion of an ideology which seeks to maintain a political and economic, as well as an ideological control over the remainder of the social formation. It is the nature of ideological control which more than any other question raises the issue of the potential within a civil society of other ideologies and ideas prevalent within those sections of the social formation, described by Gramsci as the subaltern classes, as a motor for change. If ideology forms the sphere of influence in which the ruling class achieved hegemony, so also it is in ideology that the working class can mount a counter-hegemonic assault.

It is, therefore, through a recognition of the nature of the ideological position of the subaltern classes and the understanding of the need to create a new *Weltanschauung* in which the myths, ideas and cultural values of those classes are employed as tools for change. 'Popular beliefs, once they have gripped the masses, are nevertheless material forces.' This brings the review of Gramsci's ideas to a consideration of the force and value of those popular beliefs, what Gramsci described as 'common sense', 'the largely unconscious way in which a person perceives the world'.[37]

Common sense

Just as Gramsci couldn't conceive of a non-intellectual human being, so he argued that the majority of humankind are philosophers: 'insofar as they engage in practical activity and in their practical activity (or in their guiding lines of conduct) there is implicitly contained a conception of the world, a philosophy.'[38]

This view, that all of humankind are philosophers – are intellectuals in their own right – dominated his thought, influenced his theories and directed his attention to ideas about the role of popular beliefs, attitudes and politics. As a consequence, he examined the influences of cultural traditions, symbols, myths and language. Suggesting that there are a number of forms of philosophy emerging from a popular or 'spontaneous' philosophy, Gramsci defined them as language, 'common sense' and 'good sense' and 'folklore'. The point that he was making was that implicit in the concept of hegemony is the notion that many of these ideologies, creeds and beliefs – the *Weltanschauung* or world outlook – while not necessarily political, profoundly affect the balance of social relations and the exercise of power.

The philosophy of 'common sense', described as the 'philosophy of non-philosophers', is seen by Gramsci as organic, that is, as being of, and coming from, the 'homogeneous social group' or the masses, at any given point in time:[39] 'Broadly speaking, "common sense" means the incoherent set of generally held assumptions and beliefs common to any given society, while "good sense" means practical empirical common sense in the English sense of the term.'[40]

One's understanding of the world or one's conception of it, emerges to a large extent from the multifaceted social grouping of which one is a member. Such a social grouping shares many experiences, modes of thought and methods of acting. Often it is divided and fragmentary. Salamini suggested that Gramsci 'distinguished between various levels in hegemonic ideologies ... each representing qualitatively different conceptions of the world adhered to by various social strata'.[41] But what he was also saying was that there is nothing within 'philosophy', 'common sense', religion and folklore which is necessarily mutually exclusive. There are elements of one in each of the others. Philosophy has been influenced by 'common sense' at different times. Equally there are points in history when 'common sense' is fundamentally influenced by the dominant philosophy or ideology. At those points in time, philosophy represents 'the most general, elaborate conception of the world, the most coherent systematic and rational conception developed by a hegemonic group'.[42]

Gramsci's search for an understanding of philosophy and 'popular' philosophy led him to conclude that there were in fact two such philosophies; those which 'distinguish between historically organic ideologies, those that is, which are necessary to a given structure, and ideologies that are arbitrary, rationalistic or willed'.[43]

He argued that on the one hand ideologies are 'historically necessary' in so far as they have a validity which is 'psychological', 'they organise human masses, and create the terrain on which men move, acquire consciousness of their position, struggle etc.' On the other hand, however, there are those that are 'arbitrary [in that] they only create individual "movements", polemics and so on'.[44] Because 'common sense' can provide the bedrock for a dominant ideology, it must be seen that it also contains the potential for the creation of a seed of resistance and the basis for a counter-hegemonic ideology: 'It signifies that the social group in question may indeed have its own conception of the world, even if only embryonic; a conception which manifests itself in action, but occasionally in flashes – when, that is, the group is acting as an organic totality.'[45]

There are also quite substantial tensions in the relationship between 'common sense' and the ideology or philosophy of the ruling elite which could more accurately be described as 'class contradictions' and which could only be reconciled through political action. So, because differing concepts of the world are contained within differing social groupings, a struggle of 'political hegemonies' is inevitable: 'Hence the reason why philosophy cannot be divorced from politics'. Therefore, '[t]he relation between "common sense" and the upper level of philosophy is assured by politics.'[46]

Because he was concerned about the dangers inherent in a political situation in the 'spontaneous militancy' of the masses and the equally dangerous and often undemocratic group in the vanguard of the struggle, he attempted to develop a theory which posed the question of the relationship of the two – the relationship between the intellectuals and the masses. In this he poses the dilemma of forging a union of the two by examining the relationship between 'intellectuals' and 'people-nation':

> The popular element 'feels' but does not always know or understand; the intellectual element 'knows' but does not always understand and in particular does not always feel. The two extremes are therefore pedantry and philistinism on the one hand and blind passion and sectarianism on the other ... the intellectual's error consists in believing that one can know without understanding and even more without feeling and being impassioned: in other words

that the intellectual can be an intellectual if distinct and separate from the people-nation i.e. without feeling the elementary passions of the people, understanding them and therefore explaining and justifying them in the particular historical situation and connecting them dialectically to the laws of history and to a superior conception of the world, scientifically and coherently elaborated.[47]

Clearly Gramsci had a difficulty reconciling himself to the notion of the traditional intellectual as the moral leader within society. Indeed he argued that their function throughout history was to strengthen the cultural hegemony of the ruling class:

This form of culture is truly harmful especially to the proletariat. It only serves to create misfits, people who believe themselves superior to the rest of humanity because they have accumulated in their memory a certain quantity of facts and dates which they cough up at every opportunity to almost raise a barrier between themselves and others.[48]

There is clearly a rejection of the traditional intellectual in that statement suggesting, indeed, that they have actively militated against the intellectual development of the working class, the only basis for the development of a counter-hegemony. If this is true then Gramsci is also insisting that the intellectual has played a reactionary and counter-revolutionary role within society: 'The intellectuals are the dominant group's "deputies" exercising the subaltern functions of social hegemony and political government.' These comprise:

1. The 'spontaneous' consent given by the great masses of the population to the general direction imposed on social life by the dominant fundamental group; this consent is 'historically' caused by the prestige (and consequent confidence) which the dominant group enjoys because of its position and function in the world of production.
2. The apparatus of state coercive power which 'legally' enforces discipline on those groups who do not 'consent' either actively or passively. This apparatus is, however, constituted for the whole of society in anticipation of moments of crisis of command and direction when spontaneous consent has failed.[49]

So it is the collaborative nature of the traditional intellectual in the process of social change – a recognition that they have assisted in and contributed to the process of establishing social stability – that Gramsci criticises. But he sees them not merely as people engaged in a form of mental and intellectual conceptualisation, but as functionaries – dealers in the business of 'consciousness' – sustaining and supporting the status quo. In doing so, of course, they legitimise the culture of the ruling class and are recognised in those circumstances as the 'traditional intellectual' with all of the status and power such a rank would accumulate.

The answer lay in advocating the concept that everyone is an intellectual – the basis for a new counter-hegemonic project: 'All men are intellectuals, one could therefore say: but not all men have in society the function of intellectuals. Thus because it can happen that everyone at some time fries a couple of eggs or sews up a tear in a jacket, we do not necessarily say that everyone is a cook or a tailor.'[50]

Thus Gramsci reduces the level of the intellectual to the level of a functionary and elevates the level of the functionary to that of an 'organic' intellectual:

> Intellectual activity must be distinguished in terms of its intrinsic characteristics according to levels which in moments of extreme opposition represent a real qualitative difference – at the highest level would be the creators of the various sciences, philosophy, art, etc., at the lowest the most humble 'administrators' and divulgators of pre-existing, traditional, accumulated intellectual wealth.[51]

Therefore, if we are to consider the possibility of a counter-hegemonic culture which incorporates the notion of the intellectual as cultural 'leader', there is a need to examine the possibility that it is from within the subaltern classes that they must emerge. They must be organic to those classes – they must as a consequence become 'organic intellectuals'. But what would be the purpose of such a group of organic intellectuals? In short, their function would be to broadcast, circulate and diffuse counter-hegemonic communist ideas and culture.

The central contention contained in his views on the intellectual is the attempt to rid himself of the notion that the intellectual is a higher being, a superior being: '... although one can speak of intellectuals, one cannot speak of non-intellectuals because non-intellectuals do not exist ... there is no human activity from which every form of intellectual participation can be excluded.'[52]

It follows, therefore, that if we accept the view that there are organic intellectuals within the subaltern and working classes able to diffuse counter-hegemonic ideas, there may also be individuals emerging from the traditional intellectuals who may also share such counter-hegemonic ideas. So it is the function of these 'radical' intellectuals to provide the leadership in pointing the working classes to a higher conception of life, to new meaning and, ultimately, to a new consciousness. Such a new consciousness would form the basis for the counter-hegemonic project and provide the framework for the emancipation of the working classes. It is at this point that the philosophy of praxis intervenes because it 'does not tend to leave the "simple" in their primitive philosophy of common sense, but rather to lead them to a higher conception of life'.[53]

Gramsci's arguments with the theoreticians of the Second International and those empiricists within that tradition in Italy such as Croce militated strongly against adopting positivism as a means of understanding the nature of the development of Western society. The struggles against Bukharin and Kautsky, of importance both in a historical and ideological context, only really assume a theoretical significance when we consider the arguments against empiricism as the only method worthy of consideration. In many ways, therefore, this is the central question, not only because of its intrinsic value in the Marxist dialectical tradition, but because it has implications for the development of a methodology of social and political change.

We start, therefore, from the position that an understanding of society, if it cannot solely depend on the abstract theories of the economists of the Second International, must be influenced by broader and wider strata of interests, pressures and cultural diversities. But it is Gramsci's 'absolute historicism', the suggestion that we constantly need to encompass and understand the totality of our situations, which informs the development of such methodology. Marxism, according to Salamini 'had been robbed of its philosophy and reduced to a simple method of explaining historical and political changes in terms of economic changes'.[54]

So how can a theory be appropriated which appears, on the face of it, to be rooted in the politics and social pressures of Italy in the period when the ruling class before and during the coming to power of Mussolini attempted to create their own hegemony? 'Marxism is an autonomous conception of the world, capable of explaining the totality of the historical process and engendering an intellectual revolution in all fields of knowledge.'[55]

Such a conception not only requires that a greater degree of adaptability be applied in relation to such an understanding of the world and its separate and component parts, but it demands it. This is central to his arguments. So in appropriating his concepts, is there a suggestion that the historical differences between Italy and Ireland, the United States or Romania, the subjects of later studies in this book, do not matter, or do those differences reinforce the need to ignore methods which are located in tightly controlled ideologies? Indeed the conclusion points to the absolute need for a consideration of other influences and pressures.

The fact that, for example, Italy and Ireland were predominantly Roman Catholic is insufficient reason for assuming that the ideas of Gramsci can be transported on this rather selective approach to history. Indeed, there are some others – such as the growth of fascism in Ireland mirroring that in Italy – which suggest more specific developments. But fascism in Britain under the British Union,[56] or in Romania under the Iron Guard,[57] didn't emerge organically and develop as indigenous organisations independently from the movements in both Germany and Italy. Indeed, they were, with the possible exception of Romania, by comparison, tiny organisations with little real or substantial influence. Once that threat disappeared in Ireland with the emergence of Fianna Fail and the marginalisation of the IRA, the Blueshirts,[58] shorn of their uniforms, quickly disappeared. The fact that many leading members of what became Fine Gael, such as former Taoiseach, John A. Costello,[59] applauded and encouraged their activities had no influence whatsoever on their eventual extinction. The problem, of course, lay not in the threat of a full-blown uniformed fascist army, but in the adoption of fascist ideas creeping into the body politic. Professor Joe Lee was quick to point out that these fascistic ideas were 'so effectively domesticated that they lost much of their sinister comparative import'.[60]

Apart from those peripheral developments, Italy had a strong and effective left opposition which, despite its defeat by Mussolini, represented a countrywide antagonism to capitalism, something which found no real basis in the Irish or the US body politic. In spite of the political split in Ireland into Fine Gael and Fianna Fail[61] as a result of the civil war (divisions based, to a large extent, on the agrarian separation of large versus small farmers), little of this energy was transmitted into the creation of a party founded on socialist ideas and based on an urban working class. After the death of James Connolly,[62] the formation of the Labour Party was a fledgling affair with few teeth and even fewer committed activists. Class politics, in the experience of Gramsci and post-war Italy, never really found its feet in Ireland or in the United States and the occasional anti-communist utterings of both the church and constitutional politicians, occasionally directed at de Valera[63] and the IRA, but more consistently against the small and ineffective Republican Congress,[64] were of no consequence. Even the peasantry, that most stolid and consistent of social structures, were markedly different: in Italy, the peasant was confined to a feudal pattern of living within a village and commuting to the field, whilst in Ireland the peasant – landowner or landed labourer – lived on the land itself but in dispersed patterns across the land.

Attempts to mechanically transport ideas from one historical period to another would fail if it were not for the objective social conditions in which such concepts can be applied. Indeed, it was Gramsci's rejection of the notion that there were 'iron' laws which were appropriate in every situation, which allowed for the expansion of his ideas out of the strait-jacket of abstract empiricism and sterile economism. This is not to suggest that he rejected empirical evidence; according to Carl Boggs, it was the rigid reliance on such evidence by the empiricists as the only basis for a theoretical understanding of the class forces in society, that compelled him to argue against his countryman Croce and in the Second International, Kautsky, Bukharin and Plekhanov.

Interestingly, it is the nature of Gramsci's anti-economism, his struggle for other forms of analysis, which offers the greatest opportunity of understanding the nature of our own society. The struggles of people in circumstances which do not have the immediate characteristics and force of the class conflict, as identified by Kautsky, are often rejected by the inheritors of that same rigidly economist tradition which he represented. In other words, the 'iron' laws to be applied, according to them, would be that they must satisfy certain economic conditions before they can be considered as having the potential for fundamental social and political change. In short, they must have a 'class' character. However, what they failed to understand was that wherever power exists, opposition to it will emerge. Such a conclusion would result in the view that other, less class-oriented struggles, possibly involving an alliance of several classes, are meaningless and a diversion from 'real' class struggle.

In rejecting this rigid approach to social movements and their potential for change, Gramsci pointed to the value within Western civil societies of understanding and recognising the ideological needs of other sections in society such as the peasantry and craftworkers, as well as those unsophisticated ideas located within their traditions, their culture and their consciousness. In this sense, it is not necessarily a class consciousness, or a working-class culture, but one located within their own communities and informed by a variety of influences such as land, religion, myth and folklore. Such characteristics can be found in the urban centres of Dublin and Belfast, or on the side of a mountain in Donegal or Antrim or in the dull narrow streets of Fagaras in Romania, or in the tree-lined deserted avenues of downtown Baltimore in the United States.

Thus, in seeking to apply Gramsci's ideas to examine both the practice and ideology of community development, their transportability would seem to be both appropriate and pertinent. Arising from that, a number of possibilities in Gramscian theory point in the clear direction of a methodology. Much of it emerges from what Salamini describes as Gramsci's 'sociological thought'. Salamini suggests that there are two theoretical orientations which, on the face of it, appear to be 'a contradiction in terms'. Gramsci's approach to an analysis of social phenomena is characterised by 'absolute historicism and absolute humanism'.[65] From such a point of view, society is perceived as essentially an historical process in which its 'socio-cultural phenomena' are understood as being 'historically determined'.

He adopted what became known as a 'critical sociology', which was designed to attempt to explain social phenomena and socio-political institutions in relation to their specific historical conditions. And whilst he attempted to develop a plan for a Marxist political sociology, it was left incomplete because of his premature death:

> It is necessary to study the objective formation of the subaltern social groups, by the developments and transformations occurring in the sphere of economic production; their active or passive affiliation to the dominant political formations, their attempts to influence the programmes of these formations in order to press claims of their own; the birth of new parties of the dominant groups, intended to conserve the assent of the subaltern groups and to maintain control over them; the formations which the subaltern groups themselves produce, in order to press claims of a limited and partial character; those new formations which assert the autonomy of the subaltern groups, but within the old framework; those formations which assert the integral autonomy etc.[66]

The criteria dealt with in his outline provide the first clear indication that there are methodological areas which have a resonance in relation to the study of community action. Salamini maintains that Gramsci's methodological criteria are those of 'historical materialism' and suggests further that whilst sociology considers the relationship of those elements within a social structure, it must, in addition, consider the 'interrelationship between the whole and the parts. The whole can determine the qualitative structure of the parts and the parts can determine the qualitative structure of the whole.'[67] Femia would have agreed:

> ... any particular concept receives its full meaning only in relation to the entire conceptual structure in which it is embedded, in relation to all its dimensions. Theoretical ensembles must be considered in their unity and not as agglomerations of discrete, self-sufficient elements which might be torn from their context without altering their significance.[68]

Such a method asserts that whilst each element is sovereign and independent, nevertheless they are related to each other, and to the whole – structures to structures and, subsequently, to the superstructure. Gramscian sociology, therefore, seems to suggest that a productive method of examining society is to analyse it from the point of view of its 'global development' and the development of its concrete and autonomous elements or component parts.

Unlike positivist sociology which debases social laws and attempts to turn them into 'natural laws', Gramscian sociology enhances and proclaims the importance in history of human activity. Marxist sociology recognises the function of such human activity in 'consciously shaping the development of the historical process', and as such Marxism as a philosophy is 'history becoming conscious of itself and since history is conscious human activity, man becomes the central focus of reality.'[69]

Therefore it is the centrality of human experience which points to a recognition of the value and potential for the development of a social and political methodology based on Gramsci's ideas: 'Marxist sociology of knowledge is then a form of critical consciousness, a form of ideological thought. It follows that the validity of sociological research resides not in its scientific function but rather in its ideological function, that is, in its capacity to organise the experience of the masses.'[70]

It is in the area of the organising of the masses in which sociologists intellectualise their experiences that Gramsci would have understood sociology as a 'Marxist theory of society'. In those circumstances the sociologists become not merely observers or commentators, but actors who struggle to change conceptions of the world based on a series of 'a-political, a-philosophical' superstitions such as 'common sense, folklore and religion'. The purpose? To steer the masses in a direction which would allow them to consider the world, not as a collection of unrelated parts, but as an integral and universal philosophy of praxis: 'The philosophy of praxis does not tend to leave the "simple" in their primitive philosophy of common sense, but rather to lead them to a higher conception of life.'[71]

The suggestion, therefore, that a counter-hegemonic force could lead the masses to a recognition of the prospect of a higher 'conception of life' is a fundamental and logical corollary of the proposition implicit in the philosophy of praxis.

In attempting to examine Gramsci's ideas, this book was moved by only one consideration – the problem of whether it was possible to transform his theoretical framework into tools which would allow a consideration of the issue in question, namely, the relationship between community action and the involvement of the state.

This raises the question of whether it is possible to adopt theoretical concepts and frameworks which are located in an entirely different space in time and in an entirely different historical and social epoch. Femia suggests that it is: 'Needless to say, thinkers develop their ideas in a determinate historical context and with particular purposes in mind; but it on no account follows that these ideas cannot transcend their origins.' But, Gramsci took the matter further:

> The question arises whether a theoretical 'truth' discovered in correspondence with a specific practice can be generalised and deemed universal ... The proof of its universality consists precisely in that which it can become: (1) a stimulus to know better the concrete reality of a situation different from the one in which it was discovered ... (2) when it has stimulated and helped this better understanding of concrete reality, it incorporates itself into this reality as if it were originally an expression of it.[72]

Gramsci offered a framework for an understanding of the nature of a modern, Western capitalist state through his concepts of the superstructure and the forms of civil and political society which shape its substance.

Those limiting theories of social control which are narrowly state-centred are restricted precisely because of the tendency to consider them within an urban paradigm and in a specific political/historical context. The limitations of such approaches emphasise, by contrast, the potential of an examination of hegemony for a wider under-standing of the pressures and constraints imposed by a ruling class within civil society. Those views which reduce the wider debate on the nature of social control to one which concentrates only on the economic needs of the ruling class at any given time in history, echo the already discredited arguments of those within the Second International who were influenced by the economism of Bukharin. Indeed it was the rejection by some of the role of the state, and by others, of the exclusivity of the state in the process, which force one to examine the potential of Gramsci's ideas, as a vehicle for a more satisfactory theory of the nature of social control, authority and order, within the totality of human relations which, together, constitute the social formation.

Much of the work on Gramsci's concepts concentrates on an examination of the nature of the relationship between base and superstructure in which the dominant classes create a system of control disseminated by an ideological hegemony in which 'bourgeois *Weltanschauung*' is 'diffused, popularised and finally internalised by the masses becomes commonsense knowledge. Bourgeois domination is essentially an ideological and cultural fact.'[73]

Gramsci's 'method' provides for a consideration of social control within a comprehensive and almost limitless social context. An examination of his understanding of the processes of the interaction of the twin planes of civil and political society and the nature of the ideological hegemony provides a significant and universal expression of the diverse forces and influences in the modern and complex capitalist state.

It is against this background that the use of a Gramscian analysis becomes not merely valuable but essential. In this context the acquisition of his concepts of the state, hegemony, society and the role of the intellectual and ideology and their transferability into conceptual 'tools' is of critical importance for the development of an examination of the impact of community action on the state and vice versa. But whilst few would argue with the question of whether in fact the state does have an overriding and executive interest in what happens on the ground – at the base – it is not a matter of the fact, but the extent to which its interests coincide or conflict with local communities, which must be at issue.

2
Coercion, Community and Civil Society

Social control and constraint within the modern state

'The only way by which anyone divests himself of his natural liberty and puts on the bonds of civil society is by agreeing with other men to join and unite into a community.' John Locke 1632–1704

The expression 'social control' has been eclipsed by much of the jargon now available in the handbook of the community activist, although for a period the term became one of the most overused in their vocabulary. It was even believed by some that there was a state conspiracy which was designed to neutralise the development of a new strain of community action politics.[1] But for many citizens the social problem was merely a hiccup in civil society in which the present generations with their laptop computers and mobile telephones had no vested interest or concern. So whilst capitalism became entrepreneurism and exploitation was confused by enterprise culture, the negative and inflexible social control was transformed into the positive and constructive social inclusion. In textbooks, social control is used to describe a range of processes of conformity and harmony which has implied the need for the control of crime and deviance, law and order, socialisation, incarceration, bureaucracy, disciplines and constraints, involving the press and agencies of the state, welfare and educational systems as well as the family and community.[2] The list is endless and indicates the way in which civil society responds to behaviour and those people it regards as threatening, incompatible and undesirable. Ordinarily the response manifests itself in terms which many find oppressive and undemocratic and in which deviants are locked away and categorised. Often we bow to the prevailing mood and withdraw to our own crowded corners. In Locke's words, we divest ourselves of our natural liberty and join together in communities.

Since the community movement in Britain and Ireland immersed itself in a profusion of social partnerships with the state and its representatives, all talk of social control appears to have been withered and trampled underfoot in an undignified scramble towards the 'inclusive' society. This chapter sets out to examine the origins and debates around the use of the term and its value as an explanation of one of the coercive processes of socialisation. In doing so, however, it goes further by locating it within definitions of the state and by contrasting its use as an imprecise pejorative description of state authority against the more scientifically exacting Gramscian explanation of hegemony

The volume of literature in this area invariably concentrates on issues more closely concerned with the problems of crime control and social deviancy and the relationship of the individual and the state. Few, with the notable exception of John Dearlove, have examined the issue of social control with the community as a focus of concern. Consequently, the problem of attempting to explore the issue within a community context is considerable.

Does government use its considerable resources to control, not only community action, but, more specifically action which it regards as political and a challenge to the authority and legitimacy of the state? After all, laws exist to be obeyed – a method of control acknowledged and accepted by almost everyone. We are led to believe that in a civil society only the social deviant challenges the right of Parliament to enact law. Lawbreakers are immediately made amenable to such laws through the enforcement agencies. Such is the recognised and explicit face of the state. Because the state is popularly perceived as being the embodiment of the democratic will, it is legitimate and accepted as lawful. What is less immediately recognised, or understood, apart from the fact that the state is the state of the ruling class, is the more implicit and surreptitious form of cultural control over groups and individuals which Gramsci found it necessary to describe as ideological hegemony. But to enable that to become clear we must first look at what is understood by this measure which the community radical believes is a manifestation of the coercive power of the state and which they, perhaps lazily, describe as social control.

This question is important in the examination of the relationship between the state and community action because of the belief amongst many community activists in the nationalist communities in Northern Ireland as well as some who were involved in the Community Development Projects in Britain that all community action is subject to the needs of the state. It is generally believed, especially amongst some more radical activists, that an independent community 'movement' is neither acceptable to the state, nor possible in present political circumstances. Therefore the withdrawal of funding from community groups in Northern Ireland such as those in the Bogside and West Belfast during the early 1980s, was confirmation for many activists of what amounted to a political subterfuge which was actually designed to undermine the 'community' base of the Republican Movement, so that for a brief period community action became synonymous with republicanism. Coupled with allegations of Northern Ireland Office intrigues in public statements were accusations from community groups that a system of government-inspired social control was in place in Northern Ireland. Thus, whether willingly or not, community work acquired a political dimension which forced many into positions they did not understand and others on to the sidelines of a debate they did not want.

Arising from this debate on coercion and control, two questions emerge: is it likely that government would allow public funding to be used to assist community activists develop an alternative political strategy which could potentially draw them into a confrontation with the state? Does the state benefit from a mistaken belief amongst community activists that government would act in a coercive way to protect its interests?

There are clear and unmistakable historical precedents which point to the existence of the use of extra-governmental agencies in imposing the will of the state. In his writings on nineteenth-century social and political reforms, Asa Briggs pointed to traditional models of restraint such as religion and the education system being used to enforce the values of the ruling class and counter the spread of revolutionary and seditious ideas.[3]

The pessimistic nineteenth-century romanticist view that the pre-industrial model of community had broken down with the onslaught of industrialisation, created the basis for a widespread critique of the nature of society at that time. The old forms of community organi-sation, exemplified by the Rousseau-esque view of civilisation as 'a fall from nature' became subject to the more exacting needs of a modern and complex industrial society. This view of the difficulties in the transition from pre-industrial society to the more complex industrial society in which communal authority is superseded by class antagonisms has implications for debates which exist today. The distinction between the cultural interests and living patterns of both has its roots in a long and protracted debate with philosophi-cal origins in the enlightenment of the early eighteenth century. Whilst there were many who idealised rural traditions and patterns of life based on the old 'village' form of community, a friend of Edmund Burke, George Crabbe, doctor and chaplain to the Duke of Rutland, was highly critical of the idealisation of rural work, describing, instead, its harshness:

> 'For now he journeys to his grave in pain;
> The rich disdain him; nay, the poor disdain;
> Alternate masters now their slave command ...'[4]

What was seen as a breakdown in the natural order led to a developing sense of alarm and crisis amongst the members of the new ruling elite, described as a 'fear of the town or dangerous classes'; there arose a search for new ideas and new attempts to create within the mass of ordinary people the need for self-discipline, order and a respect for lawful authority.

But new radical ideas were already beginning to take root. Inspired by the growing and developing opposition within Europe to the established order, the creation of the Paris Commune and the growth, within Britain, of the Chartist movement as well as the emergence of Fenianism, Parliament instituted a series of reforms designed to impose a control on those elements most suspected of succumbing to revolutionary influences through the imposition of what Mayer described as a 'middle class morality'.[5]

These social stirrings were to have a resonance in Ireland. Some years earlier, in a speech to the House of Commons, Thomas McCauley warned of the dangers to British society of any attempt to reject the Reform Bill (1831) by pointing to the hazards experienced in Ireland of a failure to heed the growing discontentment with English rule: 'Have they forgotten how the spirit of liberty in Ireland, debarred from its natural outlet found a vent by forbidden passages?

Have they forgotten how we were forced to indulge the Catholics in all the licence of rebels, merely because we chose to withhold from them the liberties of subjects?'[6]

McCauley, as much as any other nineteenth-century politician, was aware of the dangers of the use of coercive means of subjugation, especially in Ireland. It is a not uncommon claim that it is the peculiar historical, social and political relationship between Britain and Ireland which is, at root, the cause of many of the problems which exist today. Raymond Crotty claimed that 'the one constant feature of the relationship between the colonies and the metropolitan powers was that the former were held so that they might serve the interests of the latter.'[7]

Of course, the British establishment had good cause to fear the question of Ireland. Asa Briggs' analysis of the growth of Chartism in the middle of the nineteenth century referred to the potential for revolution amongst the mass of Irish 'navvies' who had entered cities such as Liverpool, Birmingham and Manchester 'of which it was estimated one fifth were Irish'.[8] But because of the festering grievance of the national question in Ireland, Briggs suggested that as long as O'Connell remained alive, few 'politically motivated' Irishmen would have moved towards Chartism. In this instance he argued that the drive for Catholic emancipation in Ireland virtually emasculated the potentially critical involvement of the disaffected Irish in the Chartist movement in Britain. In spite of this fact it did not deter *The Times* from a valuable story when it insisted on describing Chartism as a 'ramification of the Irish conspiracy'.[9]

There are interesting parallels between the growth of Chartism in Britain in the mid-nineteenth century and the growth of republicanism in Ireland in the latter end of the twentieth century. Both were seen as representing a threat to the existing hegemony and to the sensitive cultural balance of the established order. Both were influenced by the drive for some form of ideological independence and both were engaged in the development of a counter-hegemonic bloc through their challenge to the legitimacy of the values and power of the state. So, if all of this is true, how have these matters affected the issue of the relationship between the state and community action, particularly in Ireland, today?

For those involved in the maelstrom of Northern Ireland politics at the present time, such issues seem to be more clear. As Loney made clear in his work, *Community against Government*, politics and community action are inextricably linked. This was manifest in the problems generated by the controversy in Northern Ireland of the political vetting of some community groups. Perhaps, in the volatile and uncertain atmosphere of political confrontation, government could easily claim that it had access to information which suggested that some community groups were providing support to paramilitary organisations. It is an undeniable fact that none of this information ever reached the public domain except through oblique statements issued by the Department of Economic Development, although if true such an alliance would have the potential to provide a lethal political cocktail. But the nature of the secrecy of the agencies responsible for analysing and processing such information meant that the public did not know the substance of the allegations or the means by which the state exercised control, other than the power to withdraw their right of access to public funding.[10]

Such powers, in spite of the administration's view that they should be free to act in the 'public interest', create considerable problems for the state. There are circumstances when even government can be called to account for its actions and there are many examples of state exposure emerging as a result of community-led intervention. It follows that once community activists are able to counter a tendency towards Machiavellian and conspiratorial solutions to political problems, they will find themselves increasingly drawn towards a more constructive and interventionist form of alternative politics. But, because the community worker already identifies with the notion of social control as a part of the coercive arm of the state, it would be more helpful to locate it within the more ideologically flexible concept of hegemony in which the power of the ruling class can be identified and defined and as a result more accurately challenged.

Social control – a debate about ideological hegemony?

There are several quite different areas to examine which might assist in this. It would be important to consider the background to the issue of social control against interpretations and theories of the role of the state within a historical as well as a sociological framework. Such interpretations should allow us to probe the nature of social control, particularly from the point of view that such control has cultural as well as economic dimensions. The claims of some community groups, particularly in West Belfast, after funding was withdrawn that they were paying the price of the area's political and cultural preferences reinforce the need for such an analysis. If accurate, in that context, the concept of hegemony, rather than social control, emerges as a more reliable tool for an examination of the forces engaged in this process.

There has been a tendency amongst those investigating the nature of social control to consider it only in relationship to the changing nature of crime, psychological disorder and the occasional knee-jerk reaction of society to social problems. Mayer pointed out that in the nineteenth century control was focused not only on deviants but directed, also, against 'sub-cultural ethnic groups'.[11] Some critics of the British legal system would argue that the law, which is presumed to be neutral, becomes 'a primary mechanism of social control or social order'. The problem with such a simplistic and lazy conclusion is that, whilst fundamentally correct, it avoids the layers of cultural influences which permit us to both loathe and legitimate the legal system at the same time. Described by Spitzer as 'legally based coercion', the study of crime control and the administration of justice must be seen within a 'far more general historical process', what he described as the 'rationalisation of social relations'.[12]

But was it simply the 'rationalisation of social relations' which precipitated what became known in Northern Ireland as the programme of 'political vetting'? After all, few seriously believed that the state was interested in a handful of tiny, almost irrelevant, community groups. And yet there was a need to harmonise relations between those disaffected communities and the state to the extent that the interests of the state could also be seen as being in the interests of the community itself. In such a context the rationalisation of social relations could be seen as another euphemism for the more recently politically acceptable social inclusion. In the context of the mid-1980s the political vetting issue was merely a crude manifestation of the blunt end of the same political process, the coercive, rather than the consensual, side of the process of hegemony in which social harmonisation is a vital ingredient.

In June 1985 former Secretary of State for Northern Ireland, Douglas Hurd, responded to a question in the House of Commons from John Taylor MP, about the funding of community groups who are suspected of having connections with paramilitary organisations:

> I am satisfied, from the information available to me that there are cases in which some community groups, or persons prominent in the direction or management of some community groups, have sufficiently close links with paramilitary organisations to give rise

to a grave risk that to give support to those groups would have the effect of improving the standing and furthering the aims of para-military organisations, whether directly or indirectly.[13]

This parliamentary statement of Douglas Hurd must be seen in context. The number of community groups directly affected as a result of what became known as the 'political vetting' issue was relatively small. Some, like Dove House in Derry's Bogside, had only four temporary workers. Yet another had only one, who happened to be the son of a prominent local newspaper editor and supporter of the moderate SDLP. Out of the thousands of groups involved in accessing state funding, only a handful were targeted. It could hardly be described as a massive political issue. At its peak, there were some 11,000 people employed under the scheme designed to alleviate the effects of long-term unemployment by concentrating on the employment and training needs of people within a designated community context. The Derry group mounted a brief and highly effective campaign to have its funding restored whereas others continued to be both suspect and deprived of public funding. But whilst this is of considerable public importance, particularly to the people directly involved, it is the more general effect on those not immediately involved that is of interest as a result of the more general question of the regulation of community action.

The British government would argue that they were, after all, fighting a war against a determined and resourceful, politically motivated, armed organisation. The use of community-based groups would be a valuable and useful tactic in their prosecution of a protracted war designed to gradually undermine governmental authority. In those circumstances, the control of such groups through the provision of public funding would seem to be a natural, logical and justifiable response. It could be argued that the review of public funding is morally correct and simply the logical responsibility of a flexible and reforming government. But if in a conflict situation community action can be used to upset the status quo, the argument runs that it must be countered by the use of community develop-ment to maintain the status quo. That ultimately lay at the heart of the strategic use of state-inspired, community-based interventions in Northern Ireland.

If we were in any doubt about the willingness of the state agencies to initiate controlling mechanisms as a means of maintaining authority we need look no further than South-east Asia. James

Midgley pointed to the use of community development programmes during the war in Vietnam as a social control device and an important element in the war effort. 'American community development expenditures' he argued, 'were highest in countries such as Thailand and Vietnam which were considered to be most threatened by communism.'[14]

Some might argue that in a war situation it is morally correct to use such methods, even seeing them as necessary reforms. However, we are not concerned with the question of moral justification, but whether such control actually exists and if it does, it is managed by government as a direct or indirect consequence of it. For example, in the light of recent changes to the welfare benefits system and the withdrawal of support to the disabled, it might be stretching credibility a little to describe government representatives portraying themselves as reformers. Stanley Cohen and Andrew Scull saw such a description as a 'quintessentially optimistic perspective', change being seen as 'inherently progressive'.[15]

As an example of change, most of us acknowledge the fact that the state does intervene in our lives. Indeed, most accept it without criticism. The community movement, by and large, now sees change in that limited and narrow way. The almost uncritical, indeed enthusiastic, acceptance of 'social' partnerships in some quarters and of 'community' employment schemes, amongst many other 'community' initiatives, are heralded as examples of progressive social adjustment in which the community is seen as having a leading role. Whilst many within the community movement welcome state intervention in the area of economic development, few consider the drawbacks to such an eventuality, particularly when it is claimed that the state involvement arises from other political considerations as distinct from the purely economic one.

Could it be said that such intervention is merely another controlling mechanism of government designed to destroy community initiative and independence at a time when such independence could be exploited by groups attempting to undermine the state? These were the fears, presumably, which were expressed by Hurd in the House of Commons.

In spite of the obvious connection between the statement of the Secretary of State and the bureaucratic sharp end of authority, there are many other factors which should be considered. Some commentators, such as Asa Briggs, pointed to controls emerging through 'the intricate network of responsibilities within extended families' sometimes described as communities,[16] whilst others such as Dearlove saw control as in part the effect of the division of society into classes.[17] This question of purpose and motivation raises all sorts of difficulties. Some, such as Hofstadter,[18] consider the motive in the nineteenth century as a 'nostalgia' for a 'lost order' or, amongst some middle-class urban immigrants, a discontentment with urban life and a desire to return to the small tight-knit and secure community of their origins. On the other hand, there are those who look to the drive within the capitalist class to protect and preserve their ownership of the means as well as the fruits of production. The transfer of skills by the 'liberal' bourgeoisie to the poor as a means of overcoming the more obvious effects of social problems, particularly through programmes of public works, were described by Raymond Crotty as merely a device which continued to cement their influence, authority and power within society.[19] If this argument has any substance to it, then it is in this area of activity that we witness the origins of the benefactor – the philanthropist and the charity worker.

Is there such a quasi-legal device as social control or would it be more precise to say that we are really discussing the Gramscian conception of ideological hegemony? Dealing with such a complex problem is not merely to look for solutions as much as the need to search for the correct questions when dealing with areas of the control of certain parts of the citizens' lives. For example, who or what controls the development of community-based organisations? What is their motivation and their function? Is the concept of social control merely a manifestation of the coercive arm of civil society and is it actually being tested and put into operation not just in Northern Ireland but in Britain and the United States as well?

It was suggested in the opening paragraph of this chapter that the media is a controlling mechanism – or, at best, is used to defend other mechanisms. Anti-terrorism 'expert', Brigadier Frank Kitson attempted to justify the use of the media by suggesting, without using specific examples, that it is used to greater effect by the opponents of legitimate governments: 'From one side of the world to the other the organisers of subversion have access to the people through these means and although the same channels of communication are available to those involved in protecting the existing order, they seldom manipulate them so skilfully as their opponents.'[20]

Although Kitson's work was published in 1971, it is certain that he would have known of the extent of the government's influence on the media at the time. Since his period of service was in Africa and Northern Ireland, his own experience must have taught him that the resources of the propaganda machines of the Kenyan Land Army (Mau Mau) and the Irish Republicans were minimal when set against the vast resources of the state. However it could be argued that the insurrectionists' effectiveness says as much for the lack of quality of government propaganda as for the superior quality of the opposition. In Northern Ireland, for example, the power of the British press to sell its newspapers in the nationalist ghettos was never seriously affected by the distribution of any of the alternative socialist or republican publications in spite of the surge of opposition to the British tabloids in the early 1970s and the bombing of the *Daily Mirror* offices and printing works in Belfast in 1971. But there was a widespread recognition that the press represented, by and large, values which were not shared by the nationalist community. It was the transfer of these values which proved to be crucial in the prosecution of the long war.

Miliband argued that those in control of the media and in a position to influence public opinion are either drawn from bourgeois backgrounds or advocate bourgeois values because of the process of their own socialisation,[21] whilst Dearlove also saw the educational system as well as the mass media as crucial, contributing to the need, within civil society, for some form of social control.[22] Was this an attempt by them to define a systematic transfer of values and morals through the media? Is this what Gramsci understood by the process of ideological hegemony?

In addition to the widespread belief that some form of social control actually exists and is operated by the state, there are a number of other matters to be considered. Presumably for the purpose of maintaining an administration which is being disputed by a section of the population and in circumstances which are affected by a variety of social, economic, political and historic influences, the question of control is not a straightforward one in which controlling devices can be clearly identified and categorised. But the particular focus of all of this and the core of the issue is the fact that government operated a form of cantankerous influence through its ability to allow or deny access to public funding for voluntary organisations.[23] Some within that community would argue that such controls are directed at certain communities at specific moments in the development of their relationship with the state. This has an effect on the way in which some seemingly neutral groups reach an accommodation with central government in which, sitting on the edge of the political spectrum, they are still affected by harsh decisions taken at the centre – what could be called a 'rippling' effect.

When discussing reasons why those responsible for operating different forms of social control act in the way that they do, John Mayer raises a number of vital points which place the whole question in a different light.[24] Citing the example of the use of charitable organisations to 'dull' the attitudes of the working class, he notes that little actual evidence has been produced to prove that the working-class attitudes and/or behaviour changed substantially.

The increasing use of the term 'social control' was attributed to a number of former senior British police officers, particularly those who have had either a first-hand experience of the Northern Irish situation or with strong views on the subject of law and order. Former Chief Constables John Anderton and Kenneth Newman made reference to the need for social control when discussing the more general issue of public policing policy. Anderton was reported as saying that 'we are surely heading for a situation in which stricter measures of social control may have to be applied to stabilise society and secure our democratic system.'[25] Perhaps they were merely stating their own quaint opinions without reference to the realities of existing civil society. They were, after all, well placed to observe and reflect a more informed view of the coercive needs of the state.

Acquiring an understanding of the numerous interpretations of social control in circumstances in which most of the advocates mean something entirely different is no easy task. Clearly Kenneth Newman has an entirely different view of the operation of social control than Istvan Meszaros, whose pamphlet *The Necessity of Social Control* takes the view that whilst typically operated in defence of capitalism, it can have a positive effect on developing socialist societies.[26]

There can be no doubt that we have two different and quite diverse views expressed defending the need for some degree of social control: one advocating the need to have such control imposed from above, in the interests of democracy, whilst the other suggesting that such control is, of necessity, a part of the operation of reversing the alienating effects of capitalism. Within a socialist system, Meszaros argued, social control operates at a level which is conducive to the maintenance of the system and of its members:

> Today, however, we witness the emergence of a fundamental con-
> tradiction, with the gravest implications for the future of
> capitalism; for the first time in human history the unhampered

dominance and expansion of the inherently irrational capitalist structures and mechanisms of social control are being seriously interfered with by pressures arising from the elementary imperatives of mere survival.[27]

The contradiction of which he writes is contained in the Marxist view that such inconsistencies which already exist in a capitalist society are forced into the open by the constant struggles of the working class through what he describes as the 'elementary imperatives of mere survival'. The problem is that Meszaros argues not just that the development of a system of social control under a capitalist system is wrong, but that within the context of a socialist system, some form of social control is not only necessary, but desirable. His view raises interesting and novel contrasts with the points raised by Engels that in *some* circumstances the state can operate at times to 'harmonise' social relations and act as 'ostensible mediator'.[28] Meszaros's ideas are interesting as a means of rationalising the controlling mechanisms within a 'socialist' state although his insistence on the use of the term 'social control' to describe the process of the exercise of authority serves only to obscure the basis of his argument. Surely it would have been better served if he was to fit his ideas more closely to those of Gramsci. In other words, hegemony rather than social control as a principal mechanism of state power.

Nevertheless it did provide an interesting contrast to those who support the capitalist system and who advocate some form of social control as a function of stabilising its future. In those circumstances therefore the statements of former Chief Constables Anderton and Newman can be seen as understandable and predictable. They reflect the view of their class.

The role of the state

Several contributions have been made to the debate on social control in recent years. Most place the state at the centre of the issue. Although Spitzer argued that there was a 'tendency to overestimate the role of the state and underestimate the role of the market in interpreting how social control actually operates in capitalist societies',[29] he went further and suggested that, with the exception of South Africa, 'the advanced capitalist societies are more likely to rely on the market and private mechanisms' to achieve social control rather than look to the state and its administrative and law enforcement agencies.

The language of Orwell darkens any discussion of the state with his inventions of 'Big Brother' and the 'thought police' lurking in the deepest recesses of our collective memory. This Orwellian nightmare is a common, even predictable, one. Disagreeing with this notion, Spitzer saw it as misrepresenting what he described as the 'dynamics of coercion' in Western societies but concedes that there is a certain amount of agreement that it is 'within the state's power to manipulate, dominate and constrain'.[30] However, he takes issue with any attempt to suggest that there is a model of control on which most states could seek some common ground. Spitzer's main argument is that there are some states where the operation of control is much more effectively pressed implicitly through 'free enterprise' than through the explicit organs of the state. It isn't that he has any fundamental disagreement with the fact that social control is a real and tangible concept, but that Cohen and other 'state-centred' theorists are far too narrowly focused. To make the point he argues that free enterprise 'has penetrated everyday life far more effectively and thoroughly than the state'.[31]

Spitzer feels that the difficulty with the state-centred theorists is that their argument inevitably focuses on the link with 'political institutions'. Arguing that the differing structures of capitalist and non-capitalist societies are determined by the differing relationships between the political and economic institutions, he suggests that in the capitalist society, the separation of the two results in a more pervasive form of control emanating from the 'private' institutions. He develops this theme by suggesting that, on occasions, the 'reciprocal' relationship which exists between the two operates a form of control which is most effective when the 'economic institutions are operating smoothly'. Political controls are often only needed when the 'economic control' breaks down.

The traditional Marxist view – that political control follows directly from economic control and that the state is a manifestation of this – has its origins in the work of Engels. He argued that the state is a palpable expression of the irreconcilable antagonisms between the classes, which eventually 'places itself above society'.[32]

Here we have the argument between those who advocate the 'state' as the highest form of social organisation which assumes a total responsibility for the actions and activities of all of its members as distinct from those who look to the source of power behind the state – what Spitzer describes as 'free enterprise' – and which he identifies as the real controlling agency. This could be seen as an issue of cause and effect, with the cause of social control being 'free enterprise' or capitalism, and the effect of such control operated through the various structures of the state, with the 'executive of the modern state' acting as a management committee for the 'affairs of the whole bourgeoisie'.[33]

The state, John Dearlove announced, regards community work as being principally concerned with self-help, its proper sphere of its activity. Such a process, he believed, is seen as a form of community socio-therapy transforming activism into compliance, minimising the effect of community organisation and tending to integrate and draw peripheral organisations within the general influence of the state.[34] This view tends to predominate amongst many community-based organisations which argue for greater freedom from constraint to pursue and develop alternative forms of organisation and neigh-bourhood democracy. Such views are often regarded as a nuisance, creating problems for those in power. But are those views widely regarded as capable of creating the basis for the building of political alternatives against the interests of the ruling class? Can they mobilise sufficient resources which will pose a serious threat to the stability of the state and its dominant class? 'The trigger that sets off disorder is not economic distress itself but the deterioration of social control. To restore order, the society must create the means to reassert its authority.'[35] This view of Pivern and Cloward suggests the need when offering aid with one hand, to institute a set of controls with the other.

Spitzer sees this question of the influence of capitalism on social control, in terms of its value as something which can be bought and sold on the open market. He sees it simply as a commodity. His argument is that the issue must be linked to the need within society for some form of security which can be 'purchased in the market place'.[36] Security, he insists, is a social need using an example of the purchase of private housing as an indication of the attitude of some to the issue of security. In this instance private housing, presumably, is viewed as being more secure in terms of its value as an investment than public housing. That, therefore, is an example of the purchase of security – as a commodity.

In those circumstances such a view would make difficult the separation of the commodity of 'security' from the commodity of 'property'. This is precisely Spitzer's point. He illustrates his argument by using such examples as a way of explaining the nature of social control, by describing the more idiosyncratic influences which determine the way in which some members of the population decide how to purchase their proportion of security. The problem with this argument, is that if we accept that the principal motivation in the purchase of housing is the element of 'security' and not 'property', then such a criterion, of itself, excludes that vast ocean of people who are both unwilling and incapable of ever purchasing such security. Does this set them apart from that element of control? If so, it would, presumably, exclude a section of the population over whom the need for such controls exist – the section most likely to suffer from discontentment, frustration and anger at their condition. The reverse view of 'security' may be appropriate and seen, not as a means of controlling the individual, but as a means of control *for* the individual responsible for its purchase – as a commodity. Is the effect, therefore, an effect which is aimed, not at the purchaser but directed against those who cannot afford to purchase 'security'? Security, therefore, designed not merely to protect the consumer, but as a means of protecting the consumer *against* others? Who then is being controlled – the consumer or those against whom the consumer requires protection? This point is made in Spitzer's article. He raises the contradictions within capitalist society of the problem, for capitalism, of having to operate within a system which needs 'protection' from those who are perceived as being a threat to the capitalist interest. Clearly also, such protection brings with it a series of controlling mechanisms, which result in a paralysis of the existing opportunities for 'free enterprise'. Such stifling controls are not always conducive to the interests and development of capitalism – what he described as the 'relationship' of 'capitalist vitality' to 'growth'.[37]

The parallels with community development in Ireland begin to emerge. The injection of vast sums of financial subsidies to stabilise the local economy through the provision of welfare payments and temporary job provision create an almost entirely dependent population.[38] In stabilising volatile political situations, there is a need to increase public spending – measures which are often criticised by local representatives of the CBI as being against the commercial interests of the local manufacturer. They argue, instead, for greater commitments from government for investment in the private sector as a means of stabilising the economy, citing the process of 'rein-dustrialisation' as an example. Clearly, government is faced with a dilemma, in which the public sector emerges as the 'dominant influence in the region's economy'.[39] The withdrawal of resources from the public and voluntary sectors could result in the erosion of public confidence; an increase in localised, sectarian frustration, disillusionment and subsequent increase in support for the enemies of the state. Initiative and control, government would argue, would pass into the hands of the insurrection and decades of work would be lost.

In 'Notes towards a Working Definition of Social Control', John Mayer raises another aspect of a less direct method of control by arguing that not all aspects of control deal with the issue of deviancy.[40] However, the problem is less a question of social or political deviancy as society's perception of it. To many it is a simple matter of those who ignore or challenge the rule of law. To others, however, it is a much broader question of the predominant values implicit in the notion of civil society, often unrelated in any direct way to civil or criminal law. The question posed by Spitzer, of security as a marketable commodity, could be one example.

Mayer suggests, instead, that in 'middle and upper-class WASP [White Anglo-Saxon Protestant] culture' there is an attempt to impose their values on ethnic working-class groups in the United States through the voluntary participation of those same groups in social and economic regeneration programmes which ignore the ethnic and cultural values of their own communities. In those circumstances there are some, he believes, who *want* to have their behaviour 'influenced or changed'.[41] It is an interesting point because it suggests that those groups wanting to change their own condition are actually participating in determining the nature of their own control. Whilst this suggests that, in voluntarily participating in the mechanism of control, the group is conscious and aware and in total agreement with such developments, although there is also a possibility that the group participates without being fully conscious of the implications of its involvement.

Again, the experience of those groups affected by controls in Northern Ireland demonstrate that what Mayer wrote can be applied to several situations outside the United States. Many groups allow themselves to be controlled by the state agency, the Department of Economic Development (DED), in the belief that they are acting in the best interests of their own communities. Indeed many of them would see such control as normal and acceptable, although often this can be seen as a mask for the ambitions of either the group or the main actor within the group. Clearly, there are those who sincerely believe that conforming to the criteria of the state funding agency benefits the community they represent and so their participation is justified as being for the greater good.

But for Mayer, the important issue isn't whether such controls actually exist as much as the question of the 'functions' of the controlling device and the 'motivation' of those responsible for the control. What, therefore, is the reason for imposing the controls and how do they operate? Although, perhaps a more appropriate question would be, for whom, or what, do such controls operate?

The difficulty in asking such a question is the issue raised again by Spitzer when he discussed the differences between the 'state-centred' theorists and those who look, as he did, to the market forces as a controlling agency. The problem with asking the question 'who?' is that there is a tendency to drift towards a theory of conspiracy which takes into account, not the *function* of social control so much as the issue of *motivation*. For some the primary reason for operating some form of control is the base issue of power. In other words, society is split into the powerful and the powerless; the logical corollary being that it is the 'powerful' who act to control the 'powerless'; the capitalist versus the worker; the man versus the woman, and so on. It all seems fairly straightforward with such dichotomies representing society as we understand it. Except that the problems begin to emerge when we consider the definition of power and, more importantly, who in society has a monopoly of power? This issue raises interesting questions when we come to look at the contrasting views of Gramsci and the more orthodox Marxists on the relationship of the state to hegemony and ultimately to the freedom and rights of the individual. Indeed it is interesting to note that on the question of the classical Marxist approach to power – in other words, the role of coercion and force as the basis for domination by the ruling class within the state – Gramsci appeared close to Max Weber in his analysis of bureaucracy when Weber claimed that Marxism had 'typically ignored any form of domination outside the sphere of production itself'.[42] Gramsci regarded this as a particular manifestation of the analytical deficiency responsible for earlier failures.

The term 'social control' has become almost commonplace in society today as a means of explaining the lack of empowerment within working-class communities. However, it should be said that the problem of 'disempowerment' is often seen as a personal or individual problem which many community groups, particularly those engaged in 'women's issues', can address through programmes of 'assertiveness training' and 'personal development'. But it is assumed, because government creates structures which operate within some form of agreed order and arrangement, that government is operating a controlling mechanism which will determine the future conduct, behaviour and potential of its citizens.

The volume of literature on this issue deals, to a large extent, with the controlling elements of incarceration and law enforcement. Few deal in any specific way with the question of the control of community action. However, Marjaleena Repo did refer to it briefly, in her article, 'Organising the Poor against the Working Class', and Rolston in his work 'Community Politics', refers specifically to the state intervention in the arena of community relations in the early 1970s,[43] whilst Dearlove is much more comprehensive in his attempt to link the control of community action to the state.

The problem which Spitzer concentrates on – that the state-centred theorists ignore the problem of capitalism and the use of 'free enterprise' as a mechanism – can also be applied to the community and voluntary sector. The problem is that whilst the use of the market as a mechanism can be understood from a functionalist point of view, it doesn't entirely address or answer the question of motivation. The difficulty arises not just because the issue of function is regarded as being inappropriate, but that it becomes an irrelevance when taken without any consideration of the reasons why such mechanisms are put into operation and by whom. For example, the civil servant, as distinct from the teacher, may be unaware that he/she is involved in a controlling mechanism which restricts the independence of others. It is a matter, perhaps, of alienation – the distancing of the bureaucrat from the object of control – in the same way that the worker is often alienated from the product – the means of generating wealth and profit. The teacher, on the other hand, is not alienated in the same way from the student – the object of his/her control. However, this isn't always the case; John Fish suggested that universities in the United States are involved in a process of alienating local communities precisely because of the need to exercise some control over them. Therefore, '[o]ne cause of alienation and low self-esteem is being treated like objects, without being respected or consulted by the large bureaucracies that are supposed to be trying to "help" them.'[44]

Thus the motivation, clearly, is different between one and the other just as the motivation of the educational institution may be entirely different from the teacher. Similarly, the civil servant may be divorced from the 'object' over which a considerable amount of direct control is exercised on the clear understanding that such control is exercised with the full authority of the law and in circumstances in which the civil servant has no particular personal interest.

Stanley Cohen drew a picture of social control as a huge army of 'fishermen and fisherwomen working all day and even into the night according to more or less known rules and routines, subject to more or less authority and control from above, knowing more or less what the other is doing'.[45] In many ways such a picture accurately illustrates a view of the state in which the many involved in its processes work without any real regard, either for the implications of control, or for the motivations of the initiators. Indeed, they collect data and information, in the same way as the fishermen harvest the seas as a collective and unconscious response to the need for food – without any thought for the fish. This is an example of the dominant social class responsible for controlling another sub-group becoming, themselves, alienated from those over whom they exercise such control.

The traditional Marxist view of the state, that it is merely an extension of the power of the dominant ruling class, has been under attack for some considerable time. Often described as 'vulgar materialism', this view has been associated with those who advocate a more economically determinist perspective. It is now being argued that the state, instead of being partisan, is independent of any specific class interest.[46] It is omnipotent in that it monopolises the legitimate use of force, yet subservient in that it responds to whatever pressures are exerted upon it. However, both Marx and Engels recognised that 'as the state arose from the need to hold class antagonisms in check ... it is as a rule the state of the most powerful, economically dominant class.'[47]

This claim that the state at times seeks to rationalise social conflicts, if not to harmonise them, whilst at the same time acting in the interests of the ruling class, offers tempting hints that the view of hegemony, as a tool in understanding the nature of the state didn't originate solely with Gramsci. But this must be firmly placed within context because it would be wrong to suggest that Engels had changed his position with relation to the 'irreconcilability' of the classes within the state. Lenin however, was unwavering in his conviction that the state 'was a manifestation of the *irreconcilability* of class antagonisms' (emphasis added) and sought to make this point as a means of endorsing Engels' contribution to the issue in his work *The Origin of the Family, Private Property and the State.*[48]

It is probably at this point of departure – in other words, the relationship between the individual, the state and the process of transformation – that the question of the state and its use of the machinery of authority becomes most crucial. It is at this point that the ideas of lawful authority, legitimacy and social control begin to acquire an entirely new dimension. Hegel's view, therefore, that the individual existed only to endorse the authority of the state and that 'authority would inaugurate freedom'[49] takes on a new meaning and significance. It is interesting when contrasted against Gramsci's view that 'if you're not able to understand real individuals, you can't understand what is universal and general.'[50] Such an apparent dichotomy has implications for the more recent communitarian dogma of 'responsibilities' in place of 'rights', which is discussed later in this book. However, there exists the possibility of a meeting of minds between Gramsci and Hegel on the relationship between the state and the individual at the point when the interests of the state and the individual coincide. The anarchists Bakunin and Proudhon, in the nineteenth century felt most uncomfortable with Marx's Hegelian views of the nature of the state which they described as 'decidedly authoritarian'. Although coming from the same Hegelian tradition, Proudhon and Bakunin were inclined to believe that authority simply bred more authority. In the circumstances envisaged by them, the state would acquire greater authority and, increased power as the ruling class consolidated its control over the state – as *the* organ of class domination.[51]

This view of the state as the prime agent of the ruling class however stands in marked contrast to that of the state as the instrument of reconstruction or as a facilitator of revolutionary change. This ability within the Marxist tradition to see the state both as a theory of 'bourgeois society' or as a 'doctrine of social revolution' allows for diverse views to be considered when posing both analyses for and solutions to the means for the transformation of society. However, it is with Gramsci that we are able to consider the development of the theory of the state both as an instrument of class domination as well as a tool for revolutionary transformation and change.

This question of the role of the state dominated the ideas of the earlier Marxists, not least of all because they saw it as the 'epiphenomenon' of the class struggle. Believing that bourgeois society could not do without the state, Marx did suggest that there were circumstances when it might reduce its functions. Indeed, in spite of the period of transition from capitalism to communism when the state would 'wither away', he felt that the highest stage of communism would not be 'completely stateless'.[52] However, suggestions that the tendency to isolate single factors or elements of human existence, whether it be the philosophical 'idealist' or the economic 'materialist', according to Boggs, merely resulted in the conversion of theory into 'empty metaphysics'.[53]

There are three distinct tendencies emerging from a theoretical study which point to the areas of concern surrounding the question of the control of society and its implications for those advocating community action ideas as a method of social change. Briefly, those areas relate to society's need for controlling mechanisms, either as a basis for the stabilising of social relationships, whether in a capitalist or a socialist society, or as a means of rationalising social conflicts. What surfaces from this analysis is a recognition that the state emerges as a central agency in the development of social control theory.

One of the difficulties emerging from a study of social control is the problem of an apparent lack of ideological perspective. The views of Spitzer and Mayer, whilst argued within a broad Marxist context, are insufficiently precise for use as an analytical tool. Many are considered within a Marxist framework, but are concerned, largely, with the subjective motivations of the practitioners, rather than the objective implications for the future of the state and of society as a whole. Indeed, they are more concerned with observing the process of social control as epiphenomenon, in other words, as a by-product of the state rather than as an intrinsic element of the function of the state itself. As a consequence therefore, their arguments, directed at those whom they regard as 'state-centred' and who ignore other forces such as the 'market' and 'free enterprise' as fundamental elements in the control of society, are seen more clearly. Such arguments are not concerned with the processes of change, or with change itself.

Much of this, of course, has to be seen in a wider context. The historical origins of social control theory can be found in the development of methods of control through many of the great social reforms of the nineteenth century. A consideration of the emergence of such controlling devices must be seen against the need for greater moral stability in the light of the political problems being created by the Paris communards in France, the peasant rebellions and the growth of Fenianism[54] and Chartism in Ireland and Britain.[55] However, discontentment with urbanisation during this period, resulting in a movement anxious to retain a connection with the past and a return to the idyllic, rural delights of small, village-like communities must not be overemphasised or exaggerated. Much of this can be seen in the literature and art of the period, but care must be taken when using it as an example of Victorian opposition to the incursions of the state rather than as an effete nod in the direction of romantic nostalgia.

The emergence of charitable institutions at the same time as the creation of social reforms was seen as an attempt to 'dull' the minds of the working class, making them less amenable to radical or revolutionary solutions. Benevolent control, as a method of harmonising social relations, had its advocates amongst middle-class philanthropists of the nineteenth century, and protagonists among many of the more revolutionary thinkers of the time, who identified its negative implications. Marx saw the role of the state, in this context, as seeking to harmonise social relations by neutralising class conflict, as its primary function, and as a consequence, securing the future of capitalism.

Early in the chapter it was stated that whilst laws exist to be obeyed, it is generally acknowledged by even the most anarchic of ideologists, that they have to be viewed within the context of the state. Indeed, it is the centrality of the state and its role as the arm of the 'economically dominant class'[56] and as the 'manifestation of the irreconcilability of class antagonisms'[57] which form the core of many of those arguments expressed by those viewing it from a Marxist perspective. It is the nature of the state and, as a consequence, its role as a manifestation of such class antagonisms and not its symptoms, which formed the basis for disagreement amongst these early socialist theoreticians.

In contrast, there are those reductionist opinions which consider the processes of socialisation, peer-group pressure, public opinion and education, as the principal motivators in the implementation of social control. Against these arguments are those which point to other considerations which, whilst superficially Marxist in outlook, tend nevertheless to circumnavigate the central role of the state and look to the functions, or symptoms, of capitalism through free enterprise as having a primary function in the control of society.

The problem with those who adopt a reductionist approach is their inability to see the relationship between the state as the core and its functions. There is a constant attempt to treat them as separate and as having equal value in the process. Clearly this cannot be the case if the community activist is to accept a structuralist perspective that the state is central *because* it is the arm of the dominant ruling class, regardless of which class that may be. Furthermore, such a perspective must take into account the course of change implied through the process of community action as intrinsically linked and related to the interdependency of both the state and its base, the super-structure and its structures.

Where do these seemingly abstract arguments bring us? Change is often seen as inherently progressive. The state is viewed as intrinsically static. Some activists argued for community work to form the basis for a new agenda based on a more egalitarian approach to local development, whereas others saw it as a means of building a new socialist 'Utopia'. On the other hand, however, Dearlove saw community work as a form of socio-therapy designed to transform local or neighbourhood activism into compliance. Seen in that light, Kruss's observation, that 'the "organic intellectuals" of the ruling class have the function of organising consent, so that the people become willing partners in their own subjection', forces us to think more clearly about the role of the community activist in the estab-lishment of social partnerships with the state.[58]

The examination of those theoretical arguments which consider social control only in the context of the state from an entirely economist point of view fall short, in their analysis, of considering the broader implications of such control and the effect it has on the wider community. Equally, those who look only to the function of control miss the point of motivation and source of origin. Furthermore, such a viewpoint often locates the question of control in the valuable but narrow confines of an urban working-class context, without considering the wider implications and effect on the much more complex cultural terrain which forms the *whole* of a civil society, the rural as well as the urban.

The theoretical arguments of many of those discussed provided little in the way of clear and concise tools which would allow for the exploration of the control of radical community activity and more specifically, the relationship between the state and community action. The strengths of those arguing for a state-centred approach were weakened by their concentration on a purely economist framework. On the other hand the consideration of concepts related to the epiphenomenon of social control as a 'commodity' available on the free market reduced a consideration of its implications to abstract and pointless speculation. Clearly, what was required was a surgeon's precision, with the perspective of a philosopher's ability to consider all of the issues involved. A new approach was needed. As Gramsci observed: 'Being cannot be disjoined from thinking, man from nature, activity from material, subject from object.'[59]

3
Community as Counter-Hegemony

Community, class and empowerment

Writing in a seminal work on 'community' in the mid-1970s Sean Baine wrote of the formation of what were called 'People's Councils' as a response to the failure of the left to resolve what were being described as 'community' issues.[1] The idea that class could be replaced by community as a model for change was not particularly new, but in the 1970s and since, the attempt to provide a momentum for such a development has increased. Before the realignment of the left, in the wake of the uprisings against Soviet occupations in Hungary and Czechoslovakia, the prospect of someone on the left dropping class as a force for progress was extremely unlikely. Of course there were a substantial number of groups arguing for a different, 'alternative', perspective. But many of those frustrated by the futility of the Militant group, its tactics of 'entrism'[2] and the apparent fruitlessness of attempting to develop a mass political party on the sidelines by various Trotskyist, old Stalinist and Maoist parties, became seduced by a different perspective which focused on the separate arena of struggle within the community.

The two most significant contributors to the debate about the potential and value of such an arena of struggle at that time were Martin Loney and John Dearlove. Both examined the futility of attempting to identify new battlefields against the state and against capitalism. Describing the differences between two schools of thought on the impact of poverty, Loney suggested that they were ranged between those who argued about the effects of poverty, in other words on the characteristics of the poor themselves, and those who attempted to focus on the structures of society, in other words, the causes of poverty.[3] The concern in the mid-1970s for the individual idiosyncrasies of poverty has been replicated by more recent advocates of a 'community' approach to such problems. Those who remained loyal to a structuralist perspective of community work joined others on the left in the free-fall of socialism. Those disciples of the new way, of new age, New Labour and of community and family, clambered on to the back of poverty and began the process of rediscovering the almost forgotten image of the charity worker, as community became synonymous with benevolence and compassion, and community action replaced the need for class struggle.

Dearlove was anxious to point to the growing frustration of the poor at that time because of the belief that Labour had abandoned them. That problem was exacerbated by the continuing failure to build successful alternatives which would both highlight and address their social and economic needs. It was argued by the left at that time that only through class conflict could the issues of homelessness, unemployment and helplessness be satisfactorily resolved. Indeed, to a large extent it was the army of voluntary but vocally socialist groups consisting of those engaged in battling with authority through claimants' unions, local defence groups, housing action groups and community volunteers, who were most outspoken in their frustration with the inability of the old and new left to deal with these problems. Some of this frustration was also expressed amongst some radical social workers who struggled to change the nature of social work from one acting in defence of the establishment to one arguing in support of the poor. John Dearlove was so concerned at the increasing levels of contact between the community sector and the state at the time of writing his article 'The Control of Change and the Regulation of Community Action' as to suggest that its mere survival was dependent, to a large extent, on its ability to make adjustments and changes in its activities, although such an adjustment, he argued, would not only leave it helpless and ineffective, but would fundamentally alter its ethos of independence and autonomy. It would, in fact, become the apologist for the state, subscribe to the prevailing ideological hegemony and 'assist government in the maintenance of the established order'. It became therefore a choice between survival and helplessness, with most groups choosing the former and offering vague excuses for the latter.[4]

How is it that community, with its notion of cooperation and classlessness, was able to enter our political, social and economic consciousness without as much as a 'by-your-leave'? How was it that there appears to be little record of debate on the dichotomy of community and class amongst the theoreticians of the left, other than the few publications which have been confined to the basement stores of some university libraries?

Community 'work' became an alternative, not merely to describe the process of growth within and between communities, but also to explain a range of activities and processes in the political, social and economic tendencies of those activists engaged in this area of work. In time it came to mean different things to different interests. For many caught in the poverty trap the notion of 'community' is meaningless unless there is something tangible associated with it which gives it a force, a potential and a dynamic; in other words it lacks power as a force for change. Even those academics who emerged from the Community Development Projects experience with a radical view, but whose belief in the dynamic of the working-class 'community' fell short of a genuflection to the more generic term, implicitly recognised its limitations for real change. But if community became the battlefield on which new banners were to be struck, then community development was to become the strategic weapon in which the demand for social inclusion would emerge as the bright new slogan. But the problem with the pronouncement of such watchwords is that they also have the potential to become the banner for a range of quite disparate interests. Hence Harry Specht's endorsement to those who saw it as a vehicle for a campaign on behalf of and led by the poor:

> Support for change must involve a broad cross-section of the body politic and not just the poor. Like it or not, one of the things we can learn from the history of social change movements is that they require the involvement of a wide range of actors including intellectuals, middle class supporters, people with money, large numbers of people and so forth.[5]

Is this true in all respects? Is it too general a statement to be taken literally? Implicit in Specht's view was the belief that a movement for social change cannot succeed without those elements he described as a part of the leadership. Such a claim is problematic for two specific reasons. In the first place the initiative for social change rests solely with those in need of it; in other words it emerges organically. Secondly, it can only flourish if its momentum towards success is at all times supported by that same group. The trade unions in Britain and the 'labor' unions in the United States are examples of social movements which could not exist without the base. Although community development was often seen as a basis for action by urban-based community groups, it became, in time, synonymous with addressing economically deprived and marginalised minorities right across the spectrum of social class. But it is a long road to travel, after all, from the days of the claimants' unions and the community 'activist' to those of the community business and the community 'entrepreneur'. Interestingly, whereas Specht's view would have been regarded as a heresy in 1975, it is more relevant today than at the time he made it to the Association of Community Workers in Britain. We now live in the epoch of the social partnership – the alliance of the government and the community.

The range of definitions which are used to describe a liberal analysis of society, emphasising the need to struggle for wider democracy and accountability, can be found in the drive to resolve the social and economic problems affecting the new categories of poor, now known as the 'disadvantaged', the 'marginalised' and the 'socially excluded'. But the problem in securing a definition is that it is used so widely and amongst such a diverse range of interest groups that a common agreement and understanding is difficult to grasp. For example, the statement which claims that 'community development is about the involvement of people in issues which affect their lives' is as banal a definition as one is likely to get anywhere.[6] A still further assertion that it is 'a process based on the development of an equal partnership between all those involved to enable a sharing of skills, knowledge and experience' tells us little more. A community work course organised by two local activists, Paddy Logue and Seamus Keenan in the Bogside in Derry, during one of the most intense periods of conflict, attempted to place such work into a more explicitly political context:

> They share an anti-imperialist outlook, i.e. the ruling class in Ireland is part of an international capitalist class whose oppression of the Irish workers is economic, political, cultural, religious and military. As community workers, they see community action as part of the overall struggle of the working class to achieve liberation. It was clear to them that this overall struggle had failed to improve

the lot of the working class. In housing, health and jobs low standards and discrimination had persisted through the seventies and state repression and torture continued unabated. Mason's militarism contrasted with professional community projects financed by moneybags Melchett. The state's policy of diverting, dividing and attacking the working class with its twin tactics of the iron fist and the velvet glove was overwhelming. The efforts of the few community activists who resisted this policy were puny in comparison. Most fell into the state's trap and scrambled for Melchett's beads and trinkets.[7]

Such a view of community work was not widely shared even at that point in 1980 in the middle of considerable community turmoil and political unease. But whilst community activists were few in number then, there has been a proliferation of such workers today and of those involved in some form of political action, after almost twenty years of exposure to such ideas, there would be even fewer now who would subscribe to the view of Logue and Keenan.

In defence of community

Clearly, community work is not about division and conflict. Advocates of a community work perspective often identify as their base specific geographical boundaries or 'neighbourhoods' or 'communities'. On occasion they identify communities of 'interest' which can be related to a variety of different factors such as race, gender and class, or in the way different groups of people respond to whatever they perceive as relevant to their needs. Described as 'process', 'product', 'praxis' and 'programme', community action advocates emphasise the importance of 'democracy', in which people are allowed to participate in the developmental process, and collective, in so far as it provides for some basis of consensus or democracy in its decision making. Community work is said to be about confidence-building for the individual within the group and from the group to the individual. It straddles borders and boundaries and can involve a broad range of strategies in attempts to draw resources to communities. In short, it is all things to all men and women. Put like that it is not hard to see why it is so popular.

The principal problem with those who advocate community action as a means to solving the problem of the 'socially excluded' is the very fact of their chameleon-like ability to change and adjust to differing circumstances and conditions. More recently, community development has been characterised by a profusion of theoretical ideas and perspectives which has led to a confusion of objectives and to a variety of interpretations. In spite of the many attempts to generate networks and construct umbrella groups which can address the isolation and powerlessness of the community, most falter and gradually disappear in pursuit of their separate, if similar interests.

The problem with this is that many who attempt to define precisely what community development is, tend to avoid identifying the ideological construct in which community development rests, or indeed, specifying precisely in whose interests it operates. Perhaps conveniently the very essence of the community activist is that which allows for adjustment and compromise as the advocate of the new poor in circumstances where they are being redefined and remodelled as the 'socially excluded'. The objective of the community activist is to struggle to reverse this trend; in other words, to struggle *for* social inclusion.

Disillusionment often exposes the activist whose frustration with the slow pace of change leads ultimately to a rejection of the community-based 'process' as a basis for change. And yet there still exists that feisty group of advocates who continually argue for the 'bottom-up' approach as the development of a new and healthy form of 'democratic action'. But they are now on the defensive. The community activist is as likely nowadays to read the *Financial Times* as the *Socialist Worker*. The views of those who see it as having programmatic qualities as a method of social change and who ultimately lean towards a structuralist outlook are becoming fewer by the day.

But what has this got to do with ideology? The need to see economic deprivation as a problem of structural inequality rather than as a problem of individual poverty is an indicator of the direction adopted by those committed to a more radical approach to community action. The structuralist perspective, an argument which was dismissed by one former labour MP as so much 'left-wing blather' was based on the view that local communities had little real control over their social condition. This argument created a number of problems because the advocates of the structuralist approach saw it as an excuse for a refusal to become involved in the development of the small, locally-based community project. Working-class communities often have little real control over the activities of their 'community' representatives or of the projects organised in support of the principles of 'inclusion' in spite of the 'democratic' rhetoric:

'... structural change was not something that could be affected by local Community Development Projects (CDPs) and to adopt structuralism as a fundamental approach merely induced neglect of the possibility of ameliorating some aspects of deprivation.' In other words, to engage in debating the causes of the problem was seen by many activists almost as an abandonment of social responsibility.[8]

Those, especially in the Community Development Projects in Britain, advocating a structuralist perspective, were engaged in an attempt to establish the source of poverty by focusing attention on the imbalance of wealth in a civil society. This was most evident in the mid-1970s in the involvement, for example, of the overtly political group, Conference of Socialist Economists, in working with project activists in the publication of documents highly critical of the Labour government and public policy. But even within that group there was considerable disagreement, not only about the nature of the problem, but more specifically on the means of addressing it.

Did this suggest two perspectives, one expressing an evolutionary approach whilst the other urged revolutionary change? There is no doubt that within the dominant Marxist faction the community problems of poverty and inequality become subordinate to the 'central' problem of working-class powerlessness. 'Community' has no power to initiate or sustain change whereas 'class' for them undoubtedly had. But there was still the difficulty of convincing the minimalist constituency within the developing community movement that social change can only be dealt with at the level of the structure. On the other hand, the minimalist viewpoint was expressed in terms of immediate need. The poor could not wait for the structures to make adjustments or for the political changes to take place before their needs were addressed. So were the structuralists going to ignore immediate local needs for crèche facilities, welfare rights units and other self-help services? There was much scepticism about their approach as well as their commitment and responsibility from those who believed that the worst effects of poverty could be alleviated through community action.

Concepts and theories were believed to be of little relevance when faced with the more humdrum problems of running projects on shoestring budgets. But whilst some activists were suspected of advocating a structuralist approach to change, central government, on the other hand, enjoyed a less fragile relationship with community groups. Clearly such a situation came about because support for state strategies offered the hope of some financial reward, in spite of the fact that there was a commonly held view that regulation and control always accompany the acceptance of government handouts.

The acceptance of such handouts was accompanied by other problems for the activist. As community action moved from amateur standing to professional status, it acquired new advocates who engaged in a new modern discourse with one another in the language of the Eurocrat. For those interested in community work as a process of change which emphasises the educative as opposed to the economic, such a development was not necessarily a welcome one. The use of Freireian terms such as 'conscientisation' were replaced by others, less conjectural but perhaps more functional, such as 'sustainability', 'social inclusion' and 'additionality'. But more than simply the replacement of one set of terms for another, is the implicit meaning of changes which suggest moves away from negative concepts to those proclaiming a more positive approach to development. Whilst the objective for many involved in developmental work continues to be the raising of consciousness rather than the tangible and material consequences of the process of development, there is a distinct and tangible tension between the two tendencies. Some take a more pragmatic approach, whilst others cannot conceive of community development without a consideration of both.

In defence of change

Many of the community workers involved in the Community Development Projects in Britain still complained of a lack of theoretical perspective. Some saw a need for fundamental political change as the only means of addressing the social problem with the community development method as a means of underpinning that process. It was the classic argument between those who wanted to use community development as a tool for actual, if limited, local change and those who saw it as a catalyst for 'radical' if not 'revolutionary' objectives. One made common cause with the struggles of workers and the trade union movement at the point of production, whilst the other remained sceptical of the value of the unions and advocated instead the advantages and potential of the local cooperative and other alternative micro-developments.

Some groups such as Northern Ireland Community Development Review Group (CDRG) might suggest that in the attempt to describe community work as having three distinct areas of activity (organisation, development and action) community development provides a strategic focus for those interested in self-help processes, whilst community action depends on an almost impromptu reaction to the community problem. Within a community action perspective, the problems for the community of social exclusion and marginalisation become subordinate to the central problem of working-class disempowerment. In other words, the unemployed have no power.

The problem was that the radical approach of those arguing for a Marxist perspective failed to take account of the seduction of the short-term gain. There was a profound difficulty when attempting to apply such a structuralist critique to the practical problem of coping with the work on the ground. Opponents of the Marxist approach argued that it was inappropriate and difficult to operate and that it tended to be longer on analysis than on application.

Yet another difficulty is that many activists within the community work area regard the theoretician and the ideologue with more than a little contempt. Loney referred to this when he noted that 'in Britain "community politics" reflected an activist and atheoretical, populist approach.'[9] This is evident from the degree of suspicion which exists particularly towards those interested in the work from within university institutions. Equally, those who argue against minimalism in community work and who attempt to place poverty in a wider perspective are treated even less charitably in circumstances when concepts and theories are believed at worst to be irresponsible and at best to be of little relevance to the wider needs of the community. But in spite of the suspicion against some university institutions, it is those same organisations which are churning out dozens of young, relatively inexperienced community development graduates every year, many of them staffing local development organisations, advocating strategic and partnership approaches and at the same time promoting more 'inclusive' dialogue with local and national government agencies.

It would be quite wrong to blame the academic for encouraging the use of community as a model of social change any more than the socialist for advocating the importance of class. But where does this emphasis on 'community' as a model for social and political change come from? In more recent memory it has been passed down from those who attempted to raise the standard in Britain in the early 1970s through the Community Development Projects and others, particularly in the United States who, in parallel with the growth of the civil rights movement and the response of the Johnson administration with its anti-poverty programme, identified community as an archetype model for socio-political action. Of course it would be quite wrong to suggest that the originators saw such action coming from all-class alliances of working-class and middle-class interests, although those in government clearly saw some merit in this. But frustrations with this approach caused difficulties with, for example, one supporter of the CDP reacting to such developments and arguing for the 're-politicisation of working-class communities'.[10] This was seen as one method of drawing together the parallel developments which were taking place in both the trade union movement and the newly emerging social 'community' movement based within the geographically organised neighbourhood. For many, especially within the Conference of Socialist Economists in Britain, only a bringing together of the labour and community movements offered the prospect for real change. After all, such a partnership worked successfully in New York shortly after the First World War when the labour unions supported neighbourhood groups campaign against exploitative landlords and the imposition of high rents.

Perhaps one drawback in approaching development from this 'neighbourhood' perspective is the problem of attempting to define community as a model which consists of some kind of 'harmonious entity', distinct, that is, from the diverse and occasionally irreconcilable classes which exist within it. It is not always appreciated by some that not all communities consist solely of working-class people. Such a model is based on a recognition of community action as essentially an 'educative' process in that it deals only with the human potential rather than the class differences of its members. Such a model also implies that everyone within the community has a similar potential and that class divisions are unimportant and subordinate. Therefore, the question prominent in such a community development 'approach' is one which is related to a commonality of identity, in which everyone is equal and in which everyone acts for the common good and in the common interest.

Any view which insists that such class unity is impossible within a community wouldn't fit very neatly into such models. Claiming that much of this is fallacy, and offering the experience of a community in Toronto as an example of the difficulties facing such action, Marjaleena Repo suggested that an all-class alliance in pursuit of community objectives is virtually impossible.[11] Can there be a reconciliation between diverse class, ethnic, race and gender interests in the search of a solution to a community problem? The experience of an early Irish example of community development, Muintir na Tire (People of the Countryside), founded in 1931, illustrated a positivist view of the community development model in which class was believed to be divisive and destructive. Muintir na Tire saw their experiences of community work, instead, as a model of how they felt the wider civil society should operate, and argued for 'the co-operation of the whole community rather than the collaboration of a single class. Muintir na Tire does not seek a classless society, but what it does aim at is a society that is class-barrier-less.'[12]

However ideal the Muintir na Tire experiment in developing a classless society was, there is little evidence for such a model existing successfully in more recent years. Tensions exist within most organisations, particularly those which attempt to articulate some form of inclusive approach to decision making. In discussing the nature of community power, Nelson Polsby claimed that 'the leaders of the community are much more likely to be middle class than lower class.'[13] This is of interest in the light of the earlier discussion on university institutions producing young, usually middle-class, enthusiastic development officers. As the sector becomes increasingly more professional in its approach to development work, there is no real evidence that a local leadership is being allowed to emerge organically either from within the community groups themselves, or indeed, from within the community as a whole. Many of the development officers tend to be university graduates, often coming from a middle-class background and because of the nature of their employment contracts many of them tend to move to where work may be available. A new generation of itinerant workers has begun to emerge. Have they got the potential to play a radical role as brokers for the building of a counter-hegemony using community work as an agent of change?

Community as a model of change?

If the above observation is true – in which development workers become transient beings – how can they possibly develop long-term strategies for change, if they have little loyalty to the community in which they work or if their training is directed only at the function of development rather than to the underlying need for change? How could such a generation of activists address social inequality if the source of such imbalance is the state? Just as Marx believed that the state was the principal instrument of political change, so also, it becomes the political arm of the ruling class. Social movements which challenge the right of the dominant class to sole authority become, in effect, protagonists within and against the state. There are some political apologists for the community movement who argue that it is one example of a social movement unconsciously seeking to breach class structures and therefore, objectively, challenging the class nature of the state. But does it have the potential of translating community action into a social movement which can impact on existing super-structures and initiate a real social, economic and cultural adjustment? Does it have the potential to create the basis for a counter-hegemony allowing its principal actors, its radical intellectuals, to assume leading roles in the process of change?

The terms 'community development' and 'community economic development' have become recent alternatives, not merely to describe the process of growth within and amongst communities, but also to describe the variety of activities of those engaged in neighbourhood work. The nature of the work can provide a valuable indication of the nature of the group itself although community development associations in the rural countryside might prove to be the exception. Such associations have long histories of involvement and often represent a broad spectrum of social class and commercial interests. However, within urban districts, it is generally accepted that such development takes place within those areas described as socially and economically marginalised, working-class communities. What is the difference? Most of its theorists suggest that community develop-ment is a fusion of two principal elements or disciplines. The first is positioned within the hierarchical geographical location of neigh-bourhood indicated by an urge or impulse for social change in which the initiative is taken by those who live within it, whilst the second is often located within the horizontal area of social, technological and economic change and driven to a large extent by commercial as well as social interests. Some, however, have attempted a more complex definition:

> Community development is a synthesis of the struggles by people to obtain their rights through community action and the partici-pation of people in a relationship with the institutions of government. Community development is also about change. Change takes place in society at all levels, across community, regional, national and international boundaries: and it takes place in society in different contexts. As a concept, community devel-opment is about social justice in communities which are, in most

respects, disadvantaged, where power and the ability to influence the exercise of power is, at best, only in attenuated form. At worst it is altogether absent. In Northern Ireland disadvantage, power-lessness and change exist in a complex context of political, socio-religious and inter-community hostility, distrust and opposition, as well as of intra-community solidarity and unity.[14]

The problem in securing an interpretation is that it is used so widely and amongst such a diverse range of interest groups that a common understanding, based on local experience is difficult to grasp. Perhaps its power is in the ability and the tendency to adjust and alter its appearance; a chameleon of rational and social progress: 'Community development is about the involvement of people in issues which affect their lives. It is a process based on the development of an equal partnership between all those involved to enable a sharing of skills, knowledge and experience.'[15]

From that definition it is clearly not necessarily about division and conflict which its advocates regard as negative and destructive. Supporters of the community development process of change make a number of assumptions which do not always stand up to close scrutiny. For example, the process involves a recognition that com-munities should be consulted and should participate in decision making. The process should have a comprehensive strategy by public authorities, to ensure that this widening of democracy permeates all parts of social and economic planning and service delivery. Citizen groups should have access to sympathetic professional assistance, technical advice and advocacy, facilities, money and resources in order to participate effectively. And, finally, this process requires a change in attitude amongst professionals to assist them to be far more sensitive to the needs, concerns and ideas of local people. Much of what is contained in those assumptions, whilst laudable, is not always based on reality. But because of the apparent potential of any community-based initiative the state has taken a much closer interest in these developments. For example, local government has appointed community development workers; the Department of Health and Social Services hold wide-ranging discussions on the role of community development as a strategic option for their social work programme, whilst other government agencies engage consultants on the merits of introducing community development strategies in decision-making processes. The state agencies may not have adopted all of the assumptions about the community development process, but they have certainly brought the phraseology within their sphere of influence.

Often community development is confused with social and community work which is essentially about building relationships and confidence on a one-to-one basis, although this can often form a significant part of the approach. There are three additional principles which are regarded as central:

> People have the ability to work and act together so that they can have an influence over the social, economic and political pressures which affect their lives. It, therefore, seeks to create organisations and structures which aim to give expression to those needs by arguing for a wider sharing of resources through participation and involvement. It is about the sharing and involvement of skills and knowledge in the initiatives which are needed to respond to the problems already outlined. It is about converting or translating those initiatives into forms of action which confront the attitudes of individuals or the decisions of agencies which do not take account of the social, economic and political pressures under which disadvantaged communities have to labour.[16]

Has a community development ideology emerged from all of this? Are its adherents supported by a philosophy which identifies their background, their world-view and their position in relation to other social and political forces? The main problem is that community development has been characterised by a lack of theoretical ideas and perspectives as well as attempts by its advocates to promote a process of social change which is bereft of a theoretical base. Loney made much of this in his work on the Community Development Projects in Britain.

Community development is loosely referred to as a term which describes a range of activities as diverse as local self-help, community care, cooperation and community action. An expert in rural development and a leading authority on the community development approach, TEAGASC member Patrick Commins, identified a number of 'variants which could be "recognised in practice" ':

- The 'unit of action' is a community, i.e., people sharing a common locality;
- The emphasis is on developing the capacity of the community itself to take action to deal with its problems;

- The impetus for community development is derived from within the community, not instigated from outside;
- Following the above, local initiative and leadership are developed as the community's basic resources;
- The community development action is based on the community's 'felt needs';
- The community supplements its internal resources by drawing on external supports in such a way that the major institutions are made more flexible to fit the particular circumstances of the community (in contrast to having the community fit its demands to the rules of external institutions);
- All sectors of the community are given an opportunity to participate in the development process;
- Special efforts may be necessary to assist certain groups to organise so that they are better able to participate at a wider community level;
- The process of decision-making is rational and democratic, regulated through local structures that give all sections of the community a voice in what is happening.[17]

Commins considered two specific areas or 'components' of the model as concrete 'development tasks', the building of resources, structures and skills, or as an 'educational process' in which the building of confidence and awareness go hand in hand. It is educational in that, as a consequence of the community development process, the members of the community are better equipped to address the community problem, either at a micro level – the individual and community level at the base, or at the macro – the institutional, national or structural level.

There are few of Commins' 'variants' with which one could have any fundamental disagreements, except the suggestion that community developers, in 'drawing on external resources' are able to avoid adjusting their demands to suit the rules of the external funding institutions. This is patently not the experience of many participants and is precisely the point to be made in considering the issue of the inclusion and promotion of some employment-generating programmes in community-based activity. Is this analysis of Commins the only rationale for the advocacy of a community development perspective?

The rationale stems from two main viewpoints. One is to recognise the existence and fact of the community as a tangible social entity and the second is to position it within the social structure as a tool for change. Implicit in such a view is the assumption that there is a need for change within the community as well as the need for development. Such a view stems directly from a position which identifies the community as containing within it elements which are under-resourced, under-educated, unskilled and lacking in power – in other words, the undeveloped, the underdeveloped, the socially excluded, deprived and marginalised. Such a situation is based, not just on the lack of resources but on the need to cultivate and reinforce already existing skills and initiatives and to use the strength of communal activity, solidarity and kinship to bring these 'resources' to the fore. Such resources are often identified as local initiative, skills, leadership and people. The mobilisation of such resources is reduced to becoming a mere stage in the process of community development.

Advocates of the community development approach to problem solving within communities look to the experience of the human impulse (a sudden or spontaneous tendency to act without reflection) amongst people which can be both selfish and anti-social adding to the perpetuation of the community problem, but which can also contribute, according to Commins, to 'the processes which point in the direction of solutions'. A variation on the dialectical process, these anomalies, it is said, lead to discourse and become the dynamic and the motor within communities for change. But whilst the new community activist would probably not agree with this conclusion, nevertheless, it must be recognised that in those circumstances, conflict, also, becomes a force for change, for progress and for development.

Can the community movement accommodate the notion that a 'change agent' can create a situation in which he/she can act, not merely as a facilitator for minimal changes, but as a local leader advancing the cause for structural 'political' changes? Implicit in such a development is the suggestion, rejected by Marjorie Mayo, that the community worker 'could or should take on the leadership of local working class politics'.[18] This issue is important because it highlights the role of the community worker, not only as a facilitator *of* change, but also as a radical advocate *for* change and for seeing the issue of solving local problems within a broader political and structural framework.

Contrast this against the more pragmatic (within a modern context) method of solving problems – the tendency to look to the state as the repository of all solutions – and we can immediately see the difficulties involved in motivating communities. The results can be frustration, alienation, subordination, dependency, indecision and disempowerment.

In spite of the lip-service it pays to community initiative, government is really not interested in creating a monster which might lead to its own downfall. The prospect of having another social movement creating alternatives to the state, with government goodwill, is simply not going to be permitted. Welfare rights groups are fine, in so far as they become buffers between government departments and populace. In that role, it could be argued, they act as 'fire-fighters' extinguishing one source of potential community dissatisfaction. Self-help becomes merely a misnomer in such a situation, synonymous not with economic or political initiative, but with increasing dependency on the state through the local agency – the community resource centre. The community worker, instead of advancing an alternative counter-hegemonic agenda in those circumstances, through appeals for participatory action, becomes instead, according to Smith, 'a means of buying off working-class protest, while reforms in the fields of welfare and income inequality have the effect of removing protest without altering the power structure'.[19]

According to the CDRG, community development offers an alternative method of addressing social problems, by allowing greater participation through local democratic structures and a sense of solidarity. It is supposed to be about returning power to the community, allowing participants to have a say in decisions which affect their lives and reducing the sense of alienation and isolation forced on them by increasing dependency on the institutions of the state. It is said to respond to the needs of the community, to base its own criteria on an approach which takes account of and rests its authority and credibility on consensus and manifesting itself on the 'community-based' grouping through what is often described as a 'bottom-up' approach. But there is little evidence for some of these grand claims. Many community groups are no more representative of their constituency than other local interests. Indeed, some community groups, through the management of government funding, have become mere extensions of some aspect of the state. In those circumstances they are hardly likely to create conditions in which they are forced to bite the hand that feeds them.

Community development has also been described as 'the active involvement of people in the issues which affect their lives', although many of its advocates tend now to avoid most of the manifestations of conflict, evade confrontation and refuse to become embroiled in controversy. Whereas the somewhat ambiguous definitions probably represent the mainstream view of the community development movement, they are after all no more than mere aspirations. However, interestingly, they also reflect local government policy which tends nevertheless to reduce community development to no more than a 'service which seeks to act as a bridge between the local authority and local communities'.

Broady and Hedley's list of 'interpretations' tends to confirm this view by suggesting an approach which does not see economic development as the only priority and, in spite of concessions towards 'democracy', minimises the role and potential of collective action. As described, this approach is essentially about service provision:

1. Community Development as liaison with Parish Councils
2. Community Development as the self management of buildings
3. Community Development as consultation and participation in service delivery
4. Community Development as co-opting voluntary organisations
5. Community Development as local welfare planning
6. Community Development as general support for the voluntary sector
7. Community Development as extending democracy
8. Community Development as direct support of neighbourhood groups.[20]

Of course there have been considerable adjustments to this view, especially since the development of the social partnerships initiative introduced as a result of European Commission intervention. But Broady and Hedley confirm the idea that local government asserts its right to a central role in promoting community development. In doing so, they tend to avoid a number of charges which suggest that extending democracy was, in reality, a euphemism for extending the services of local government into the neighbourhood with the help and support of the community group. That may not be such a bad thing, but in many ways it marks a serious difference between those who see neighbourhood as a constituent part of the broader community and those who argue that each community has a dynamic of its own, without reference to local government boundaries or electoral wards. It is perhaps also a reason why most local government community service departments are more concerned with the single-issue approach to community work rather than the integrated one favoured by most community associations. The last thing the local politician or civil servant would want is a localised political alternative community structure. In other words, community groups which want to feel free to engage in any activities which are seen as necessary, particularly those which are seen as strengthening the 'sense' of community, which enhance their understanding of the 'cultural' values and which provide substance and meaning to the notion of the significance of neighbourhood, could be viewed as potentially threatening. The community development approach in taking account of such understandings of community underlines the importance of 'neighbourliness' as an opportunity to escape from the grey uniformity of present-day living in a modern industrial society. It offers a distinct, if diverse, approach to living 'enriched by local cultures, values and traditions'. It is believed that such traditions and values can be reinforced through the educative processes of community development.

In defence of local resources

The differing attitudes of those who regard community development as a 'process' can be identified as those who see the educational opportunities arising from such development and those who argue that it is the changing 'attitudes' which are important rather than the tangible and material consequences of such a process. Changes in attitude become the criteria. Does it affect the individual or the group? Can the search and the struggle (process) for the material benefits of community development strengthen the solidarity of the group?

Community development as a programme, method, movement and philosophy provides us with a dilemma. It can be both 'process' and 'action'; educational goals – awareness, and concrete results – bricks and mortar. But is that how it is seen on the ground? Is the practitioner concerned with forms of community action which are only about conscientisation? Would it continue to survive in those circumstances and if so, would government continue to subsidise its activities, or must it contribute to the development of the superstructure? Further, is it regarded by government as now fundamentally necessary to the continuing health and well-being of civil society? Must it make the passage to community 'economic' development in order to survive, and if so, does this mark the turning point in the transition from community activism to community compliance?[21] Community development is often seen as representing two distinct and separate tendencies: radical action and education or training, leading to economic independence. The report of the ESF/Magee Community Economic Development Innovatory Training Project saw one as 'intrinsically related' to the other.[22]

The model of community development that looks to the need for action as a dynamic of the developmental process – 'learn through action', or, 'education through participation and involvement' – is often based on an understanding of the limitations of a consensual approach to working with communities. The question 'Why won't the whole community get involved?' is on the lips of every community activist. Implicit in such a question is a recognition that there are sections of communities which are organised more easily than others, seeing some sections or groupings within the community as 'allies' in struggle.

The growth and proliferation of the 'community resource centre' with its focus on 'community care', 'cooperatives' and 'welfare rights' is a response to the inadequacies of the condition of society. This present situation is seen as affecting only those on the economic edge and is often regarded as nothing more than a local response to the perceived needs of the overall community. Hence the series of networks which spring up based on a series of interest groups. But the community activist appears to have a more global view of the current situation now than he/she would have had twenty years ago. Community becomes a defence in the struggle to find solutions to the decline of local economies by responding to their economic needs and, arguably, acts as a defence against what is seen as the gradual erosion of the Welfare State. But there is also another dimension to their activity in which the community is also seen as the defender of local values and local culture. Increasingly the local activist who adopts traditional political tactics to publicise the problems affecting his/her own community is seen as taking part in a wider political activity. Networks of community activists across neighbourhood and geographical barriers are now a common feature of such work, although their political impact is minimal, representing a substantial number of activists, sometimes acting as a conduit for information to those engaged within community groups in the struggle for continuing financial support.

Paradoxically, it is at this meeting point – the relation between action as educator and education for economic development – that the lines separating the community developer and the community economic developer become a little confused. Does this dichotomy mask the difference, within a community development context, between those who argue for a radical agenda and those who seek to provide a balance between street and state in what they believe to be the best interests of the local community? So how do the community developers see the importance and significance of economic development in the context of their own work with their strong emphasis on educative and cultural values? Can they create a radical agenda?

Recent changes in the way in which institutions relate to 'community' provide strong indications that a shift in government and European Union policy has taken place.[23] A more confident community sector argues that an acceptance by government that the major problems cannot be solved at the centre implies that the burden of responsibility for economic development must, of necessity, shift on to the voluntary sector. This is seen as an argument for greater resources. Government, on the other hand, has been suggesting that such a shift is an indication of the need to move away from centralised control and to concentrate more resources within the local community providing opportunities for greater initiative.[24]

In many ways, of course, local economic development is determined by the range of, or lack of, resources which are available. Perhaps that is why greater emphasis is placed on economic development in a rural context, precisely because the prospects for the exploitation of natural resources are much higher. The question about what constitutes an urban 'resource' becomes slightly more problematic.

There is the common belief that the one advantage communities have which determines the nature of any economic development is that they are instinctively cooperative and promote self-help, a view which has become elevated to a position of doctrinal principle. The notion of self-help, incorporated and enshrined in the constitutions of community development organisations everywhere suggests that the collective determination of every community can make things work. Such values, it is often said, are indicative of the cultural strength of some communities. However, such a view is not shared by everyone. Dearlove was critical of the notion of self-help, suggesting that it emerges as a form of 'community socio-therapy' transforming 'activism into compliance' and reducing it to 'community disorganisation' and integrating 'marginal groups into the established order'.[25]

But these issues do raise some interesting questions about the connection between cultural values and economic development from a community perspective. Such descriptions of 'community' might be regarded as entirely inappropriate in that all of those negative peculiarities can be identified in each and every community development association. Described as the 'cultural obstacles approach to problems of development',[26] such observations tend to add new dimensions to the reasons why economic development in urban working-class ghettos has not been as successful as some might suggest. A report in 1988 identified six groups in Belfast as having created some economic enterprise, although only one, Glencairn Co-operative Enterprises continued to trade successfully.[27] Is that because of resistance from within, or is it purely the consequence of what is essentially a structural problem typical of the fate of small enterprises?

Community economic development or community enterprise has become increasingly popular as a means of local 'community' expression. The initiative in setting up the Local Enterprise Development Units and Enterprise Allowance Schemes, whilst not specifically designed to meet community needs, looks to community development projects as their principal clients. The more recent emergence of a rash of community cooperatives must be attributed, at least, to the fact that there is now some sort of financial backing for those interested in entrepreneurship as a means of addressing problems of their own unemployment. However, it is also seen by some as 'legitimising the claim that the unemployed are responsible for their own condition'.[28] These developments cannot be seen in isolation from the growing sense of despair which exists in almost every disadvantaged community. It is no coincidence that the growth of such initiatives has come at the same time as unemployment levels rise.

One of the difficulties in terms of the measurement of the success or failure of a community enterprise, of course, is that it cannot always be determined by the number of jobs created. The quality of the job is debatable and the relative increase in the circulation of money within the community is depressingly small compared to the effort and investment in terms of time, energy and enthusiasm. Successes, therefore, are best measured in other ways which, it could be argued, reflect the educative, rather than the economic, dimension. The problem, however, is that such educative experiences can degenerate into apathy and disillusionment as much with the process as with the outcomes.

So what is the state of the community development movement now? Is there a meeting of minds between those who advocate such development as a process of change which results in confrontation with the state or those who see the need to take the state on at its own game and on its own terms by building economic infrastructures using the community as the primary resource? There are those who feel this to be something of a wasted, if not a counter productive exercise: 'Small community enterprises may be free to establish any business they please, but they will have little impact on the overall development of the economy' and suggest further, that it is designed to 'manage the unemployed by taking relatively small numbers off the register'.[29]

However, the suggestion coming from sections of the trade union movement in particular, that some community economic development within a broader regional strategy is desirable, suggests that the view of local economic regeneration as some form of back-door 'Thatcherism' is now no longer as bitter a pill as it was when first proposed.

Finally, it would be worth noting some of the points raised by Gaffikin and Morrissey: when they outline some of the risks of 'reproducing many of the limitations of community development raising unrealistic expectations; indulging in generalised rhetoric; disavowing the need for rigorous evaluation; enabling government to shed its responsibilities for alleviating poverty and unemployment and offering small scale projects to counter large scale structural decline', this suggests that the 'educative' process has been singularly unsuccessful.[30]

For all of the arguments at the moment in favour of community enterprise, this one persists as disadvantaged communities attempt to breach the impenetrable wall of structural poverty. Perhaps it really is a problem of unrealised ambitions, fought out on the streets of community action, which creates the biggest barrier to working-class communities making the transition from community protest to community development through local enterprise.

But this question does raise certain questions about the nature of such development and the wider implications of the contrasting approaches. For example, if we are to contrast community development with community economic development by investigating the practice, it would first of all be necessary to look at the origins and underlying principles which determined its growth and popularity. The emphasis and direction of community development has changed in quite fundamental ways over the past twenty years from development as action for change, with the community worker acting as advocate on behalf of the poor by challenging institutions, to a more pragmatic approach based on the provision of services, liaison with agencies and the encouragement and stimulation of local economies through the development of local partnerships. Does this suggest a change in ideological direction? Much of this can be found in the contrasting approaches to community development in Britain and the United States, where the co-option of radicalism is at a much more advanced stage.

4
The Co-option of Radicalism

Concepts and controversies

The late 1960s and early 1970s were stimulating periods for those anxious to pursue a liberal agenda in community activity. This was the time of the Paris student uprising; of the emergence of a civil rights movement in Northern Ireland, the internationalisation of the anti-war movement and a realisation in the United States amongst establishment conservatives that there would be no turning back on the issue of the rights of black people. It was also the period in which much concern was expressed about the futility of a politics of the 'left' in which class provided the motor for change. Slogans announcing 'power to the people' replaced those of 'victory to the working class' at demonstrations across the country. It was a period in which the suppression of dissent became a norm for regimes as far apart, geographically if not ideologically, as Northern Ireland, Chile, West Germany and South Africa. It was also the beginning of the end for Stalinism. In France, crucial social adjustments were taking place with large numbers of workers leaving the countryside to take advantage of the increasing industrialisation of the large urban areas and, whilst it would be an exaggeration to suggest that France had lost its substantial peasant base, there is some evidence that the 'garden of Europe'[1] was also in the process of fundamental change.

Across Europe and the United States, profound social adjustments were taking place. In setting out to acknowledge the importance of these changes, this chapter explores one important aspect which forced the problem of poverty back to the top of governments' lists of priorities. In addition, it examines the varied responses to this problem particularly those tendencies within the labour movement in Britain which fought to undermine the arguments for a planned economy by adopting minimalist and futile community development strategies. The enthusiastic adoption by some on the 'left' for these new developments resulted in the gradual erosion of any attempt to build a serious opposition within Labour and the eventual co-option of their zeal for radical change.

In Britain, a struggle for control of the 'heart' of Labour was being waged in the corridors of Westminster between the pragmatic Home Secretary, Jim Callaghan, and the 'left' intellectual and Secretary of State for Social Services, Richard Crossman. The Labour government in the latter end of the 1960s was just as torn with personality and ideological clashes as the 'New' Labour administration of thirty years later. Arguments about the nature of the welfare state were just as prevalent, and as damaging, then as they are now.

Central to some of the debates in the labour movement was the argument put forward by G.D.H. Cole that whilst socialism *implied* a welfare state it was not in actual fact *the* welfare state.[2] This view was crucial in the arguments which have raged before and since. The notion of welfarism being at the heart of a socialist state became both a rallying cry for many of the Fabians in the Labour Party and at the same time a point of considerable disquiet amongst those who had been arguing for a socialist programme for decades. Anthony Wright in his article 'Tawneyism revisited: Equality, Welfare and Socialism', pointed out that 'socialism was stuck at the stage of welfarism and economic management, whereas the great task that lies ahead of us is that of passing beyond the Welfare State, in which people get given things, to the kind of society in which they find satisfaction in doing things for themselves and for one another.'[3] Any self-respecting community activist of the late nineties could not have put it better. Crossman was a little more precise: in *New Fabian Essays* he wrote that a system of 'welfare capitalism' was being created which emerged from a reworking of capitalism rather than from any tendency to seek an accommodation of socialism *and* capitalism.[4]

Much of the language of that period can still be found in the current literature of the community development movement. The notion that the 'process' implicit in the community development method, suggesting an innate satisfaction associated with 'doing things for others', is one which can be found in the constitutions of myriad community groups throughout the Western world. Indeed, one of the fundamental beliefs of the communitarian movement, particularly in the United States, is the overarching sentiment of a selfless approach to human development and human relationships. Interestingly, the doyen of the liberal 'left' in Britain and closet 'New' Labour supporter, Roy (now Lord) Jenkins enthusiastically endorsed the idea of welfare capitalism in the same volume of *New Fabian Essays* when he claimed that 'great numbers of people will consider welfare capitalism a comfortable and stable form of society and will be in no hurry to change it.'[5] Jenkins may well prove to be more of a prophet than even he had thought in 1952 when he penned those words. One is unlikely to see much light between the columns of 'New' Labour and the standard-bearers of the community movement in their respective visions of a new classless society, unless the view expressed by British Prime Minister Tony Blair that doctors, teachers and nurses are rewarded by what they do, as distinct from what they are, is evidence, perhaps, that communitarian ideas are seeping into the Labour political establishment.

Underpinning much of the debate on welfarism was the belief that new forms of democracy and accountability could be encouraged on the ground through the processes of community involvement and participation. One of the unstated objectives of those who initiated the community projects which emerged from the Committee on Juvenile Delinquency under President Kennedy and the Ford Foundation was the emergence of an enthusiasm for a form of pioneering social and economic improvement. Their view was that changes in social conditions to a large extent would depend in part on the range of reforms as well as on the levels of coordinated planning and, in particular, on a clear understanding of the needs of the recipients.

What was interesting was the decision to describe the programme as an experiment, first of all because it suggests an insight into the problems facing those who designed the programme, but also because it provides an interesting example of the problems facing the 'liberal' lobby in the United States at that time. Clearly, there were a number of problems emerging, not only from those traditional conservatives who argue against state intervention, particularly in the area of social reform, but also from those local politicians who identified any attempt to increase local accountability as a direct attack on their personal power base. Describing the projects as experiments enabled the promoters to justify their decision to spread resources selectively. Peter Marris suggested that there were a number of other reasons for the decision: 'who can object to finding out, or attack the endeavour before he knows the outcome? To call a reform an experiment postpones the hard questions of political interest while its principles have a chance to take root. Conversely, it allows government to entertain ideas of reform without commitment to them.'[6]

What is interesting about both responses to the resolving of social problems at the base is the fact that they emerge as initiatives by the state or its representatives. In so far as they represent a 'top-down' approach, each demonstrates a particular regard for the needs of their respective administrations rather than the needs of those for whom each is responsible. Whether the issue was one of differences in ideological approach, as it was in Britain, or the specific problem of a local political agenda, as it often was in the United States, the fundamental difficulty was a serious disregard for the real problem of a lack of accountability on the part of the state as well as an ongoing neglect of the obstacle of endemic and structural poverty which at root was seen as the result of unbridled capitalism. The axiom which turned the spotlight on the poor by making them responsible for their own poverty and therefore responsible for finding solutions to that poverty provided a godsend in the shape of 'self-help' and 'entrepreneurship' through the classless and inoffensive medium of community. Democratic development *through* the community became the guiding philosophy as community development became its standard.

The genesis of community development

What are the origins of community development? Where did it come from and what is its focus? It is difficult to provide a precise date or location for its origins especially if we were to apply one of the many definitions. Such definitions could easily apply to many of the social movements in the early to mid-nineteenth century, including the utopianism of Owen in Britain and the cooperativism of Plunkett in Ireland. In the twentieth century, its genesis could be located within the British Charitable Organisation which focused on the regulation of the charitable activities of the wealthy or the University Settlement movement which was interested in the general improvement of the poor through the promotion of role models and examples of good practice of self-help. In India, there is some evidence of rural reconstruction with a strong community dimension taking place at the beginning of the century with Mahatma Gandhi emphasising the centrality of the community or 'village' as a force for regeneration. The many developments in adult education, especially the Workers Educational Association, are also examples of early initiatives. In many ways, these early organisations are concerned not only with material advancement, but with the problem of establishing clear understandings and an acceptance of the rights and responsibilities of citizenship. Not unusually, therefore, Africa becomes the testing ground for a British concept of citizenship with its concentration on loyalty and responsibility becoming the determining criteria.

Community development originated in the notion, based to some extent on British colonial experience in Africa, that loyalty to the state, and a recognition of the significance and importance of 'citizenship', begin in the small social unit where day-to-day activity manifests itself in strengthening human relationships and developing common interests. Much of this was based on the widespread adult literacy programmes in operation at that time. This resulted in a recognition that the use of new ideas in adult literacy, coupled with developing work in government departments, would lead ultimately to discomfort at the use of the term 'mass education'. This was eventually replaced by the new term 'community development'.

It is difficult to pinpoint the precise origins of community development as we understand it today but as a term it was probably first mooted at the Cambridge Summer Conference of 1948. Much of the conference was taken up by reference to the problems of African administration. There was some concern from the delegates, mostly colonial civil servants, who balked at the term 'mass education', defining it instead as:

> ... a movement designed to promote better living for the whole community with the active participation and, if possible, on the initiative of the community, but if this is not forthcoming spontaneously, by the use of techniques for arousing and stimulating it in order to achieve its active and enthusiastic response to the movement.[7]

A booklet published by the British Colonial Office noted that as the participants did not unanimously agree on the use of the term 'mass education', they opted instead for the alternative term 'community development'. Others such as E.R. Chadwick described his activities in Nigeria during the Second World War as experiments in 'communal development'.[8]

In the areas of social policy, the members of the Seebohm Committee were strong advocates of the importance of the local government social services having a community work focus whilst the Gulbenkian Foundation were responsible for producing substantial and influential reports in the areas especially of community work training. Much of this precipitated a sea-change in thinking into the value of public participation in areas of public life. Both the Skeffington Report on planning and the Maud Commission on the reorganisation of local government began to move decisively in that direction. A *Community Development Bulletin* was produced by the Mass Education Clearing House after its inauguration in 1949. The training of officers in community development techniques was carried out and conferences in community development were organised in Malaysia in 1953 and in Ashbridge in 1954. Clearly the basis for a firm footing in this new model of social and economic improvement was being laid, with the bedrock of the welfare state providing a solid foundation in the struggle to eliminate poverty.

By contrast, in the United States, the view during the post-war Eisenhower period was that the sheer momentum of economic growth would, of itself, create the conditions for the steady erosion of poverty and inequality. There was a firm reluctance to go down the welfare state road taken by Britain's Labour Party, although the spread of mass public education and expanded welfare services combined to create an impression of a nation getting to grips with the more extreme incidents of poverty. However, as the post-war boom gradually settled into long periods of recovery and recession, the divide between those well-off citizens and those at the bottom of the heap grew wider.

It was the increase of concern with the growth of the social problem in the United States that resulted in the emergence of what became known as the 'Grey Area' Projects of the Ford Foundation and which probably marks its beginnings as a clearly identifiable formation. But it was in Britain that we see the more active use of the term 'community development' as a strategy for social change. Indeed it dawned in a British colonial context, first of all, in South Cameroon in 1948 as a consequence of the inadequacy of existing forms of education to meet the growing needs of the colony's native population. There were a number of reasons for this apparent interest in the needs of the colony's inhabitants. As the former colonial power, Britain was concerned to minimise any negative effects of a transfer of power to the local inhabitants. The inevitability of national independence on the part of the African and Asian nations resulted in a recognition of the need to ensure that any subsequent administration would be one which would be influenced by the Western democracies rather than by the Soviets. In order to achieve that, however, there was also a recognition that education in a newly emerging nation had to take account of much more than basic educational needs. Poverty was widespread, inter-tribal conflict was endemic with political factions basing themselves within the extended families and their respective tribal communities. It was felt that any successful programme had to move beyond the conventional school system by emphasising the importance of 'community' as a medium for social and economic change within a newly emerging nation: 'The concept of community development originated in the search for a program to compensate for the limitations of the conventional school system and to enable education to provide for the progressive evolution of the people.'[9]

A Colonial Office memorandum drew attention to the problems of the conventional school system by suggesting, initially, that the objective of education should be 'to promote the advancement of the community as a whole' and drew on a range of issues which hitherto had never been seen as the brief of the educational system by including in the curriculum 'the improvement of agriculture, the development of native industries, the improvement of health, the training of people in the management of their own affairs and the inculcation of the ideals of citizenship and service'.[10] Yet another, even earlier, British Colonial Paper of 1925 entitled 'Education Policy in British Tropical Africa', suggested that 'education should be adapted to the mentality, aptitudes, occupations and traditions of the various people concerned.'[11] All of these aims would be regarded nowadays as synonymous with the goals of most Western community development groups and associations. But equally, as education was increasingly seen as inseparable from this process of community development, conversely, community development was also identified as essentially an educational process.

It must be recognised that the British experience was based entirely on a pragmatic response to colonial needs in Africa principally because of the mounting difficulties in coping with deficiencies in the areas of health, welfare and education. After all, these were vital areas of concern, not only to the Colonial Office, but to those Africans able to look more critically at the state of their country, especially those in the vanguard of the new independence and national liberation movements. Perhaps it was with this in mind that shortly after the end of the Second World War, the Colonial Office had begun to recruit a number of specialists in community development with the general aim of a programme of development based on some form of community education. There was a tendency during this period to look away from more institutionalised forms of education and development to less formal models based around projects such as the creation of adult literacy projects. To a large extent, however, the entire programme was a little like closing the gate after the horse had bolted.

It is important to make a clear distinction between what we have so far described as community 'development', which can probably be traced back to the period already described as that influenced by the activities of the British Colonial Office in Africa, as distinct from community 'action', which has a much longer history and could include social protest movements on a range of issues from mass campaigns for civil rights to less vocal protests in support of the establishment of a crèche in a local neighbourhood. What makes each related to the other, in the first place, is the common denominator of community whilst in the second place there exists a general understanding of the extra-parliamentary nature of the work.

Whilst it could be argued that the bulldozer of African nationalism was unstoppable and that the clamour for independence was growing ever more loud, resulting inevitably in the gradual, often reluctant, colonial withdrawal by Belgium, France and the United Kingdom, the experiences gained through the Colonial Office experiment in far-off Cameroon were not entirely lost on those in government who looked a little anxiously over their shoulders at the growing threats from within their own inner cities.

There was a belief amongst some community workers that as the problem of poverty became more of a crisis for those on the receiving end, it became less of a problem for those in government. This became especially clear when it was stated by Anthony Crosland in 1956 that: 'we have now reached the point where further redistribution would make little difference to the standard of living of the masses; to make the rich less rich would not make the poor significantly less poor.'[12] This acknowledgement of the impotence or more accurately, reluctance, of the state to address the problem, to some extent established the pattern for subsequent Labour administrations and allowed succeeding Tory administrations to get off the hook of spiralling social security expenditures. Arguably it also lays the foundations for the arguments of Thatcher and her myopic vision of a self-contained Britain. Nine years later and the problem was brought back into focus after the publication of Abel-Smith and Townsend's work *The Poor and the Poorest* which made the startling claim that in 1960, a mere four years after Crosland's statement, the estimation of those living in or around the poverty line was seven-and-a-half million.[13] Yet another publication which undermined the case against welfarism was that produced by Titmus who argued that 'it was assumed too readily after 1948 that all the answers had been found to the problems of health, education, social welfare and housing, and that what was little more than an administrative tidying up of social security provisions represented a social revolution.'[14] The great problem in examining the case *for* welfarism in the context of an examination of community development is that many advocates see their projects acting as substitutes for the deficiencies of the welfare state.

How were those experiences gained in a British colonial context and the lessons learned from the United States to be applied to a British domestic setting? Described as the 'most ambitious action-research programme'[15] of its time, the Community Development Project originally conceived by Derek Morrell, an Under Secretary at the Children's Department of the Home Office, consisted of twelve local projects in different parts of Britain. Each had an action team of three members and an additional research team of approximately the same number. The action teams were responsible to their relevant local authority, whilst the research teams were hired by a local university or other third-level educational institution. The 'action' part of the project was 75 per cent financed by central government through a special Urban Aid Programme budget, announced by Harold Wilson in 1968, whilst the balance was borne by the relevant local government authority. The entire cost of research was carried by central government and paid to the university through the same Urban Aid Programme.

The projects were sponsored by a number of different government departments responsible for child care, welfare, housing and education. Administration for the project was the responsibility of the Community Programmes Department of the Home Office. It was designed to meet the need for assistance for projects in areas of social need and government was expected to respond to local CDP findings – all of which were to be monitored by inter-departmental committees of ministers and civil servants. The project's aims were summarised by Greve: to improve the quality of individual, family and community life in areas with high levels of social need ('multiple deprivation'), through programmes of social action related to local needs, resources and aspirations; to increase the range of social and economic opportunities available to people living in the community; to increase individual and communal capacity to create or take opportunities and to make effective and rewarding use of them, and to increase the capacity of the individual and the community to exercise self-determination of their own lives and control over the condition and use of the environment.[16] However, according to the authors of *Gilding the Ghetto*, there were also a number of assumptions on which the aims were based:

> Their brief rested on three important assumptions. Firstly that it was the 'deprived' themselves who were the cause of 'urban deprivation'. Secondly, the problem could best be solved by overcoming these people's apathy and promoting self help. Thirdly, locally-based research into the problems would serve to bring about changes in local and central government policy.[17]

The title *Gilding the Ghetto* comes from the minutes of a 1969 conference called by Harold Wilson to discuss US and UK poverty initiatives: 'Miss Cooper, chief inspector, children's department, Home Office, said: there appeared to be an element of looking for a new method of social control – what one might call an antivalue, rather than a value. "Gilding the ghetto" or buying time, was clearly a component in the planning of CDP and Model Cities.'[18]

Most of the projects were located in larger urban areas, although two, Cleater Moor in Cumberland and Glynncorwg in South Wales, were in much smaller communities. Most of the areas shared common characteristics: they were highly industrialised, with similarity of incomes, education and physical environment.

The CDP produced a large number of reports examining local problems, some more substantial publications under the auspices of the Centre for Environmental Studies of the Central Information and Intelligence Unit, and a series of final reports representing the evaluation of many of the projects' activities.

After the first year of operation the inter-departmental structure disintegrated. The creation of a consultative council in 1972 and in 1974 of a CDP workers' organisation resulted in a review being carried out by the management services division of the Civil Services Department. There was a growing concern at the Home Office that the project was beginning to move in a different direction from that originally intended. A more radical approach was being promoted. This first appeared in the Inter-Project Report in 1974: 'Analysis of the wider context of CDP areas has led us to recognise what many social scientists have been reasserting in recent years: that problems of multi-deprivation have to be re-defined and re-interpreted in terms of structural constraints rather than psychological motivations, external rather than internal factors.'[19]

One example, Coventry, was believed to be evolving through two distinct phases. The first identified what has been described as a dialogue model of social change which directed its activities to diagnosing solutions to local problems identified by members of the community. The second phase resulted in a move away from the local, neighbourhood, level by looking towards government 'as the source of problems and the locus for organisational and operational change'. Obviously, different approaches were gaining ground. Local project groups were beginning to assert a certain independent road to development and the identification of the source of social problems as well as the means of addressing such problems. Two perspectives appeared to be taking shape.

Some considered the need to exert some influence on the 'decision-making structures' of local government to be paramount, whilst others believed in the need to 'develop a radical critique directed at a wider audience'. Increasingly, the staff of the projects were beginning to look at the development of the CDP from entirely different standpoints. Thorny questions on what was described as the 'deodorising and confusing concepts of community' were raised once again. Community, it was said, was being substituted for issues which should have been driven by considerations of class. Arguments raged from whether the problem of poverty stemmed from the locality or neighbourhood itself, rather than that urban inequality was the result of a much wider problem which was 'rooted in a global market system'. For some the solidarity implicit in the community was simply not enough: 'Groups representing a number of local projects began the process of working towards publications on unemployment and council housing directed at working-class audiences and informed by an increasingly socialist perspective.'[20]

The new radical initiative being taken by the local project groups marked a distancing from the interpretation of local development by central government. There were other changes taking place. Responsibility moved from the Home Office to the Department of the Environment whilst the change from the small innovatory project to the larger 'partnership' and institutionalised programme was located in a number of selected local authorities. Clearly government was unhappy at the developments taking place on the ground.

Why was there a need by government to change its emphasis from the 'small' neighbourhood-based project to a larger 'institutional-centred' approach? Did this escalation of community work projects result in a correspondent need for employment in the community development sector? Observers such as Waddington argued that there were two forces at work: the first was that there was an increasing urgency to deal with the pressures of poverty from people below in the shape of an increase in self-help groups as well as the emergence of a proliferation of 'urban-protest' movements. The second was that demands from the institutions for change resulted in a growing recognition that in order that they might operate on a national scale more effectively, there was a need to adopt new structures and create new alliances with communities – described by Bryant as 'social planning and service development'.[21]

Letting the poor manage their own poverty

A less cynical observer might suggest that in the circumstances it would not be difficult to recognise that the state sees the promotion of the community development approach as one way of releasing the pressures on the civil service to deal with other issues. 'Let the poor manage their own poverty' is one way of phrasing what Gaffikin and Morrissey described as 'privatising poverty'.[22]

What were outlined as 'innovative' experiments to deal with residual deprivation in the marginalised and peripheral regions of Britain and Northern Ireland were to have a lasting effect on the future of community development for decades to come. The Community Development Projects are still regarded by some with enthusiasm, and by others with horror and loathing. The Community Worker Research Project in Northern Ireland, and its predecessor, the Community Relations Commission, are still remembered with considerable suspicion and scepticism several decades after their work. The principal common factor in the separate initiatives outlined is the dominant role of the state, first of all, in initiating the projects from above and secondly in attempting to influence their subsequent development. All of those who were actively engaged in those initiatives enthusiastically adopted what they all described as a 'community development approach' to the specific social problems identified as their reason for being involved. However, almost all of the projects collapsed in an atmosphere of distrust and disillusionment. The CDP report was to claim that 'the state's fight against urban deprivation has been exposed like the "emperor's new clothes" as empty rhetoric.'[23]

The problem, explained the authors of this report, was that the 'basic dilemma' remained the same: 'how best to respond to the needs of capitalism on the one hand and maintain the consent of the working class on the other'. Little has changed. It is often said that these are dilemmas faced by community development workers in most areas in which the twin problems of apathy and social deprivation are being confronted by those with too few resources. However, the problem is that few of them ever really confront these surface dilemmas and rarely face the more fundamental issue of state control, much less question the nature of the dominant hegemony.

Are there any similarities between those issues discussed above? What conclusions could we come to about the nature of community development in what could be described as two entirely different social, economic and political settings? The two areas in which the separate projects were located in Britain and Northern Ireland were different in two material aspects: their economic condition and political autonomy. Northern Ireland was heavily dependent on the British subvention and after 1969 was becoming increasingly unstable because of the gathering political conflict. Britain during the Harold Wilson era was faced not only with a number of serious economic and political problems, but also the fact that the Labour administration was substantially compromised because of its coalition with the Liberals. Government was moving towards what were described as 'quasi-corporatist methods of economic intervention' by arguing for greater and closer involvement in government by the trade unions as a means of introducing an incomes policy. Martin Loney cautioned; 'what concerns us here is the possibility of the Government attempting to find new ways of strengthening the bonds which held society together into the field of urban policy.'[24] There were clear hints of a government project aimed at a strengthening of the existing hegemony. It was also a period in which the 'new left' had emerged as a decisive force in European politics, arguing for new methods and new strategies of confrontation with central government.

The initiatives, taken by the British Labour governments under Wilson in 1968 and Callaghan, in the Northern Ireland Office in

1978, must be seen against a background of considerable social, political and economic turmoil in addition to the growing problem of racial discrimination and ethnic frustration resulting in riots raging in Britain's cities. There were clear reasons why government should decide to establish these experiments in social policy. The projects in Britain and Northern Ireland had some obvious similarities.

Twelve community development projects were located in Britain and after a period of ten years, fourteen were established in Northern Ireland. Both programmes had an element of research written into their proposals. They were to address the problems of social need by improving the quality of life and increasing social and economic opportunities. Almost all were located in urban areas which shared common characteristics such as level of income, education opportunities (or the lack of them), but with some exceptions, such as Glynncorwg in South Wales and Omagh and Crossmaglen in Northern Ireland, which focused also on physical environment. There were a number of other similarities as well. Community workers and researchers on the ground in Britain were having to come to terms with the philosophical and ideological constraints of locating their practice within what could be described as a piecemeal and a reformist tradition.

But, in so far as there were some obvious advantages and similarities between the two projects, there were also some obvious dissimilarities. The nature of the two economies, the dependence of one on the other, made the effects of the economic crisis seem much worse in Northern Ireland, where unemployment in some nationalist areas was worse than anywhere else in western Europe. The response in the north was minimal in comparison with the efforts in Britain.

Attempts to cater for a larger number of projects in Northern Ireland really couldn't be compared with the more widespread and concentrated effort put into the earlier experiment in Britain. Whereas an equivalent British project had no less than three action team members and an additional three researchers, similar groups in Northern Ireland had only one. Of course, we are dealing with markedly different areas and with different sizes of populations. In Britain the community development projects were designed to act more as facilitators of existing or new community initiatives, whereas in the six Northern Ireland counties the project workers – acting both as animateurs and researchers – were attached to those existing projects which had successfully applied for assistance.

Community relations and co-option

Whilst the question of race relations had a substantial influence on the development of the CDP in Britain, it didn't have a major impact in Northern Ireland, which had its own peculiar condition of sectarian discrimination, mainly against Catholics, to contend with. In Northern Ireland the question of community relations was fundamental to the Community Work programme and crucial to its future development. Paradoxically, the disbanding of the old Community Relations Commission under Maurice Hayes provides some limited evidence of this.[25] It was felt that the attempt to create an independent agency which would have to deal with an institutionalised problem such as sectarianism – because it was separate from government – would fail. The only way that such a problem could properly be addressed, they believed, was when there was a closer liaison, leading to a permanent and concrete bridge between community and executive. After all, this was a society in which the only apparent unifying factor was a begrudging acknowledgement of the state's functions and responsibilities for both communities in the field of social welfare.

It seemed as if the state project was an unashamed if extremely limited attempt to establish the civil society in all of its forms, manifestations and structures. But to complete such a project successfully they would have to, in the first instance, establish the nature of the ideological hegemony in the particular and separate political contexts of Northern Ireland, on the one hand, in addition to its political parent, Britain, on the other. The question was, which one was to come first. Presumably that which was most dominant in their minds, that which was most dangerous: the Irish question.

Clearly the separate approaches manifested in two distinct perspectives were informed by divergent views of the state and its relationship with local working-class communities. The twelve projects in Britain rejected establishment explanations of social and economic marginalisation and declared for a more radical critique of the reasons for the impoverishment of local communities. For those in Britain attempting to develop alternative forms of opposition to state intervention, class continued to emerge as the principal dynamic for change, whereas in Ireland 'community' continued to mature, in part because of the lack of a traditional working-class base, as the only viable social structure with anything like a sense of the communion necessary for any form of combined social or political action. To a large extent this *a priori* determining of the battlefield decided the nature and the extent of the conflict.

In Britain, much of that opposition was filtered through existing political organisations such as the Labour Party whereas in France it was the Communist Party and trade unions. However, in Northern Ireland, political opposition would find expression in either the Republican Movement or the now expired Nationalist Party and its successor the Social Democratic Labour Party (SDLP). The Unionist Party was not regarded as a sufficiently sympathetic political grouping within which civil liberties could be raised. Indeed, its record has been a dismal history of antagonism to anything which addressed issues of poverty and discrimination especially if they were raised within the minority community. With the obvious exception of Northern Ireland, and because of the peculiar political conditions which existed there, all of the other activists in the British Community Development Projects found that either their energies dissipated under the weight of the dominant political groupings, or that those attempting to develop an alternative method of protest found themselves swamped in the overwhelming weight of public and media opposition to extra-parliamentary activities.

Just as with the Home Office experiments in the late 1960s, similar attempts to probe the issues of poverty and exclusion in the United States were made during the Kennedy and Johnson eras. There had been a long tradition of community involvement in issues in both rural and urban protest movements. Indeed the community dimension of the mass popular movements was central in the United States from the period immediately after the end of the Civil War and the rapid spread of industrialisation. With the exception of those on the left or liberal wings of the Democratic Party, there were few national structures through which the anti-war movement, civil rights and anti-poverty movements could channel their activities. Unlike Britain, the US labour unions did not have an equivalent TUC and were more prone to periods of conservatism, especially where foreign policy was concerned.

The economic problems emerging from the American Civil War period, particularly in the countryside, generated a range of difficulties for farmers dependent on bank loans and overdrafts. Much of this resulted in farmers either being forced off their lands or becoming chained to the dictates of the money-lender. As a response to these problems farmers set about establishing a number of self-help organisations, with one of the most prominent at that time being the National Grange.[26] Although this new experiment in cooperation was an interesting example of self-help, its influence waned because of the innate fiscal conservatism of its members and it became marginalised to the status of a social network and educational association acting for the benefit of the more affluent farmers. But there were earlier developments and other experiments in the United States. The influences of European utopianism and religious radicalism emerged in the shape of a variety of organisations such as Oneida which was established in New York in 1848 by a group describing themselves as 'communists' or 'perfectionists' and later, under the influence of Dorothy Day, the Catholic Worker Movement.

In those early developments of the nineteenth century, much of the protest was confined to agrarian issues related to farm production and land ownership. The organisation and eventual social stratification of the large urban areas only really emerged as a feature of the end of the last century. But the gradual confinement of larger numbers of urban residents, partly accelerated by the massive increases of European and Asian immigrants as well as a movement of the rural population into the cities, resulted in the now familiar problems of overcrowding, insanitary living conditions and economic exploitation. For many leaving even worse conditions in their native homelands, especially in Europe, the United States offered fresh opportunities and heightened expectations. But for those who joined the exodus from the countryside in the hope of finding greater security within the new industrial conurbations, there was much to protest about. For those used to building their own homes and living on their own land, they now had to cope with slum conditions, often having to pay a rent to landlords they rarely saw. Similarly, with those who grew their own crops and produced their own food from the land, they too had to deal with a new situation of having to pay for it. For most, the only marketable resource they possessed was their ability to sell their willingness to work and the time to spend working for others. And yet, in the anonymity of the urban slum, there existed the basis for a community solidarity located mostly in the ethnic groupings which did not exist to the same extent in the American rural landscape and which clearly could not have existed amongst the disparate and confused migrant masses pouring in through Ellis Island.

What is especially interesting is the nature of some of the responses to these social problems. In their interesting work on the social protest movement in the United States, *This Mighty Dream*, Madeleine

Adamson and Seth Borgos suggest that whilst there were clear demarcations of interest on the part of both the labour and neighbourhood protest movements, there were points during which the distinctions were barely discernible. They record one incident in which the labour movement became involved in the housing issue by demanding that the mayor and governor halt evictions of the unemployed for non-payment of rent. According to AFL President Samuel Gompers, this action served as a model for the New York labour movement, 'followed in practically every succeeding crisis'.[27]

There is much evidence of widespread support for these kind of actions, with organised boycotts of high-priced foods becoming a feature of the struggle of those living in poverty attempting to redress the imbalance. Adamson and Borgos record the extent of the protests as, on one occasion, a boycott being supported by '150,000 families on the East Side' and, in the case of the Lower East Side, rent strikes attracting some 13,000 supporters. Whilst many of the leaders of these protests were working-class women, much of the responsibility for them was ceded to activists from within the fledgling revolutionary movement such as the Socialist Party.

Of course there were other developments taking place. Whilst much of the leadership for the protest movement against living conditions came from within a combination of trade unions, revolutionary groupings and residents of the affected neighbourhoods, there was also the attempt to introduce a form of welfarism through the inauguration of what became known as the 'settlement houses' in the slum areas of Chicago and New York. In some ways, the settlement houses were the forerunners of the resource centre of today, engaging in the provision of elementary adult education, providing play areas for children from poor families and offering basic health care. Many of them were staffed by middle-class women who were themselves interested in community improvement schemes as well as political reform and to some extent represented a much more genteel response to the problems of the day. Unlike the more militant activities of their counterparts in the 'labor unions', the settlement house supporters were more interested in manipulating the press and organising the political lobby. They were responsible for some basic reforms which incurred the contempt of those on the revolutionary left who accused them of treating the symptoms rather than dealing with the root causes of the social and economic inequality. But whatever the reason for their interest in such problems, Adamson and Borgos suggest that these 'genteel reformers shaped the development of community organising in two important ways: by legitimising a new set of public issues, centred in the neighbourhoods and at City Hall, and by defining a new vocation known as "social work", which took the improvement of urban slums as its charge.'[28] Their pioneering work had a lasting effect on community work for many years to come. Indeed, unconsciously they almost certainly laid the base for what we now understand by urban-based neighbourhood organising or community work and probably provided the watershed which formed the core of ideas on which Saul Alinsky based his seminal studies *Reveille for Radicals* and *Rules for Radicals*.[29]

Of course, hidden within the course of these interesting historical experiments in reform and welfarism are the philosophical questions of morality and conscience. Whether the organisers of the settlement houses were well-meaning radicals or middle-class reformers is neither here nor there. The principal question is what motivated them and what was their ultimate intention? Were they interested in engaging with the problem of inequality, exploitation and poverty from the point of view of addressing such problems because they were inherently immoral or were they interested in addressing the structural causes of such problems? These issues throw up some interesting comparisons with the dilemmas faced by the activists of the Community Development Projects in Britain and the community workers' projects in Northern Ireland in the early 1970s. They are especially interesting because the latter two found their source of inspiration in the experience of community-focused activity in the United States, particularly in the struggle against poverty of the Kennedy and Johnson period.

The view of those in the Eisenhower administration – that the strength of the economy would, of itself, create the conditions for the eradication of poverty and a gradual reduction in the gap between rich and poor – would have been sorely tested in a United States suffering from the ravages of a fluctuating economy and the growing disenchantment of a black population weaned on discrimination, marginalisation and racism. Peter Marris and Martin Rein drew attention to the massive flight of blacks from the South to the more affluent areas in the North and West.[30] According to them almost one-and-a-half million fled between the years 1950 and 1960. This movement resulted in the replacement of the white population of the inner cities with an overwhelmingly black population. The inevitable cycle of poverty became the most dominant feature of their landscape. Poor education and a lack of skills contributed to the lowering of expectations as the black population struggled to find and keep the most menial of jobs. Education within those areas suffered as the black student body became more frustrated and more distanced from the, mainly, white teaching staff. By contrast, the white population, now comfortably secure in the suburbs of the major cities, came to represent and highlight the worst manifestations of the increasingly separate existence of the two communities. Growing frustration amongst the black community with their sense of inadequacy and failure only served to emphasise what they believed to be the inherent racism in US society.

Although there were a number of projects which attempted to address some of the manifestations of black frustration under President Kennedy, it is only really when the specific problem of poverty came to be considered as a matter of national social policy under Lyndon Johnson that we begin to see a more coordinated and focused response from the state.

There had been a sustained attempt through the Housing Act of 1949 to get to grips with one obvious source of racial inequality. But the view that the expanding economy could also sustain growth and have a positive effect on the imbalance of wealth persisted well into the early 1950s. The suggestion that a slum population relocated into better housing would begin a process of social adjustment, even of reconciliation, was probably a little optimistic. Some of this was based on the notion that a renewed inner city, free of the ghettos of the past, would allow for a process of revitalisation in which the local economy would be given free rein to encourage enterprise with a subsequent rise in taxation revenue used to offer and support services for those in need. Of course it was a pipe dream. The movement of relocated slum dwellers amounted to little more than an occasional shift to similar ghettos on the other side of the block. Getting away from the dreariness of discomfort and unemployment was going to be much more difficult than that. It was down to the Ford Foundation to provide the most immediate response in the shape of what became known as the 'Grey Area Projects'.

The principal issue confronting the Grey Area Projects, as with the later Kennedy and Johnson anti-poverty programmes, was that the impetus for the initiatives came not from those most in need of them, but mostly from a range of key personnel in the federal administration. There was little real grass-roots participation in the process of development in the United States, or indeed in Britain during these early days of community-focused experimentation, in spite of the exhortations of theorists such as the Biddle brothers.[31] The contexts for these developments were being laid out by the sociological research and subsequent pessimism of Harrington in the United States and a little earlier by Titmus in Britain. On the other hand, there were others such as Daniel Moynihan who claimed that the search for solutions was almost at an end when he announced that 'we may now turn to issues more demanding of human ingenuity than that of how to put an end to poverty in the richest nation in the world.'[32]

Was the problem of poverty one which could be addressed at the level of the individual or could it only be addressed at the level of the structures? These were dilemmas faced by many involved in the poverty and community development 'industry'. There was a clear and unmistakable reluctance or refusal to consider more fundamental solutions which addressed the problem of poverty as one over which the structure has an influence. In the United States, Michael Harrington described the extent of the problem as being 'somewhere between 40 million and 50 million citizens of this land. They were poor. They still are.'[33]

The notion that community development offered its exponents and practitioners an alternative tool which would address the problems of social and economic marginalisation is seen most clearly in the contradictions which emerged as a consequence of the conflict within those programmes established from the 'top-down' initiatives of the separate Harold Wilson and Kennedy/Johnson administrations. The difficulties emerge, not just in the belief that such programmes can actually and constructively address the problems described above, but in the contrasting philosophies of those who see 'community' as intrinsically more positive than the potentially divisive social structure of 'class' as a vehicle for social change. The problem, therefore, of community development in which social marginalisation was addressed, without reference to the class basis of such deprivation, created an insurmountable barrier to those who argued for a community development strategy as a means of addressing those social inadequacies.

The notional view of community development as having the potential to straddle all sections of society and international boundaries is presented as an argument in favour of it being used as a strategy for change. The numerous definitions emphasising the involvement of people in a partnership of cooperation are underpinned not only by the recognition of 'community' as its ideological 'touchstone', but in reality also by the supervision of the state. As such the implied centrality of community is both symptomatic of a rejection of class as a vehicle for change, as well as an attempt by its some of its advocates to strike new colours against the frustration of past failures.

In the British experience, the creation of the Community Development Projects, as well as those of the United States initiative, the Grey Area and Poverty programmes, was marked by a conflict which developed out of the apparent polemical dichotomy of community and class. The emergence of a structuralist critique of community development frustrated those with a minimalist approach who regarded such debates as political navel-gazing. All of this, coupled with an almost traditional suspicion of government intentions and those university institutions engaged in supervising the progress on the ground, resulted in widespread disillusionment. Debates such as those already described, inevitably degenerated into futile arguments between those who saw community development as a process involving the participation of communities of people and those who saw process without tangible results – the product – as time-wasting and irrelevant.

The arguments about the nature of community development in the 1960s and early 1970s were not without their significance in terms of the debates which also raged about the nature of the state, dismissed by one frustrated Labour Party observer as 'all the blather of a few radical poseurs', but which highlighted the debate, not only over the ideological basis of community development, but over the role of the community development worker, either as an agent working with the state, or as a revolutionary working against it.[34]

There was a belief that the civil society which existed in Britain and the United States at that time and already under severe pressure from social and ethnic conflicts, was gradually eroding the hegemony enjoyed by their respective ruling classes. Some within the community development movement clearly saw an opportunity to intervene in that process. Many within the British Community Development Projects saw such an erosion as offering a supreme opportunity to advance an entirely different agenda based on the presentation of an alternative project. But, in spite of their good intentions, they were unable to bring such a project to fruition.

Interestingly, Lewis Corina, the research director of one of the more moderate projects based in Oldham, wrote of one of those projects regarded as more radical: 'It is interesting to note that the final report of the Hillfields Project highlights structural factors but then proposes measures similar to those to which Oldham CDP has given attention.'[35]

Ironically, the report highlighted the futility of both approaches to community development as a means of drawing the 'community' and the existing ideological hegemony together as a means of addressing social and economic marginalisation. Furthermore, it illustrated the considerable degree of naïveté which existed amongst those at that time who argued for community development as having the potential for the creation of a new counter-hegemonic project. At the end of the day, the proof of the pudding is in the eating: a decade and a half after the initiation of the CDPs the conditions they attempted to resolve are qualitatively worse. Poverty has not been eradicated either in the United States or in Britain and certainly not in Northern Ireland. Nor has a counter-hegemonic project developed to any substantial degree, except in Northern Ireland where at least amongst the nationalist community, the opposition to unionism, frustration with endemic unemployment and the political and military involvement of the British state, resulted in an explosion of self-help groups, a massive swing of support for Sinn Fein and a gradual undermining of the localised unionist hegemony. But it was no thanks to the leaders of the maturing and burgeoning community development movement.

5
Community, Catholicism and Communitarianism

The influence of the Catholic ethic and the struggle against social conservatism

The older generation can still recall the Victorian era in which cities were growing, bustling and proud places. The Empire was expanding and most people, even the poorest, were confident and purposeful – their doorsteps were polished, and extended families and good neighbours looked after the children, and gave them love and a secure start in life. Great entrepreneurs and politicians from Matthew Boulton to Joseph Chamberlain developed a burning sense of civic pride. They harnessed steam, built sewers, schools and town halls. They shaped events. These were inspiring days of individual progress, enterprise and collective care.[1]

The communitarian influence

At the opening of a conference in Birmingham in November 1994 to discuss the problems of the breakdown in community and the imagined weaknesses of modern-day family life, Dick Atkinson, regarded now as the leading British communitarian advocate, painted the optimistic and light-hearted picture above of Victorian Britain which was a gross distortion of the reality of life in that period. This isn't the stuff of sound social comment: it is nothing more or less than an abstraction based on a distorted and disingenuous nostalgia for a society which never really existed. But it is an important statement because it fulfils the need of so many of those of a conservative disposition who ache for a *volkisch* society free from the complicated influences of modernisation and based on vague notions of a simpler and more ordered civil society in which every individual knew their place within the community hierarchy.

In drawing together the principal ideas associated with community, Catholicism and communitarianism, this chapter sets out to probe some of the common characteristics which advocates tend, perhaps conveniently, to neglect. However, it is important to fully understand the nature of the moral imperative implicit in the notion of community, not merely to expose those who confirm its introspective and philosophical symbolism, but to confirm its more explicit political and social significance. So whilst the correlation between community and communitarianism is almost immediately obvious, the underlying principle of subsidiarity and its origin within Catholic social teaching is not always fully recognised.

What is especially interesting, quite apart from the remarks of the participants at the Birmingham conference, is the range of political influences of those who attended this meeting. For some, it must have been merely the climax of years of struggle to open up the communitarian debate, whilst for others, such as Labour MP Frank Field and the Liberal Democrat leader, Paddy Ashdown, it must have seemed like a breath of fresh air in what they undoubtedly believed was a period of political confusion. After all, Field was forced to resign his ministerial position without being offered the senior post left vacant by an even more confused Harriet Harman, whilst the muddled attempt to abandon old Labour, with its emphasis on a working-class constituency, merely confirmed for him the need for a new Labour project to build a fresh ideological constituency which would breach the hoary old class barricades. Riding high as one of the modern intellectual 'right' in the Labour Party at a time when it hadn't quite made up its mind about whether it was still old labour or whether it had been reborn as new labour, Field lamented the decline of western Christian society in which the consequences have resulted in a shattering of the 'moral order'. Citing academic Edmund Leech, he said: 'If the general rules which define right and wrong, clean and unclean, cease to have a universal operation in the community, then the community feels itself under threat.' Field went on to say that 'we now know you cannot, over a long period of time, have an agreement for a moral framework unless there is some acceptance of that dogmatic faith underlying it.'[2] There is nothing specially unique about such statements as they probably represent the view of most of those sitting on the benches of the House of Commons. But what is important is the fact that they also represent a growing tendency amongst many who subscribe to the centrality of the community and the family to the stability of their 'civil society'.

But is this true? Is the moral framework of civil society about to collapse because of the expansion of civil rights? Not so, according to Rodgers: 'In the 20th century, the growth of the welfare state and the wide range of professionals charged with the responsibility of attending to social and health problems in society has given rise to a greater sense that social and moral behaviour is subject to surveillance.'[3] The fact that our lives are becoming increasingly dominated by a complex network of functionaries and apparatchiks is now a major factor in our lives. Rights are being dramatically eroded whilst even the individual right to decide on an appropriate level of responsibility is being taken away. This is a crucial issue, but not the only one. How has this come about?

There is little which marks a clear division between those who argue for a community development approach to the need for social change and those who see it from what is called a communitarian perspective. It is really a question of scale. For example, in tune with many community development efforts in the United States and elsewhere, communitarians view the rebuilding of community as a process of social organisation involving self-help, cooperation, institutional integration and consensus-building. They argue for an end to the dependency culture and the promotion of individual initiative. Advocates of a more community-action model argue that communitarian conceptions of community building, in so far as they rule out the political articulation of rights-based demands, provide a weak theoretical foundation for community development. This chapter sets out to take issue with this viewpoint, arguing instead that both the community-action and community-development models are little different from their communitarian cousins in that their understanding of the centrality of community as a social construct, *a priori*, excludes any prospect of real and lasting social change. But where the ideas behind the communitarian movement make a significant contribution to the dearth of theoretical work in this field is in the attempt by American sociologist Amitai Etzioni and his colleagues to develop a concept of social change which does not set out to include class as a principal dynamic.[4]

In response to what the conservative right of US politics sees as the gradual invasion of liberal theory and practice, communitarianism emerged as a new rationale drawing together the ideas of individual rights and social responsibilities. The suggestion that as individuals we exist as autonomous beings is dismissed by the communitarians as a nonsense; we cannot exist in isolation and separate from the wider influences, values and culture of our communities.

The development of a culture of 'rights' associated with liberalism and those on the left became one which, the communitarians believed, instead of strengthening, sought to undermine the foundations of the democracy. Indeed, in spite of the attempt through the promotion of subsidiarity to create the foundations for a new philosophy, communitarianism has, instead, become the basis for a general critique of liberalism and an onslaught on what they describe as the 'rights' agenda of the left. The 'critique' has been reduced in Britain and the United States to one accompanied by complaints about the need for serious reforms in the welfare state which would inevitably result in opposition, for example, to payments for single parents and so on.

The central pivot of community is essential, in their understanding of the structure of human society, as a means of avoiding the problems associated with 'special interests' and the ongoing political struggle for power. In such a struggle, the 'negative discourse' on 'rights' tends to overshadow what the communitarian would describe as 'real' political discourse in which the business of compromise, of give and take, would be a principal casualty. Indeed, in pursuit of their claim that individual responsibility is one of the causes of the failure to reach compromise in the political world, they have argued for a 'moratorium on the manufacture of new rights'.

In response to what conservatives on the right of US politics saw as the gradual invasion of liberal theory and practice, communitarianism emerged as a new rationalisation of conservatism at a time when it appeared to be on the defensive, if not in actual retreat. The 1997 general election saw the most important defeat, in Britain, for political Conservatism since the Attlee government of 1946, even though its more seemingly innocuous manifestations continued to be represented in the social policies of the New Labour administration.

Writing of communitarianism, *The Economist* in March 1985 claimed that 'Mr Etzioni and his disciples are not content to preach good citizenship, to be ministers in a secular communitarian church.

They are driven to merge their church with the state, and so shape public policy.'[5] At this point communitarianism divides sharply into two schools: one led by Mr Etzioni that is regarded by some academics as relatively harmless because it gives an appearance of being almost barren of real content; and the other with 'authoritarian leanings that has plenty of content, but is a real danger to civil liberty'.[6] The latter element suffers from the very real pitfall of having attracted to its banner some of the strange examples of religious conservatism peculiar to the United States.

In 1996, the Reverend Samuel Trumbone of the Unitarian Universalist Fellowship of Charlotte County addressed his diocese on the subject of communitarianism and the dangers associated with the promotion of progressive ideas:

> Some progressive thinkers believe our community is being harmed by all of these new rights and freedoms. We have moved from a national value consensus held at the end of World War II by most Americans to a time of value crisis and reformation. We have moved away from a more patriotic culture where police and government officials were trusted to a suspicion and lack of respect for authority. The decline of participation in organised religion has often replaced traditional community centred religious values with self centred acquisitive ones. The values at the top controlling corporate board rooms more often than not are unbridled self-interest and greed rather than harmonising profits with the public good. The glow of pulling together for the good of all which helped us win the great war and keep the Communist menace at bay has gradually dissolved as each pursues his or her own interests and concerns.[7]

But whilst the authoritarian wing of communitarianism contains all of the oblique reference points to the bad old McCarthyite days of the Cold War about the 'communist menace', it is not the most dangerous. Communitarianism provides the ideological bedrock for a quite dangerous mixture of authoritarian politics, religious fundamentalism and sociological tendentiousness. But there is more to these views than a simplified and apparently uncomplicated response to the growing problem of crime and disorder and a concern for the imbalances of society. At its base, such views reflect the growing militancy amongst many on the right of the political spectrum and some naive camp followers who describe themselves as being on the 'democratic' left such as Frank Field and others within New Labour. There is little fundamental difference between the narrow exhortations of the Unitarian cleric on the failure to limit the extension of rights and freedoms and the odd statement of Frank Field that the decline of politics is related to the collapse of some vague and intangible moral order.

The problem with the individual, from a liberal standpoint, according to the communitarian, is the notion of the independent person as a disembodied entity separated from his/her community, without cultural understanding or sympathy either with or for their neighbour. The problem with 'rights' is the belief that they exist as incorporeal objects, without form, material substance or essence. The need for 'rights', for the communitarian, must exist only in relation to the parallel communal insistence on 'responsibilities'.[8]

Such a view of the individual, when seen in this context, assumes a tension for communitarians when confronted with their understanding of the meaning 'community', although communitarians claim that such a tension does not assume that there is a disagreement on the notion of the traditional community in which the twin symbols of the 'majority' and the 'family' become the foundation stones of their civil society. They claim to be critical of community institutions that are both authoritarian and restrictive even though they are opposed to the dispensing of too many freedoms. Consequently, they continue to find fault with any who advocate an extension of rights for the individual in a range of social issues. Is this also symptomatic of the direction taken by New Labour? 'Communitarian ideology has been afforded particular significance by political commentators in Britain who see it as a ready-made theme for the new leadership of the Labour Party.'[9]

When making reference to the community and the nuclear family, New Labour appear to be taking their cue from the communitarian movement. Amitai Etzioni and his colleagues presented the basic foundations of the movement in the leaflet *Responsive Communitarian Platform*. Its view was that the basic building-block and the vanguard of civil society is the nuclear family in which the provision for a 'morally' educative atmosphere must prevail. In such circumstances, the idea of divorce is anathema: the basic priority is the support of the children. The position of the rearguard is bolstered by the attempt to revive the moral fibre of the nation, whilst supporting such worthy virtues as tolerance of others and the application of basic principles such as hard work and thrift. In this atmosphere, communitarians argue, the creation of social partnerships involving state agencies and the community will inevitably result in the eventual devolution of powers to the community. Inevitably, such ideas have been accepted with considerable enthusiasm by both politicians and academics. Communitarians envisage the creation of a social movement equalling that of the Progressive Movement in the United States in the earlier part of the twentieth century.

Although he was the founder of the communitarian movement, Amitai Etzioni did not specifically attempt to address his analysis of society from a distinctively Catholic perspective; underpinning many of his theories is the single dominant view which focuses on the family and the community as the most important foundations and therefore the stabilising factor of modern civil society.

In spite of the modern gloss we know that the ideas behind communitarianism are not so new. It would be a relatively simple task to establish sources and reference points for the ideas of communitarianism amongst the writings and public statements of most of the political parties of Europe in the twentieth century. Joseph Lee has already hinted at the inclusion and absorption into the body politic of the early Irish Free State (Saorstat na hEireann) of ideas initiated by the fascist Blueshirts. The language of European fascism is not in some circumstances dissimilar from that of the democratic parties as they all searched for ways of addressing the social problems arising from the great depression of the 1920s. In his pamphlet *The Greater Britain*, former Labour Member of Parliament, founder of another new party and minor member of the British aristocracy, Oswald Mosley, referred to the need for a reorganisation of British society in the 1930s along the lines of a society freed from the constraints of class struggle and in which the emphasis for national regeneration is placed on individual responsibility in which initiative would be rewarded.[10] There is nothing especially unusual in these views, it has to be said. There is much evidence of these opinions being stated in the relatively moderate conservative parties throughout Europe and the United States as well as other elements of the more extreme radical right. They could also be those of the political cheerleaders of communitarianism in Britain.

Having said that, there is some confusion both as to the origin of communitarianism as well as to the practical application of its ideas. For example, it is not uncommon within the European assembly to hear members of the Strasbourg parliament refer to communitarian ideas, policies and programmes. The use of the term in that context is not intended (in so far as one is aware) to make reference to the ideas and theories associated with those of Etzioni, but to make a simple allusion to the European Union and its Commission. The communitarianism of Etzioni does not refer merely to the relatively limited geographical base of the community as we have come to describe a neighbourhood, but to the wider community within the nation state in what he described as a 'supracommunity, a community of communities – the American society'.[11] Any attempt to define this community, even that within the wider community, as based on, for example, the anarchic or communist notion of commune, or even that of the collective, cooperative or kibbutz, would ascribe to it a form of leftist political baggage which Etzioni would regard as inappropriate, even unpatriotic.

In attempting to define the idea of 'community', writer, teacher and unreconstructed communitarian Charles Handy provided a complex matrix of communities in which groups of people are stratified and categorised according to their place in society, in the world of work, a 'fun' community, a 'kinship' community, 'city' and 'nation' and so on, leading, ultimately of course, to the Etzionian, 'community of communities'.[12] In one sense what Etzioni and his friends are saying is that in the struggle for the communitarian ideal, the principle of voluntarism is its most valuable component part. Within a volunteering ethos, payment for work is dismissed as vulgar materialism and inconsistent with the spirit of giving – the basis on which a recognition of responsibilities rests. The notion of voluntarism with its emphasis on good works, charitable enterprises, sharing, though not necessarily in the cooperative sense, has its roots firmly embedded within the western Christian tradition. This is not to suggest that such virtues do not exist in other religious societies. Clearly they do, but for those who promote such values, the moral tradition which drives them and acts as the motor is reflected, for example, in the appeals for greater charity expressed by Christ in his Sermon on the Mount or in the expulsion of the money-lenders from the temple. Both of these biblical occasions have been liberally interpreted to suggest that Christ's values are located within the spirit of charity asserted through voluntarism and expressed through generosity, benevolence, compassion and tolerance. The concept of voluntarism is a basic maxim associated with the idea of charity and with community work. In consequence, therefore, voluntarism is a fundamental element of the communitarian faith. Equally, however, it is a dangerously patronising doctrine which offers no more than a compassionate and condescending benediction when faced by the kind of social problems normally confronted by the average community organisation. In short, it avoids the question of who or what is responsible for the human condition of poverty:

> An individual who loses a job due to technological change should not be forced to bear alone this 'price of progress'; society must continue to share these burdens and some welfare state must exist to provide the mechanism to do that ... as communitarians see it, a strong but scaled-back core of the welfare state therefore should be maintained. Other tasks, currently undertaken by the state, should be turned over to individuals, families and communities.[13]

Gramsci referred to the notion of voluntarism in his *Prison Notebooks* by providing a definition, as well as noting its special position within society:

> Obviously, 'volunteers' should be taken as meaning not the elite when this is an organic expression of the social mass, but rather those who have detached themselves from the social mass by arbitrary individual initiative, and who often stand in opposition to that mass or are neutral with respect to it.[14]

Constant exhortations from those leaders of the community 'movement' for a break from the past associations with dependency is now reflected in a growing enthusiasm by the voluntary sector for the responsibilities which, until recently, belonged firmly in the realm of the state.

There is no question that the communitarian movement is a labyrinth of contradictions. Etzioni, presumably in common with others of that persuasion, subscribes to the view that society can no longer sustain the massive injections of financial support necessary for the maintenance of the welfare state. Indeed, the very mention of an association or connection of 'welfare' to the 'state' conjures up, for them, visions of a form of benign bureaucracy which casts its shadow on individual enterprise. Etzioni, for example, considers the notion of a welfare state as problematic. Whilst he acknowledges the fact that 'citizens, by and large, like the idea of a system to assist them if they fall on hard times', he issues a warning of even harder times to come because of the increasing costs of maintaining such a system. He warns both the left and right of the political spectrum that their solutions are no longer sustainable, although in truth it is to the left that he directs his most severe criticisms. And whilst he refuses to accept the legitimacy of the arguments for a serious overhaul of the structures of the state to resolve the problems of unemployment as 'unsustainable', he is forced to fall on his own sword when he admits that those on the right 'must face the fact that there are socio-economic conditions that nobody can control which exact undue human costs.'[15]

How is this dilemma to be confronted? 'By applying the principle of subsidiarity', is Etzioni's reply. What can he possibly mean by this statement? His belief is that the responsibility for any problem belongs to those who are closest to it. Only when an individual cannot solve the problem should it pass, logically, to the family, thence to the local community and then only, still unresolved, should it go to central government. He constantly makes references to anecdotes or simplified examples as a means of illustrating his point:

> Suppose that as a result of a car accident a paraplegic is confined to a hospital bed. All he can do is operate a pencil-like stick with his mouth, with great effort, to turn the pages of a book. Should we assign to him a nurse's aide to help turn the pages? The communitarian view is that we should expect the confined person to do what he reasonably can, for reasons of both the dignity that comes with making a contribution to one's well being and the accompanying reduction of burden on others.[16]

There is no mention of the principle of subsidiarity in this passage unless Etzioni is attempting to reduce such a principle to its most basic form by placing the responsibility for the paraplegic's fate in his or her own hands. It is difficult to see how he can be making a serious contribution to the debate about subsidiarity by drawing on such examples. In this particular instance the question of responsibility is a valid and pertinent one if not one that was intended. If the disabled person cannot turn the pages, who must take responsibility? If he or she cannot communicate satisfactorily, who must assume a responsibility for interpreting his or her needs? If he or she simply wants to watch television, who switches it on or changes the channels?

In the light of this confusing set of impressions, one is prompted to ask the question, what is communitarianism? Why has it enveloped some sections of the body politic in a way which has prompted some within the social sciences to consider rewriting their original ideas on the nature and the responsibility of society as a whole? Communitarianism has been discussed in academia for years, after first being popularised by Amitai Etzioni in his book *The Spirit of Community*. Communitarians subscribe to some old-fashioned ideas of community and social responsibility which locate many of their sources in the ideas of the French philosopher Jean-Jacques Rousseau, as well as the Papal encyclicals of Pope Leo XIII, *Rerum Novarum*, and Pius XI, *Quadragesimo Anno*, in which the ideas associated with man falling from nature emerge as a direct result of encroaching industrialisation and modernisation.

Communitarians often refer to the importance of the principle of subsidiarity in their appeals for greater attention to be paid to the problems of a society which refuses to face matters of mutual and personal responsibility. For them it is a fundamental question of the demarcation of accountability. Who can be held to be responsible for the disparate range of activities characteristic of modern civil society? It can only be dealt with at a level commensurate with the system of subsidiarity, they would argue. Field makes the point in relation to the welfare state:

> We ought to look at local ways by which we can enhance self-improvement. At the present time, the whole community care budget is used to destroy the natural local pattern of self-support and self-improvement. Much of the welfare state has operated to destroy that most natural and important of human self-help and self-improvement impulses.[17]

Frank Field's argument is that the delivery of community care should be undertaken by individuals in the community rather than by the state. Such a view could be a seductive one for many community workers who might be deceived into believing that it is another way of producing a 'bottom-up' approach to development. Field obviously agrees with Etzioni that Western societies can no longer afford to support the aged and the infirm, the young and the poor. But in this case it is not simply a question of the increasing scale of the problem, it is also a matter of the philosophical principles underpinning the whole idea of the communitarian movement.

On one matter Etzioni comes close to the underlying principle driving the communitarian movement when he refers to subsidiarity. The idea has now been firmly established in the more macro-political atmosphere of the European Commission than at any other time. Paul Spicker suggested that in a European Union context it refers to 'the need to ensure that political decisions are not taken at any higher level than they need to be'.[18]

Liberalism versus communitarianism: a false debate?

What characterises communitarianism more than anything else is its almost ceaseless and implacable opposition to liberalism. In so far as it exists as an attempt to deliver the basis for a theory of social change, communitarianism has emerged instead as a reaction to the existence of other models of society. The popularisation of communitarianism through the support of Tony Blair with his call for a 'stakeholder society' and Frank Field with his appeals for a form of moral rearmament, as well as its more erudite advocates in academia, has resulted in a persistent and unremitting attack on anything which hints of a liberal agenda. But is that the real focus of their attention?

The problem with liberalism, they continue to insist, is that it focuses too much on the rights of the individual and not enough on his or her public responsibilities. Much of this is manifest through the arguments of more recent defenders such as Atkinson of the Phoenix Centre in Birmingham and, more recently, the former leader of the Liberal Democrat Party, Paddy Ashdown, who constantly attempts to invoke a vision of a society in which the guiding principle of 'small is best' represents all that is finest in a new Britain. Such supplications to a return-to-nature Britain in which self-sustaining communities live idyllic lives surrounded by happy, smiling children and dancing maidens is reminiscent of the vision of a Gaelicised Ireland represented by the former President of Ireland Eamon de Valera. It is also suggestive of another era as well in which such appeals for social responsibility had a more sinister dimension:

> It is neither privilege nor place for those who seek to live on the efforts of others without giving anything in return. So the British Union system of heredity is accordingly designed on the one hand to encourage to the utmost the initiative and enterprise of the individual not only in working for himself but also in deep and human motive in working for his children.[19]

It could be argued that Mosley's arguments in his propaganda piece *Tomorrow We Live* are merely absurd propaganda points, and that they were made at a time when Fascism was rampant throughout Europe and when its British section was able to claim that their political rallies in Earls Court were the biggest public gatherings ever. But it is also reminiscent of some of the less erudite statements of those who subscribe to communitarian ideas.

Frank Field's challenge that we must somehow 'agree a new public ideology or a new public moral order' is inspired by his claim that the moral framework of society has been undermined by the disintegration of the religious foundation supporting it. In addition, according to some communitarians, the liberal preoccupation with individualism undervalues what some refer to as 'the importance of a moral environment' and what Field hints at as 'the disintegration of our moral order'.[20] In other words, society will not be served well if individuals are only concerned with pursuing their own interests and the protection of their rights without reference to the welfare of the wider community. Is this why we are suddenly confronted by systematic assaults on the single parent, the removal of the right to silence and the imposition of stringent regulations controlling the right to unemployment benefit?

The communitarian platform, which was approved by a large number of prominent academics and politicians carries an endorsement from Vice President Al Gore: 'I believe very deeply that you're really on to something.' Hardly surprising perhaps as the leading communitarians Professor William Galston, and Amitai Etzioni, are advisers to the President for Domestic Policy. Bill Clinton regularly refers to the potential value of community in the process of national regeneration. In one State of the Union address, he declared, 'Our problems go way beyond the reach of government. They are rooted in the breakdown of our families and our communities.' Some years earlier on 3 November 1992, the President-elect said that 'we need a new spirit of community, a sense that we're all in this together. If we have no sense of community, the American dream will continue to wither.'

Catholicism and communitarianism

Much of what we have found associated with communitarian philosophy can be found in Catholic social teaching. In that context the Papal encyclicals are without parallel in the area of church response to social policy. Gioacchino Vincenzo Pecci, later to be known as Pope Leo XIII, laid the foundations for modern Catholic thinking in this area. As Papal Nuncio to the court of King Leopold I (1831–65) he was highly critical of the educational system in Belgium at that time, a view which resulted in him being recalled to Rome. Still later as Bishop of Perugia he protested strongly against the annexation of Perugia by Sardinia (Gramsci's place of birth) and the programme of secularisation which followed. He modernised the curriculum of his seminary, and founded the Academy of St Thomas Aquinas in which he encouraged the revival of Thomism. During that same period he advocated a rapprochement between Catholicism and contemporary culture. So if any Pope could be described as having contributed to a sea-change in Catholic social teaching it must be Leo XIII. Whereas there were some advances made by his predecessor, Pius IX, particularly the relatively bold step in appointing Leo as caretaker, it was Leo XIII who tried to draw the Catholic Church closer to the process of modernisation which was taking place throughout the Western world at that time. Although he realised the importance of making an accommodation with the forces engaged in this process of modernisation, he continued the deeply conservative policy of attacking socialism and communism, most notably in his encyclical *Quod apostolici muneris* (1878).

In a later encyclical, *Libertas praestantissimum* (1888) Leo proclaimed the church as the custodian of liberty whilst he recognised the legitimacy of government as long as he was satisfied that it guaranteed the general welfare of the citizen. But it was his support for the right of the individual to hold private property, the argument for a just wage and the right of trade unions to exist which earned him the title 'Workers' Pope'. These questions were raised in the most famous encyclicals, *Rerum Novarum* (1891) and *Quadragesimo Anno* (1931) and it was those pronouncements which led to an understanding of the meaning of subsidiarity:

> As history abundantly proves, it is true that on account of changed conditions many things which were done by small associations in former times cannot be done now save by large associations. Still, that most weighty principle, which cannot be set aside or changed, remains fixed and unshaken in social philosophy: Just as it is gravely wrong to take from individuals what they can accomplish by their own initiative and industry and give it to the community, so also it is an injustice and at the same time a grave evil and disturbance of right order to assign to a greater and higher association what lesser and subordinate association can do. For every social activity ought of its very nature to furnish help to the members of the body social and never destroy or absorb them.[21]

The underlying principle associated with the idea of subsidiarity is the belief that the intervention of the state is generally unacceptable, particularly with regard to the rights and responsibilities of the individual. It could also be argued that it is a statement in support of decentralisation as Spicker explained: 'the justification for subsidiarity can be seen in terms of a defence of the liberty of the individual and the preservation of personal independence.'[22]

Describing the process of complex networks associated with the conservative view of society in the book *How Conservatives Think*, Clarke revisited the traditional *gemeinschaft* model of community by suggesting that even at the present time: 'Man is born into society, into a family and a nation, and, by the mere fact of existence, assumes inescapable duties towards his fellows and is endowed with the rights of membership of that society.'[23] The suggestion by Clarke that there are inescapable duties implicitly suggests an element of coercion, whilst the endowing of rights also proposes that they can be withdrawn; precisely what was being proposed by Mosley in his arguments for 'The People's State – a Classless System'.[24] But whilst it is often suggested, particularly by the advocates of communitarianism, that the notion of constraint is one involving a voluntary agreement to restrain one's intuitive and instinctive reactions, Durkheim provides a definition which is quite different in that he suggests that a person's will is constrained by the application of sanctions, in other words, that he is coerced.

Central to the liberal–communitarian debate is the contention regarding the human being as a free and autonomous entity in so far as he or she can be sovereign and have independent choice. But whilst the notion of the free spirit has a force of argument both in philosophical and political literature and has formed a basic assumption of the liberal democracies it has, traditionally, until now been the political forces of conservatism and reaction which have seriously challenged this basic hypothesis. The advocates of the liberal position have argued that an organised nation drawing on its resources provides a background of order within which the individual can pursue his or her respective goals and objectives. Within such a framework the law guarantees varying levels of equality. Far from embodying a particular substantive conception of the good life, the law must instead afford all lifestyles and belief systems equal treatment. In that situation the state merely acts to provide the framework for such a development, allowing for the widest possible application of the principle of individual freedom 'consistent with the exercise of that same freedom by others'. This qualification, of course, is central to the debate because freedoms in the context of the state can only be relative freedoms. If that is true one can therefore conclude that the liberal–communitarian debate is really a superficial one. Indeed, Grasso believes that communitarianism is merely the 'fine-tuning of modern liberalism', with which many on both sides of the argument would have no real quarrel.[25] It might explain the apparent alliance between New Labour and the Liberal Democrats, or at least that version of it which made itself manifest at the meeting in Birmingham in 1995 in which the dominant theme insisted on an understanding that rights must at all times be seen as commensurate with responsibilities. It might also explain the muted response from the liberal lobby to the more recent assaults by the Labour administration on some of what were regarded as basic principles of this 'liberal democracy'. The current dogma therefore is that the notion that one can have both freedom and autonomy is a nonsense in the context of the modern Western democratic state. If such a viewpoint becomes common currency, as inevitably it must, then it heralds an extension of the hegemony, and the sharpening of the coercive element of civil society, especially in Britain, that has not yet been experienced.

Against that background, communitarianism emerges as the new guardian of the public freedom focusing on humans as social beings rather than as individuals, of the importance of communal life and of participation and fellowship. But more importantly, in the case of some of its adherents, communitarianism is not simply seen as a reactionary catharsis of the body politic, but in fact as a development or evolution of the liberal project. The belief in the individual as a free and independent being with unlimited rights has been translated into a question of relative rights and unlimited responsibilities.

Where this problem falls most acutely is on what some commentators have described as the great American democratic experiment. Just as rights may be, for some, a relative question, so the democratic experiment for others in the United States amongst the urban and rural poor, and those in the Third World affected by American foreign policy, is a relative one also. Arguments about the rights of the individual fall on deaf ears when addressed to those without jobs, food or shelter.

Such emotive images create problems for anyone attempting to engage in a critique of the liberal–communitarian debate. It is true that the poor have difficulty in contributing to debates which, on the face of it, do not directly affect them and the conditions in which they live. Individualism and rights have little contribution to make, in their view, to placing food on the table or to building much needed housing. Grasso's question, 'how can a theory of politics centring upon the good of the community rather than on the rights of the individual serve as the moral foundation of a free society?', is important in so far as it is addressed to a particular interest community.[26] Many Europeans emerging from the disaster of defeat in 1918 and subsequent collapse of their economies were little concerned for the rights of the individual. When they heard the fascist call for national unity and for the recreation of a distant folkish society, based on appeals to 'kith and kin' they listened and voted. Anything was better than what they had experienced. The community that the fascist referred to, it will be claimed, was a corruption of that understood by the communitarian today. But it was also one which was readily accepted and exploited by the fascists of the 1930s and based on a recognition of the importance of the community in suppressing individuality.

What much of the debate tends to ignore is the central influence on our lives of the state – that amorphous, conglomerate super-structure dominating our individual private as well as our public lives and functions and which is neither benevolent nor magnanimous, considerate or generous. It is none of these things because, by definition, it cannot be. It is what Gramsci described as 'the apparatus of state coercive power which legally enforces discipline on those groups who do not consent either actively or passively'.[27]

Communitarianism: a conservatism ideology

This brings us to consider just precisely in which direction the communitarians think they are going. The *Economist* was clear in its understanding of that direction: 'They are minded to merge their church with the state and so shape public policy.' But if that is true and if we accept Gramsci's understanding of the role and function of the state, then the communitarian perception must be one in which they recognise the coercive nature of the state. Such a view, it could be argued, is corroborated by their insistence on the need for a full recognition of the importance of responsibilities implied in the notion of citizenship. So the additional view of the *Economist* that, of the two schools of communitarianism, the one led by Etzioni is a harmless one, is really not accurate. Indeed, there may well be amongst those of the more authoritarian school of communitarianism elements who do pose a threat to the rights of the individual and do present a 'danger to civil liberty', but it is really a dubious point. Instead of strengthening the democratic base by widening the parameters of debate and reinforcing the rights of minorities and of individuals, both sides instead contribute to a whittling away of the foundations of the democratic project by turning the argument on its head. If the state and civil society are one and if we acknowledge the coercive imperative of the state, we must also, by definition, recognise the coercive nature of civil society.

This is an important element of civil society which is ignored by the communitarian school of thought as, indeed, it is rejected by many who wear the mantle of liberalism. To some extent, it is located in the view that the family as a stabilising force is both a central building block in the superstructure of civil society as well as a classic example and source of the principle of subsidiarity. Christopher Wolfe refers to it as that 'area in which men and women naturally learn to be sensitive to the indirect effects of the exercise of authority'.[28] But Engels had an entirely different view, both in historical as well as in sociological and, ultimately, in political terms. Whereas Wolfe points to the educative processes which take place within the family, Engels would have testified instead to the socialising and subsequently harmful effects of family life and the dependency on the family as a social unit. In *Origins of the Family, Private Property and the State* he cited American historian Lewis Henry Morgan's (1818–81) view that the family is 'the creation of the social system and will reflect its culture'.[29] But while Gramsci made no specific reference to the family, he did in passing argue that 'the stabilisation of sexual relations within the monogamous family, with the full support of religious dogma behind it, was central to creating a work force that is efficient and obedient.'[30] Boggs forms some important conclusions about Gramsci's contention which have a direct relevance to the arguments, both about the centrality of the family in communitarian mythology, but also about its coercive role in the context of modern civil society: 'In this sense the family constitutes the basic social unit of civil society, and puritanism is its underlying ideological justification.'[31] This is an extremely important assertion, not only because it sets out clearly the Marxist position both in relation to the historical as well as the contemporary role of the family, but it also exposes to some extent the reason why those within the communitarian movement are its most ardent advocates.

There is little real evidence for the complaint from Etzioni and his friends that the two-parent family is in serious decline, particularly in view of the fact that in any case, historically, it is a fairly recent phenomenon. The communitarians go so far as to argue that such a decline lies at the very heart of the degeneration of Western society as a whole. What is interesting from their perspective is that, whilst they acknowledge that changes and adjustments within the conventional family structure are taking place, they refuse to budge from their position with regard to the importance of the two-parent family as the template, so to speak, of civil society. It matters not that social and economic conditions, as well as political reforms, have forced fundamental changes in that structure. Women are now more likely to want to go to work. Men stay at home more than they ever did before, either as a result of unemployment, job sharing, or in some minor cases, as a consequence of a decision taken by husband and wife, or partners, that the women has more earning power. In any case there is no evidence for the assertion, hidden within their argument in favour of the two-parent family, that the one-parent family is either unstable or incapable of meeting its obligations to the wider society, something with which the National Council for One-Parent Families would concur.

The problem with the communitarian view of family and community is that neither is located in anything like what we understand the world to be or to mean. In truth, the belief in a community some distance away in our collective memories never really existed. What we have come to understand of the community today, based on a neighbourhood model, bears little real comparison to the vague and indistinct recollections presented as alternatives by the communitarians. The 'community' today is a complex matrix of intense competition between contesting groups, often class-based, struggling for a slice of the social and financial cake. Witness the internecine battles which have taken place within the community and voluntary sector over the distribution of funding from the European Commission, not only between communities, but also within communities. Jack Demaine pointed to the problems emerging from opening the lid on community competitiveness when, in quoting Pahl, he said that not only will 'the activation of community spirit frequently reveal a can of worms, it can also set community against community.'[32]

What is interesting from this discussion on family and community is the fact that in spite of its obvious shortcomings the focus on community, especially, has revealed numerous contradictions and miscalculations. Politicians on both sides of the Atlantic have suddenly revealed a predilection for ideas which, until recently, were regarded as conservative, just a little old-fashioned and more than a bit quaint. Suggestions that the politicians are anxious to find some middle course 'between the public and the private' really isn't good enough. Indeed, it might even be described a trifle naive. Politicians, local or national, have never really been too concerned to step over the middle line whenever they feel it to be in their best interest. The opportunities suggested by the term 'community' might offer a number of escape routes for the politician today, but tomorrow is another day and yesterday's harmonious and vigorous community might easily become tomorrow's social problem.

What will prove interesting over the next months and years is how the politician–communitarian will translate this notion of community, or its extension into nation–community, into social policy and hence into practical programmes. What will prove equally interesting is how the community movement, that mass of people engaged in the promotion and development of actual projects, reacts to these developments. Much is talked of this. Jack Demaine asks pointed questions about what kind of practical programmes will emerge from communitarian conjecture whereas, from a completely different position, Pahl admits to such optimism as problematic. Such problems highlight the failure of the communitarians to admit either that their aspiration is located in mere speculation, or that the failure to link such ideas to practice, unlike the process of praxis, results in it degenerating into mere propaganda. Unlike praxis it cannot be used as a tool for understanding and development.

Perhaps at the heart of this debate is the question of citizenship. What is citizenship and how can it be applied? Marshall referred to it as having a status which recognised an equality both in terms of rights as well as of responsibilities.[33] Interestingly, according to Demaine, Marshall saw the difference between citizenship and social class as irreconcilable in so far as it took 'the form of a conflict between opposing principles'. But the whole point which is being made and reinforced by those who argue this communitarian view is that the notion of citizenship is only about responsibilities within civil society. Gramsci's understanding of civil society as the embodiment of the ideas and values of the ruling class *imposed* through their ideological hegemony immediately raises questions about both the nature of that civil society as well as the role of the citizen within it. As far as Etzioni is concerned, it can only be about the responsibility of the citizen to the wider community. Within such a relationship, rights are a relatively minor consideration in which the community, just like the family, becomes a controlling and dominant ideological structure. Within that structure the dominating ideology inevitably emerges as that of the ruling class within it.

So the announcement by former Conservative Prime Minister, John Major, that he was going to introduce a 'citizen's charter' really wasn't such a surprise after all. There is little doubt that he was engaged in a hasty and undignified process of disengagement with any or all of the negative inheritance which passed to him from his predecessor. Indeed, it could be argued that this was the only serious attempt by the British government to implement a programme which came close to the communitarian notion of the rights and respon-sibilities of citizenship. That may be true, but it is just possible, as well, that it was all simply a cynical exercise on Major's part to both distance himself from Thatcher and all that she represented as well as a dubious and unscrupulous tinkering in party political propaganda.

But the introduction of the ideologically conservative *Parent's Charter* which focused attention on the role of the parent in building their new civil society, highlighted for many precisely the problem which existed in extending the civil society through the schools and into the home. In such blatantly obvious circumstances, the school becomes the agent of the state in allowing for an extension of its hegemony. Commenting on Adam Smith's eighteenth-century 'civil education' solution to questions raised by a hypothetical 'commu-nitarian republic', Michael Ignatieff described them as a 'pious gamble on the capacity of strangers to build a common language of civic commitment'.[34]

The conservative language of subordination, in harmony with sub-sidiarity, also becomes the language of communitarianism. Subordinating or reducing social problems to an insistence on the need for rights to take second place to the stranglehold of 'respon-sibility' to the wider community is tantamount to a demand for an acceptance of an extension of the regulation of human behaviour. Is this an overstatement or an oversimplification?

Every aspect of our lives is determined now by the moral as well as the practical authority of the state. We are ruled over and regulated from morning until night. The values implicit in 'majoritarianism' are imposed systematically through the media in brutal as well as in subtle ways. Even our sleep is governed by the exigencies of the state. Shopping times are regulated and public houses are observed as places of overindulgence and subjected to police surveillance. Films and books are censored. Cannabis is outlawed. We are required to emerge from our homes to work without reference to our right not to work should we so desire. If by chance we cannot work, we are required to sign statements to that effect, or provide proof that we are incapable of so doing. It is not enough to find the means to purchase a television, or radio, without, also, acquiring a licence thus permitting us to watch or listen to them without fear of punitive action. We are restricted from parking our car on double-yellow lines, drinking alcohol in licensed premises after the permitted hour, taking our dogs for a walk without purpose-made plastic bags, building extensions to our homes without planning permission, smoking cigarettes without being informed of their harmful effects, having sex without being made aware of the need for a condom, or working for a period of time appropriate to our material needs. In every aspect of our lives we are obliged to adopt the prevailing moral authority as our own, and if we do not, we are controlled. We experience every aspect of the dominant ideological hegemony without reference at all to our rights as individuals to the point when even our ability to respond to the need for responsibility is taken away from us. When the state is dissatisfied with our individual understanding of the meaning of responsibility, it replaces it with regulation. The state has imposed a heavy price for our 'liberty'.

Now we can see rather more clearly the basis for the views not only of Etzioni but those of Frank Field, Dick Atkinson and the British Prime Minister, as well as the President of the United States. The great moral advance of New Labour on behalf of the community has produced a counterpoint to the conservative crusade of the Thatcher and Major period, which was predicated on the importance of the family and their self-serving interpretation of the 'classless society'. In truth, both New Labour and the old Conservatives sing from the same hymn sheet in which the communitarian movement provides the orchestration whilst the rest of us provide the chorus.

Part II
The Case Studies

6
Northern Ireland: The Evolution of a Counter-Hegemony

Community conflict and the growth of a culture of resistance

Early in 1965, during the campaign to have a second university in Northern Ireland sited in the second largest city, there was a clear indication that a popular movement was beginning to emerge which would include the middle class of the nationalist community. The Derry-based campaign was one of the few genuine cross-community popular developments before or since the advent of the civil rights struggles. But whilst there is some evidence that community-based campaigns on social and economic issues were quite common in all of the nationalist communities, there is little to suggest that, with the possible exception of the poor-relief marches of the 1930s, common cross-community activity located within exclusively working-class communities was a feature of the society that was Northern Ireland. The campaign against the siting of the university in Coleraine, a provincial, largely Protestant town, was seen as non-confrontational, in spite of the sectarian undertones of the decision, because it was designed to address the relatively safe and non-contentious issue of higher education. Furthermore, the Lockwood Committee which made the recommendation was entirely made up of representatives of the Protestant community.[1] There were many more serious structural issues to address such as high unemployment, and sectarian discrimination in housing, local government and employment; these were issues which would have to be dealt with in an entirely different way, perhaps using novel means and addressing an entirely separate constituency. There would be a point, inevitably, according to Marxists such as Eamonn McCann and a few 'left' Republicans, when the middle classes would withdraw their support from the battle. But to a very large extent, the early history of community action combines a history of nationalist working-class struggle in Northern Ireland, both for the fair allocation and equal distribution of resources as well as for the demand for changes to the unionist-dominated local and regional government.

There has been a dramatic increase in community-based activity in Northern Ireland in the past thirty years. The growth and expansion of the community movement during this period were probably due to a number of factors. The emergence of a broad-based, grass-roots movement, which articulated the political demands of a substantial minority of the North's population, provided an initial stimulus to those who recognised a need for a wider response to poverty and inequality. In the volatile atmosphere of politics in Northern Ireland, such demands were easily translated into an attack on the state by unionists, whereas many socialists and republicans quickly concluded that the state was irreformable.[2] Such a development, when seen against a background of considerable social, political and economic instability and the subsequent withdrawal of large sections of the community behind barriers and barricades, resulted in a recognition by many, especially within the nationalist community, of the need to search for local solutions to local problems, as an extension of the quest for wider solutions to more general political questions.

There are two distinct phases which could be described as being related to the development of community action if we see it as a response to and progression from the political conditions of Northern Ireland. The first is that period marked by the apparent lack of government or state involvement in community initiatives prior to the period of civil rights agitation but in which the growth of enterprises such as the credit unions and housing associations were significant community-based initiatives. The second is the subsequent involvement by government, in response to the post-civil rights agitation, through a Community Relations Commission which was initiated as a clear response to the political problem and social manifestations of sectarianism. In short, the first phase took place before the outbreak of the present cycle of troubles and the second represents those developments which have occurred since. As such, 1968 – the beginning of civil rights agitation – marks a watershed in community development thinking in Northern Ireland today, not only because it represents a substantial adjustment in the perceptions and confidence of the nationalist community, but also because it indicates the change in direction in government policy about the potential as well as the deep-rooted dangers of such a development.

The community relations dimension

Whereas the first of those developments was to create a lasting impression on many of the principal actors in community activity, it was the latter which would mould their practice and in which government would intervene and affect the process, through the creation of a Community Relations Commission as well as the direct control over the distribution of finances and other resources through the Departments of Economic Development, Health and Social Services and a range of other quasi-governmental agencies.

It is interesting to note both the method and the focus of this state intervention. Because it was felt by those in government that the 'Irish' problem was essentially one of community conflict, the solution, logically, was to intervene in a way which would address the issue of relationships. But of course the problem was and is much more complex than that, and as a consequence, the Commission was not to last very long. Headed by Maurice Hayes, it was formally wound up in the course of the speech to the Northern Ireland Assembly by the former Minister of Community Relations, Ivan Cooper, when he announced the creation of a new and larger agency. But before such a decision was actually taken and legislation introduced to the Assembly which would dispatch the Commission with some credit, the Northern Ireland Assembly itself was prorogued in May 1974.

The decision to wind up the affairs of the Commission was taken for a number of reasons: it was created in the post-1969 era when independence from government was considered a prerequisite for effective work in the community and it was believed that greater, rather than less, contact between government and community was becoming increasingly recognised as necessary and desirable. There is perhaps another, if unstated, reason which suggests that the objectives of the Community Relations Commission to create bridges between the two communities through the adoption of a community development strategy ultimately hastened its dissolution. It was believed that the organisation of campaigns around social and economic issues, in addition to an understanding of the common experience of poverty, would ultimately draw the warring factions together. Gaffikin and Morrissey believed this was predicated on a failure by the British especially, to appreciate the complexity of the political crisis in the North, which also had a historical/cultural dimension to it. However, according to Ivan Cooper, the Commission was a lame duck from the start and wasn't likely to achieve very much in its existing form because of what he described as the 'congenital conservatism' of the Commission members. Furthermore, in spite of the view held by many that Ivan Cooper was primarily and solely responsible for the closure of the Commission, it was Cooper who pointed a finger of accusation at the former Commission chairman Maurice Hayes and director Hywel Griffiths as being involved in advising him that the Commission should be brought to a speedy end.[3]

The power-sharing Executive's decision which would bring the Commission to an end was ratified by Parliament. In December 1974 the Minister of State at the Northern Ireland Office announced that the Department of Community Relations would be subsumed into the Department of Education. He also announced that local government authorities would be encouraged to adopt a more constructive role in the development of community-based activity. The new relationship of local government and the voluntary sector was to be provided with the resources to enable some limited financial aid to assist community groups with their administration costs.

Within its short history, the Community Relations Commission provided a hint that a different approach to the problems of Northern Ireland might offer some hope. That different approach was to be based on a recognition of the value of promoting a community development programme. What influenced this apparent change in direction? Dr Maurice Hayes spent some time in the United States and was influenced by the community development method employed in the Johnson poverty programme as a means of both bringing separate communities together as well as raising within them a level of confidence in the prospect and the possibility of change. As a consequence, Hayes convinced the Commissioners of the value of this approach and argued for the appointment of a Director and a number of field workers who were to be described as community development officers.

There was little to indicate that the Community Relations Commission was markedly different from most other state-sponsored organisations interested in a community development strategy. Their understanding of the meaning of community development offered little that was unique or different, nor were they able to offer anything that might tackle the serious problem of institutionalised sectarian discrimination.

A number of strategies were adopted. In the first place, it was assumed that the field workers would identify existing community groups, offer support and encourage the growth of new groups in those areas where such a tradition did not exist. This seemed particularly important in those loyalist areas which had little experience in community development. It was felt that government needed to engage in dialogue with community groups and that this process would allow for channels of communication to emerge.

In so far as it attempted to deal with the problems afflicting the community as a whole through the community development approach, the Community Relations Commission had much in common with the Community Development Projects in Britain. However there were a number of quite substantial differences of perspective. First, the Commission wasn't established as an agency which would see as its primary task the creation of a community development office. Furthermore, it was compromised by the fact that some unionists saw its objective as providing a form of redemption and impunity for rioting nationalists. The efforts of some in the Labour Party to highlight the nature of the structural problems were often dismissed casually by the leadership of the party as well as by those on the opposition Conservative side of the House of Commons. Northern Ireland was not regarded as high on the list of priorities of either side in the Commons. However some more seasoned observers identified the main problem as one of the alienation of the nationalist community. And whilst, even then, it was not openly regarded as the main source of grievance, there were many who privately acknowledged this. The appointment of Maurice Hayes was seen as a deliberate attempt to send signals to the nationalist community that it was time for them to come in from the cold. Objectively, it was a discernible attempt to legitimise the state through the integration of the nationalist community, by appointing a former senior Catholic civil servant. In more recent times it would be described as the social inclusion of an already socially excluded group. But was it an attempt to extend the hegemony to a section of the community which was in the serious business of political transformation? Did government recognise the signals? This view was confirmed by Ivan Cooper: 'That's the reason why the Department was set up in the first instance. The Department of Community Relations was created to try to keep us quiet. That it had an independent veneer. It was seen by unionists as a sop.'

There were a number of problems which arose because the Community Relations Commission was conscious of the dangers to the process of such an approach as well as the fact that they were also aware of the difficulties of not being properly resourced for the task. The community development officers (CDOs) believed that they had on the one hand to be independent of the Ministry of Community Relations and on the other to have access to resources which would enable them to fulfil their role. It is almost certainly true that some senior civil servants in the Ministry were suspicious of the role of the CDOs whilst at the same time anxious to take advantage of any information which would be available to them from community groups on the ground.

The principal uncertainty affecting the work of the CDOs was the dilemma of facilitating local groups in their attempts to establish a presence by supporting and improving access to resources, whilst at the same time ensuring a degree of independence from government institutions. In other words, should they act in a traditional role as extensions of the civil service or as radical agents of change? This was especially important at the time because of the extent to which the nationalist community was becoming alienated from the Northern Ireland state and the degree of suspicion which had saturated the entire community against anything which made them mistrustful of government involvement. They had an additional problem with which to contend. Because of the terms of the Social Needs Act (1970), grants were available to community-based projects. However, the Community Relations Commission, with its limited powers, could only offer recommendations and support for those who wished to apply. In truth, the Commission had very few real powers at that time.

The increased intensity of the political conflict, with a dramatic rise in violence and the movement of sections of the mainly nationalist population, following the introduction of internment without trial, resulted in widespread disruption of local and statutory services. In response to this, the CDOs organised emergency centres providing help and assistance to many of those residents under threat of intimidation, especially from gangs of loyalists. The inevitable result was that the credibility and independence of the Community Relations Commission, already regarded with considerable cynicism by members of the majority unionist community, were to become firmly established within a number of the embattled nationalist communities. As a result, it was argued that leave should be sought to enhance the programme by increasing the level of support for the project areas, from ten groups to thirty, as well as a substantial increase in the appointment of CDOs.

The response from the Ministry of Community Relations was to ignore the request. It was felt that this rejection resulted from a fear within the Ministry that the CDOs were developing signs of opposition to the state, or that they were perceived as having the potential for doing so. This action forced Maurice Hayes to submit his resignation, followed two months later by the director, Hywel Griffiths. The effect was to result in the eventual closure of the project and the shelving of any future plans for the creation of a community development programme. Those who replaced them attempted to steer the Commission away from the community development direction towards a strictly community education and community relations approach. According to Niall Fitzduff, this was an attempt to de-radicalise the field workers.[4]

The appointment of former civil rights leader and prominent Protestant member of the SDLP, Ivan Cooper, was thought to further advance the cause of those who advocated bringing the nationalist community closer to the Northern Ireland state. It was felt that such an appointment, coming from the newly-formed power sharing executive under the leadership of Prime Minister Brian Faulkner and Gerry Fitt would result in legitimising the Northern Ireland state with a consequent reduction in community tension. However, in April 1974, Ivan Cooper announced the disbandment of the Community Relations Commission, adding that no additional programmes dealing with this area were being planned. The community development functions of the Commission would be passed over to the newly formed Education and Library Boards and district councils which had been created in the wake of the reorganisation of local government in Northern Ireland in 1973:

> I could have decided to keep the Commission and expand its budget, I would have had great difficulty in getting that through because the Commission members themselves would not have

wanted to spearhead that campaign. As far as they were concerned they wanted to keep the Commission at the size that it was. I couldn't have forced a budget over their heads if they weren't prepared to do it.[5]

While there were some who wanted to further expand the power of the Community Relations Commission, others in the Commission itself wanted its powers strictly curtailed. The problem was that the Community Relations Commission laboured under a number of uncertainties. It was said that nationalist politicians were suspicious of its role, believing it to be an extension of government whilst at the same time it had the potential to undermine their own delicate relationship with their communities. The SDLP were in a relatively strong position in the North, especially amongst the Catholic middle class, but they were beginning to look nervously over their shoulder at a strengthening Republican Movement. Hywel Griffiths believed that the real reason for the creation of the Community Relations Commission was that the Catholic community had become so alienated from the Unionist establishment that a conduit was needed which would facilitate the process of drawing that community into the body politic and subsequent dialogue.[6] The Commission was seen by some as meeting that need. But because of the demand by a small number of senior civil servants within the Commission such as John Oliver, for a greater and more autonomous role it was felt by the establishment to be threatening. Cooper on the other hand dismisses the view that the Commission and its field workers threatened the base of the SDLP in any way:

> The facts speak for themselves. If you look at the election results of 1973 SDLP politicians polled extremely well in every single area. Take my own constituency; from memory I polled 12,000. It [the Community Relations Commission] was discussed very little in the SDLP. Hume was preoccupied with his Department which was Commerce, Currie was preoccupied with his Department, Devlin was preoccupied with his and we didn't see a great deal of each other at that particular time. The only person that I was getting hassle from was Peter MacLachlan the Unionist.[7]

There are a number of different views on this issue of the role of the Commission and its community development officers. Griffiths felt that the Ministry of Community Relations was concerned about the affirmation of independence by the field workers and their ostensibly radical approach, most notably during the period immediately after the introduction of internment. In an unpublished paper, University of Ulster lecturer Dr Bill Rolston argued that there was little that was truly radical in so far as their battles were confined within the Ministry of Community Relations, and to a lesser extent, directed against the Commissioners. This was confirmed by Niall Fitzduff who didn't see their primary role as having a radical focus even though there was some disquiet expressed by those nationalist politicians who saw themselves having to face a growing threat from community groups, particularly those within strongly republican areas, in the process of asserting themselves and flexing their muscles.

Cooper saw the work being carried out by people like Fitzduff, Joe Mulvenna, Rosie Toland, Gerry Finnegan and others as essentially undermining the power and authority of his civil servants. Their problem was that they were fearful of the emergence of a nucleus of local leaders who appeared to have the potential of effectively replacing the elected political representatives. Ivan Cooper was explicit in his statement in Parliament which brought the Commission to an end:

> Another factor which led me to the same conclusion is the concern which I expressed over the lack of contact there was between some community groups and the elected representatives of their areas. There was nothing in the present Commission structure which would help to counter that tendency. I was anxious, therefore, that the advisory body which replaced the Commission would provide opportunities for the closer involvement of elected representatives.[8]

Derry community activist Eamonn Deane provides an insight into the problems which local community leaders were posing both for the Power Sharing Executive and local elected representatives:

> There was a meeting with Ivan Cooper, and Paddy Doherty, Terry Doherty and myself going to a meeting when he was Minister at Stormont. He knew all of us very well and he would have civil servants there taking notes of the meeting so we decided that we would be very formal and deal with the matter which would allow them space. There was a proposed community centre to be built at Pilots Row and the proposal that was on the table was pretty

much the same community centre that was at Brooke Park. We went in to say that we didn't want that and that we had alternative plans which were very elaborate, much more elaborate than at the moment, but what is there now happened very much as a result of these negotiations. So we went in very formally and presented the case. 'Mr Minister we represent the Bogside Community Association ...' He interrupted and said 'Would you three ... shut up. Who do you think you are talking to?' It was quite embarrassing. He said 'I know the hearts and minds and needs of the people of the Bogside more than anybody in this whole wide world and I don't need this.' He told us to get out. Not long after this Ivan Cooper announced that he was doing away with the Community Relations Commission.[9]

The problem was that the Commission did not carry out its primary function. It could not draw the Catholic community closer to the establishment. Instead, it gave an appearance of having actually created the potential for another layer of leadership between the elected representatives and the communities engaged in struggle. However limited the community development programme initiated by the Community Relations Council, it was such that in the context of an ensuing conflict, it was perceived by some civil servants as having the potential for a drawing together of those forces opposed to the state. Networks were being created, communities were beginning to assert themselves and government, however reluctantly, was furnishing some of the resources. That was believed by many within government such as the senior civil servant, John Oliver, to be an intolerable state of affairs:

> A well meaning but dangerously vague concept of community action is offered as a replacement (to party politics). Potentially more dangerous still is the astonishing new growth of community associations, some with dubious connections, but nevertheless intent on imposing their will on housing, roads, redevelopment, community halls, libraries and so on to the virtual exclusion of elected politicians ... The alternative to elected representative government can only be anarchy or tyranny in the long run.[10]

The debate which flourished amongst some of the community development workers in the post-Hayes Community Relations Commission and the Commissioners, over the potential of a community development strategy which concentrated on the value of community action as a means of addressing the political manifestation of the breakdown in community relations, turned instead to issues related to community education.

This strategy was seen as non-threatening, avoiding the embarrassing confrontational problems associated with community action and initiating a broader-based body which would be more representative. The purpose of this new body would be to take responsibility for the old Community Relations Commission's advisory role, with the executive functions being transferred to other agencies.

In the final Evaluation Report (1982) of the Community Worker Research Project, it was stated that the decision to terminate the Commission took cognisance of a number of factors. First, the Commission was viewed as a necessary invention of the 1969 situation when independence from government was considered a prerequisite for the Commission being able to work effectively within the community. There was now no need for any section of the community to feel excluded from government or to feel that government might be unsympathetic to them. Second, more direct contact between government and people was construed as the way forward. The buffer function of a Commission structure could not counter the increasing tendency towards deteriorating relationships between community groups and locally elected representatives.[11]

There was every reason for the community to feel that government was unsympathetic as evidenced by the events after the demise of the civil rights movement. However, before legislation could be introduced into the Northern Ireland assembly at Stormont to wind up the affairs of the Commission, the assembly was closed down

A Joint Working Party was set up in January 1975 between the Department of Education and the Association of Local Authorities. Representatives were to include the Clerks and Town Clerks of six district/borough Councils and representatives of the Department of Education. The Report from the Working Party addressed four specific areas: the provision of facilities, community centres, assistance to community groups and finance. These were as follows: district councils should make facilities available for community centres, provide grant aid for any groups wanting to build such centres, provide advice on 'establishment' grants to groups dealing with statutory bodies, and employ community service officers and pay grants of up to 90 per cent for the salary of organisers of those groups deemed capable of coping with such an appointment.

After consulting with a number of agencies such as the Association of Local Authorities for Northern Ireland and the Interim Standing Advisory Conference of Community Associations, the Minister of State accepted the Report in principle. Recommendations of the newly created Advisory Conference of Community Associations (ACCA) that an independent institute of community development be established were not, however, accepted. A suggestion that such a body could be created as a 'researcher for government' was received with considerable suspicion by the community associations. In 1977 the government announced a new community worker research project (CWRP) and a community education forum to meet new recommendations by ACCA that money should be made available to enable some community groups to employ a full-time worker and that money be made available for the education and support of these and other workers.

The new body claimed to offer support to community-based development projects and announced that it would produce a research evaluation report based on an assessment of the contributions of individual project workers. This report was to be directed at government so that a decision could be made about whether it should continue or disappear. It was also to have a steering committee nominated by the Minister of State, the Association of Local Authorities and ACCA.

The Community Worker Research Project was to be funded by the Department of Education for Northern Ireland (DENI) for three years. The first chairman of the steering group was Professor Hywel Griffiths, professor of social administration at the New University of Ulster,[12] and former director of the Community Relations Council. It had responsibility for the selection of projects, for establishing training programmes for the workers and the setting of salary levels and other financial matters. Forty-seven applications were received by the steering group from community organisations involved in a range of activities from working in housing issues to the care of pre-school children. In total, 14 projects were selected for funding under the community worker research project. As an initiative by government, it was a typical top-down approach to community development. Groups selected for funding were to include community associations from both unionist and nationalist, Protestant and Catholic, sections of the wider community.

On the face of it the groups would have had little, ideologically, to separate them. But the Report identified a number of different political approaches. For example, one application centred on methods of combating vandalism whereas another viewed vandalism in a wider political context. The problem of providing a welfare rights service – believed by some activists to be nothing more than an extension of the DHSS bureaucracy – was countered by those within the claimants' union movement who fought for a greater degree of involvement of the claimants in confronting the civil service for benefits. One argued for the provision of a service to an embattled community, whilst the other saw mere service provision as counter-productive and contrary to the real needs of getting to grips with the source of the problem and the scarcity of resources. Clearly for some the problem wasn't viewed only as a question of poverty, which was seen as a symptom of the problem, but of structural inequality. In other words the state was the obstacle.

University of Ulster academic Dr Roberta Woods insisted that the projects which were seen as successful were those where the community worker had a specific role and a set of clearly defined tasks relating to the provision of a service. Of those, Craigavon, Sandy Row, Ballybeen and the Media Workshop were believed to be the most prosperous, partly because of their ability to fix the limits of their roles, but also because they were able to revise their goals and subsequently revise their activities. In short, they were able to adopt a more flexible strategy.[13]

However, a number of questions emerged when activists attempted to confront serious problems such as unemployment. This proved to be difficult because of the marginalisation of community work during this period, but perhaps primarily, because of the shortage of resources. Some groups such as Dove House in Derry and Conway Mill in Belfast attempted to develop their own sources of income from the United States. Attempts to address the problem of unemployment were faced partly by a level of apathy as well as fatalism within their communities, but also by levels of cynicism by the agencies. In truth, the local communities were hardly likely to swoon with delight at the prospect of a localised response to unemployment and poverty. There was little confidence in such a process.

However, these were not the only predicaments facing the local community activist. Questions such as isolation, displacement, the management committee's amateurishness, personal jealousies and petty political squabbling as well as the unenthusiastic involvement of some of the district councils contributed to the uncertainties experienced by the community workers projects.

Woods saw the problem of isolation as a recognition of the low level of support coming from their own communities as well as from the management committees. A number of other projects such as Crossmaglen failed to meet their own objectives, partly because they were too ambitious, but also because they were unable to affect the decision-making apparatus, both locally and nationally, which had power over the distribution of resources.

Much of the work undertaken was decidedly too ambitious, creating problems both for the various management committees as well as for the community workers. Often this relationship was strained, resulting in conflict, mismanagement and a consequent failure to meet even the minimal goals set out by some of the organisations. According to Woods, whilst most of the district councils cooperated with the projects, only in three cases was such cooperation followed through by tangible action and support.[14]

Attempts to initiate self-help projects received little support and the district councils concentrated future funding on service provision rather than on support for single-issue campaigns. Whilst the councils had an opportunity to influence the development of community development work from that time on, most opted instead to avoid providing support for community action and development activity.

Some of the issues which emerged, both from the experience of the Community Relations Commission and the later Community Workers Project, such as community relations accountability, lack of resources, women, rural development, poverty, personal development, and education and training for employment raised questions about the commitment of the state to local development, accountability and independence. It was thought that there was a need to review the existing state of community development on the basis that there had been significant structural changes in the previous decade. However, it barely touched on the political issues on the ground which forced such changes. For example, the issue of the origins of sectarianism and religious discrimination was one which affected all nationalist communities.

But what were these structural changes which had taken place and which necessitated a review? Both regional and local government had been dramatically affected by the political events which had occurred in Northern Ireland since the prorogation of the Stormont Parliament. The ten years prior to 1989 had seen the re-emergence of the hunger strike as a weapon in the armoury of republican prisoners in which ten had died. The consequences, for the development of republican politics, had been profound. There was a growing recognition, particularly since the emergence of the 'ballot paper in one hand and armalite in the other' strategy of Sinn Fein, that a form of limited power lay in the streets and the hillsides of Ireland. As a consequence, the Republican Movement adopted a new and dramatic strategy which resulted, in the aftermath of the election of hunger striker Bobby Sands, in the election of 48 local government councillors, and a recognition of the value and political potential of community-based activity.[15] At the same time, the Northern Ireland Office initiated a community employment initiative, the Action for Community Employment programme, which allowed for local employment to be based on community projects.

Issues related to the need for an extension of democracy and local empowerment became the subject of discussion at most conferences on local development. These had implications for the future of community work as a profession between those who were engaged in such development at the pit face of community work and those who were responsible as policy makers for the provision and distribution of resources. The Department of Health and Social Services established a Voluntary Activity Unit (VAU) at its headquarters in Stormont with a brief to encourage and develop community-based strategies for local development.

The authors of a report on community development in Northern Ireland held the view that community work had become fragmented in the late 1980s and early 1990s, had lost its focus and that individual community workers were having to work in isolation. The report represented a clear recognition of the reality of a changing situation as well as an understanding of the increasing marginalisation of the liberal agenda originally implied by the community development method of grass-roots democracy and accountability.[16]

A Community Development Review Group (CDRG) pointed to the lack of support for such work amongst district councils and noted that even within those voluntary organisations most associated with such work, community development had acquired a low priority. The review group pointed to what it described as the honourable history of community development and its involvement in issues ranging from childcare to welfare rights and from housing repairs to opposition to sectarianism. However laudable the sympathies, the group omitted to mention the somewhat less than honourable history of a gathering reluctance to become embroiled in religious discrimination issues, whether in jobs and the allocation of housing, as well as the repressive measures adopted by the state in particular in most nationalist ghettos.

Only once, in passing, did the CDRG mention the creation or the promotion of alternatives to existing structures. In attempting to define the meaning of the term 'community development', the group examined both its historical origins and its current status as a means of addressing its relevance to the situation in Northern Ireland. It concluded that community development existed as a process which combined community work, community action and community organisation into an integrated whole. But the group went further, in arguing that it saw community development as a union of community action and state sponsorship or intervention, drawing them together in an alliance or in a partnership. Indeed, the review group in concluding a report on funding and support admitted that whilst there was a real problem of a lack of inter-agency cooperation, there was also a well-grounded belief amongst many community organisations that identification with campaigning would only serve to alienate potential funding agencies. Little was offered by way of leadership from the group whose members probably regarded themselves as representative of the intellectual traditions of the movement. Such a way of thinking might be taken to infer that the only way forward was to cut and run, ignore the broader issues and get on with the business of acknowledging the primacy of the state.

In fairness, the CDRG did argue in its recommendations for a greater input in the provision of resources in addition to admitting that the group recognised a lack of clarity from government about its responsibilities in relation to the development of local communities. But what was not made explicit was their understanding of the level of government responsibility in this regard, or the degree to which the local community should be involved in exposing the government's indolence or reluctance to deal with the structural problem of poverty.

Six major recommendations were made by the working party on community development in Northern Ireland, which covered areas related to an insistence that government recognise the potential and value of community development as a regenerating force and commit itself to a policy which accurately reflected that view; that such a policy be also reflected in the relationships between local government and the community and voluntary sector; that voluntary organisations adopt clear guidelines to provide a framework for their relations with community groups; that centres for the promotion of community development be established in both urban and rural areas, and that a financial commitment be made by the state, both for seed as well as core funding for community development.

These were ambitious proposals and some gains were made. The government allowed the initiative for a rural centre to become a reality with the establishment of a Rural Development Council to be based in Loughry College, Cookstown. It participated in the creation of the Northern Ireland Voluntary Trust, although before the recommendations of the Review Group. Government and its agencies had already made some commitment to community development through its involvement in the Community Relations Commission in the early 1970s, the Advisory Conference of Community Associations (ACCA) in 1975 and the Community Workers Project initiated in 1978. The promotion of the Action for Community Employment (ACE) programme was regarded by many community leaders as a significant contribution to local development, both as a training scheme, and as a contribution to local employment. On the other hand, there is much to suggest that the use of the ACE programme provided an excellent opportunity for the state to counter the growing influence of Sinn Fein on the streets by instantly neutralising selected community groups and rendering them ineffective as a focus for local political activity.[17]

Other adjustments were also taking place. At a time when the Rural Action Project, with its origins in the EC-sponsored Second Combat Poverty Programme, was beginning to shed one mantle and assume another in the shape of the Rural Development Council, the Review Group were making significant recommendations on the issues of rural poverty and rural development as a countering measure.

Indeed, it is the specific reference to a lack of inter-agency cooperation in community development which most marks the contrast in strategies between the models of development proposed within an urban context, as distinct from the rural situation. The adoption by most rural community groups of an integrated strategy of development is the single most important departure in developmental terms, which contrasted sharply within the single-issue focus of many urban-based groups. This issue was most evident in the criticisms raised by the Community Development Review Group. So what were the practical effects on the ground of these recommendations? If it could be argued that the community sector in an urban context, had been weaned away from the radicalism of the 1960s and 1970s, could the same be said of those engaged in such work in a rural setting?

Furthermore, did it succeed in drawing the rural community away from the economic–cultural margin and integrating it into the broader ideological hegemony of the state?

The responses from most rural communities to their condition are often marked by a tendency to see their difficulties as less of a structural problem and more a simple lack of resources. But two agricultural economists, Mike Murray of the University of Ulster and John Greer from Queen's University, Belfast, were of the opinion that there was a problem facing both the rural community and the state. Their view indicated that the dependency relationships of community to the state show little sign of weakening: 'Government has set an agenda on its terms and is operationalising a process of change which may do little to advance the greater independence of rural communities.'[18]

Undoubtedly, there was a difficulty in defining rural poverty and yet there was a recognition within Europe that it was one of the most troublesome problems the European Commission had to deal with. Speaking on the importance of rural development to regional policy, Philip Lowe, then Chef de Cabinet to the European Commissioner for Regional Policy, said that 'the ability of rural inhabitants to protect and develop the area they occupy will be paramount.'[19] The extent of the problem world-wide is well documented, but the responses from agencies and academics are, at best, ill defined, and at worst, inadequate. The extent of the problem is almost immeasurable. The World Bank has estimated, for example, that about 85 per cent (550 million) of those throughout the world living in absolute poverty (defined as an annual income of less than US $50) reside in rural areas. There was a tangible feeling amongst community activists that, compared to other more affluent countries in Europe, extreme levels of poverty also existed in some of the more remote areas of the Irish countryside, North and South.

In the context of examining the hegemonic relationships within Northern Ireland, such figures are crucial to an understanding of the problem. Whilst accepting that the European Community does not have a direct responsibility for finding a resolution to the problems of the Third World, it is widely accepted that the response to the social problems of rural Europe is less than satisfactory. Claiming that he proposed an integrated rural development programme for Northern Ireland in 1984, leader of the SDLP John Hume argued that the tendency towards a drift into the cities resulted in the erosion of traditional communities, the breakdown of order and an inevitable upsurge of anti-social behaviour. Such communities, he suggested, hold people together in a relatively harmonious equilibrium, through a network of family and community constraints and pressures which generate socially considerate behaviour.[20] This was a communitarian view of society in Northern Ireland, it could be argued, some nine years before Etzioni's book, *The Spirit of Community,* offering simplistic, yet compelling arguments for those who subscribe to a community perspective of the developmental needs of people living in poverty in both urban and rural areas of Ireland.

But some groups adopted an alternative perspective. The proliferation of community activity in the absence of state responses to poverty included organisations such as the Bogside Community Association and its successor in the same area. Both were built on traditions of self-help and initiative at a time when unemployment and emigration were almost the only options left open to men during the bleak periods following the Second World War. Housing committees, credit unions and tenants' associations were early initiatives which responded to need. But in the wake of the political crises after 1969, when social problems reached boiling point, the creation of organisations aimed at working-class empowerment rather than dependency gave a distinct and for some in government, ominous appearance of being politically motivated. One such group was known as Dove House.

Dove House Community Trust

Dove House was built in the late 1960s as an attempt to meet the growing needs of the elderly in the Bogside.[21] Whereas the locality now has a much reduced population, in the 1960s it was a densely populated area with a confusion of houses, lanes and streets and an elderly population far in excess of that which lives in the area now. The house was purpose-built to cater for six elderly people and two staff. It was thoroughly inadequate and lasted a mere six years, after which it was used as a hostel for alcoholics, and, during the crisis period of the early 1970s, especially during Bloody Sunday, as a first aid centre. It lay derelict for a number of years until Mary Nelis, a local community activist, now a Sinn Fein Assembly Member, with some assistance decided to squat in the building, carry out essential repairs and open it as a meeting place for youth and as an education centre.

Some of the Dove House members recognised and identified other local needs linked to issues such as poverty, women, unemployment and culture. The members were of the view that they had a keen understanding of the social, economic and political pressures involved in the creation of their community. They were conscious that a great deal more was needed to redress the problems which had forced people into the poverty trap. It was felt within the group that if Dove House had anything constructive to offer, it was probably because, in the face of considerable opposition from establishment figures and central government, it was prepared to make a stand and side with seemingly unpopular causes. Therefore it decided to state its support for the developing interest amongst some sections of the Bogside community in what many were convinced, because of the daily occupation of the streets by troops and the daily diet of British and American television, was a declining and disappearing Irish culture.[22]

In spite of the fact that it was an area of considerable deprivation, neighbours looked after neighbours, particularly during times of personal stress. Family ties were close and it was regarded as a matter of honour for people to look after one another. Cooperation on a variety of activities, ranging from street games to indoor snooker to festival committees, was considered almost as a community duty. It had all of the ingredients for what some believe to be the ideal urban community.

Before 1969, there were two secondary schools. Several small community-organised halls catered for a range of activities including films for children on Saturday mornings, Irish language classes and schools of music. Small industries thrived as did pubs, snooker halls, barbers and corner shops. It had one RUC (police) station, staffed by two officers, which was closed in 1966 officially because of the rationalisation of the force, but believed by the population to be because of a lack of crime in the district. It was an area which respected the need for law and order, but, because its people lacked respect for the RUC, authority rested on the esteem many ordinary people had for one another. But it was also an area categorised by grinding poverty, emigration, sectarian discrimination and congestion.

It is against this background that Dove House became not merely another resource centre, but an initiative by the community which attempted to draw together two seemingly separate areas of activity – the social and the cultural. The resulting connection with Conradh na Gaeilge (the Gaelic League) began partly because of that Irish language organisation's need for premises and partly because it was the expressed wish of the Dove House members that some response be made to the growing interest in the Irish language. A significant and unique relationship grew out of the separate, if complementary, needs of the two groups. For a brief time it stood alone as a serious attempt to provide an independent and radical alternative to community work in the early 1980s.[23]

There was little in the aims and objectives of the organisation which offered clues to the origins of such a relationship, such as the promotion of individual and community self-sufficiency through the integration and exchange of community skills, and the provision of premises, expertise and resources to foster the development of community enterprises. There is little to suggest that Dove House had any ideas, pretentious or otherwise, about Irish culture. Their activists used to respond that Conradh na Gaeilge was simply a community resource which catered for and encouraged a particular skill. It is difficult to make a judgement on such a statement. Its members believed that it ought to respond to needs, perceived or not, political or otherwise, which were expressed in any way by the community. It was felt by everyone associated with Dove House that we are all constrained by a cultural tradition of some sort, the community worker no less so than the Irish language activist.

However, a consideration of the work of Dove House and a search for the threads which drew the groups together helped to identify at least three areas of interest which were common to the Resource Centre and to Conradh na Gaeilge: community, class and ideology.

The political and military conflict in Northern Ireland brought with it pressures which divert communities into either accommodating those forms of coercion and adjusting their ideas, or using them as a means of expressing their own particular view. Work arising from such a view could be described as representing a distinct culture of resistance. In a divided society, the possibilities of a working-class culture emerging which is common to all across the community divide are uncertain. But, evidence does exist of a tendency at certain times for members of the working class on both sides of the divide to seek common cause. Those experiences hold out some hope.

Community, class and ideology

It was often felt by the group that if Dove House didn't have the community to provide it with sustenance and support, there would be few Irish language units and community resource centres at all.

Was there a connection between the work of those engaged in social action and those involved in the promotion of a minority language? The view that there is a relation between social class and Irish culture must be drawn from more than one example. Indeed the fact that Irish language activists work amongst the working class, or any other specific class for that matter, does not, of itself, establish a connection.

So what was the connection between class and culture in the Dove House experience? Class was seen by Dove House, perhaps simplistically, as being connected to poverty, unemployment and political oppression. The Dove House group didn't attempt to formulate the question of class in Marxist-terms, even though some of its past members might have described themselves as such. The manifestations of class conflict, as they understood it, related to poverty and political oppression. Furthermore, culture was defined also by a need to identify and separate themselves from those whom they perceived as the oppressors. Those oppressors were identified without exception as arms of the state, whether they be soldiers, police or the representatives of the DHSS.

What did they mean by community in the context of an area such as the Bogside? It was an issue which arose within the group in discussions on the role of the separate organisations such as Dove House and Conradh na Gaeilge and the effects such a role would have on their developing relationship. But that role arose out of their own individually developing attitudes to issues as they emerged and not as any clear form of common denominator. In other words, even their attitude to the question of the Irish language, which may appear to some to be the only real and tangible basis to that relationship, arose as each group responded in its own way to the cultural demands of a local community which defined culture as a means of laying claim to a hitherto unclear and indistinct 'Irish' identity. Their respective roles were as promoters of the language and as facilitators in the removal or eradication of social and economic inequality. Their relationship was derived from a common, if independently held, assessment of those two factors. In this context, the community became the common denominator.

There is a perception amongst some activists that community can be a substitute for class, as a model for social change, and as a means of social action and protest. Deep within this is the assumption that its substructures are of little importance. In those circumstances and against that sort of background, the community acquires a different significance. Class becomes less important and subordinate to the more 'important' one of resolving the 'fundamental' problems associated with the wider community.

Such attitudes can also be found amongst those community workers who promise a romantic notion of the past, of warm affectionate relations and neighbourliness, and who advocate the creation of almost medieval conceptions within a modern urban environment of a clannish approach to society with cities containing small village-like communities which are insular and independent. Traditionally ambiguous and antipathetic to industrialisation, such groups see the answer to social problems on a much more parochial and molecular scale than the Marxist, who has a wider and more global understanding of the social and economic problems facing communities.

The crisis of the older community after the introduction of Direct Rule in 1972 and the creation of a Northern Ireland Housing Executive with widespread and sweeping powers to demolish old buildings and erect new houses, caused considerable confusion amongst people who had found a certain security in the maze of small streets and alleyways. Even today, decades after the decision which resulted in the inevitable dispersal of the Bogside population, the local newspapers contain appeals for housing from people who want to return to their old area. There still appears to be a compulsion to return to the community roots from some within the broader dispersed 'Bogside' community.

The situation in Northern Ireland reflects a series of subcultural differences related to social class. For example, the separate attitudes to politics can be identified by the differing approaches to what normally appear to be fundamental questions of Unionism. It is perceived, for example, that Gregory Campbell of the Democratic Unionist Party in Derry represents the interests of the loyalist working class, even though in reality his interests are much wider than that.[24] The same pattern could also apply to the nationalist community where the main parties vie for a slice of the same nationalist cake. Leading Sinn Fein member, Martin McGuinness, is perceived, also, to represent the republican working class.[25]

The differences which exist between the nationalist and unionist communities are regarded by some as unique in the context of a Western industrialised modern state on the European periphery. But, within those two separate groups there also exist more traditional differences. There was a time when those differing attitudes could quite easily be identified and differentiated according to their attitudes to what are euphemistically described as 'class issues'. However, within their respective communities, both unionism and nationalism in Ireland realistically reflect the sectarian equivalents of an all-class alliance.

The constant reliance on state benefits, a recognition that high unemployment will always be with them, a tendency to encourage each other to 'work the system', disseminating information about welfare benefits which result in a network of welfare-rights offices create a sense of interaction and an interlinking within the community of people who depend on the state for support.

There are aspects of what Oscar Lewis calls a culture of poverty.[26] Impressions of marginalisation, male chauvinism and parochialism could easily be applied to the community. Of course it would be wrong to attach to the community an entirely negative impression. There are sections within it which accommodate the idea of a working class aspiring to higher status levels. Some might suggest a form of embourgeoisement. But is this the same as their wanting to be a part of the middle class?

There is clear evidence of dependency although paradoxically that is not necessarily expressed in terms of helplessness. The many community enterprises such as the credit union, several cooperative ventures, the Bogside Community Association, Dove House and numerous other local initiatives are a testament to community initiative and inventiveness. The community 'spirit', as some have described it, in which some members of the community who are in a slightly more vulnerable position than others but who are able, tra-ditionally, to rely on the more fortunate to help them out, acts even now as a relief valve which helps to neutralise their frustrations and their militancy. Such an observation might suggest that a Marxist view of class in which the contradictions and the frustrations can be harnessed to enhance and develop class consciousness is way off the mark. There is a growing recognition that the welfare state in an eco-nomically depressed area such as the Bogside creates a dependent and passive community. However it is also understood that community initiative can result in an energetic if distracted community.

To counter this, local inhabitants have developed a series of sophis-ticated defence mechanisms which assist them in coping with the problems of poverty and deprivation. Working in the black economy, in spite of the recent concerted attempt by the government's drive against it, has become a norm. Just as elsewhere, many families would find it difficult to exist without it. It is no accident, therefore, that community groups respond to such situations with the creation of welfare rights groups which specialise in making the welfare state more accessible than it has been. But some argue that such an approach merely reinforces the already deeply entrenched sense of dependence on the state. Does such work actually contribute to the growing group of dependants who are being increasingly marginalised? Do groups such as Dove House actually contribute unconsciously to the notion that within the Bogside there is a developing culture of poverty?

The question of identifying culture in the context of any working-class area such as the Bogside is difficult not only because of the different social groups within the area, but also because of the confusion of cultural interests resulting in part from the community's attitudes to their enthusiasm for the 'national' culture as well as those influences arising from the control of their present cultural interests by external interests and values.

If one were to accept that the most important feature of a community based on a geographical location is the incorporation of varied and diverse interests, and subsequent rejection of class distinctions, then examples of such diversity must avoid the stereotypes associated with social class such as the trade union movement. The history of the trade unions in the Bogside is limited. The labour movement has very little influence in the area. Politics are determined by one's attitude, not to the interests of one specific group, but to the overall interests of several, under the all-embracing banner of nationalism. Thus local nationalist politicians have little difficulty in explaining that their political aims are based on the interests of all, rich and poor. The same can also be applied to those within unionist communities. The problem though is that there are very few who could be described as rich in the Bogside and far too many who know the meaning and the experience of poverty.

A culture of resistance

It is not unusual within embattled communities, particularly those which develop a sense of resistance to the state, to see the development of ideas, habits, opinions and modes of dress which in some way reflect an ethos of opposition or resistance. There are numerous examples of this which if taken by themselves do not specifically indicate a clearly identifiable cultural form – the Tartan gangs of the early 1970s might be one. That response by some young loyalists didn't noticeably affect the general cultural environment of the community and lasted at most two or three years. Furthermore, its origins to a large extent lay outside their own neighbourhoods and had as much to do with the issue of popular music than with any specific indigenous political or religious traditions. But they helped to identify and explain distinct groups.

Areas like the Bogside, on the other hand, have also developed a series of attitudes, ideas and modes of living which are developed from the traditions of a community used to looking to its past as a means of responding to the problems and issues of the present. The well-developed interest in Celtic art and music amongst the whole community may be a useful example. Furthermore, there is ample evidence that the growing enthusiasm for the Irish language, the popular interest in Irish music and other artistic forms as a result of the community's response to its political difficulties have their origins in a period free from the more obvious manifestations of the conflict. After all, the Bogside, prior to 1969, was an area which had its fair share of Irish cultural interest groups. Whilst there were probably as many active enthusiasts in the 1950s and 1960s as now, it is the extent of the broader community's identification now with what is perceived to be 'their' culture that marks the difference. In that context it would be difficult to separate such developments from the peculiar political conditions of the post-civil rights generation.

The identification with Irish music amongst large numbers of young members of the community must be seen against the background of the present conflict. The age of musical groups such as the Dubliners and the Wolfe Tones may have passed, but the legacy of what they represented to those who listened to their music, as a symbol of resistance, isn't too far removed from the present.

Interestingly, in the Dove House experience it was those at the bottom of the status ladder who generated the greatest interest in the Irish language, art and music. This isn't surprising. The maintained school system concentrated in the past on a range of 'Irish' subjects in its curriculum. Irish history and an insistence on the Irish language prepared generations of local men and women for the political upheavals of the 1970s and 1980s. Irish culture and language therefore became synonymous with nationalism and with Catholicism, rather than with class. Indeed there would be many who would argue that it has identified itself more specifically over the last twenty years with republicanism.

The suggestion that the Republican Movement draws its base of support from the working class is only marginally correct and a little misleading. There is some evidence that the Republican Movement not only do not see themselves exclusively as a 'working-class' organisation, but have no overriding ambition to allow themselves to be marginalised in that way.[27] In spite of the rhetoric, they base their appeal to a wider constituency, recognising perhaps that the road to victory must straddle more than one restricted and limiting approach. Perhaps that is why the ambiguous concept of community appeared to gain much more ground inside Sinn Fein than the slightly contentious issue of class.

The lack of support for a class-based political organisation such as the Labour Party might provide further confirmation of a reluctance for locals to see themselves only in class terms. In spite of the fact that community organisations such as Dove House often refer to class, both in their everyday work as well as in publications, there is a tendency to be a little ambivalent about it. The unifying image of community, rather than class, suggests the crossing of class barriers and fits much more neatly into the funding criteria of the major funding institutions such as the NIVT or the Community Relations Council.

This issue of culture in the Bogside has been considered from what anthropologist Edward Tylor (1832–1917) described as the 'complex whole', rather than from the narrow view of language.[28] The fact that substantial numbers of young people emerged from the North's prisons with an enthusiasm unparalleled in the history of the Irish language movement is indicative of the struggle by sections of nationalist working-class men and women for an identity which has been swallowed up in a wash of twentieth-century media pulp. But such influences cannot be separated from the social and economic problems which affect nationalist communities. The fact that the Bogside is at the forefront of such a movement of resistance consisting almost exclusively of young active and economically deprived working-class people illustrates the point. The growing and developing movement for the establishment of the Irish language, equally, cannot be separated from the social, historical and political problems associated with the present conflict.

Its views, as well as its activities through the promotion of alternative ideas brought the state down on Dove House in 1986. For a brief but critical moment, it lost its funding support from the Department of Economic Development, and a widely supported and successful campaign was mounted to have funding restored. Shortly afterwards funding was not only reinstated, but with an increased allocation. Instead of using such a victory to increase the intensity of its criticisms of the state, the group sought justification for a pause, if not a reversal, of its previous positions.

Many groups such as Dove House have moved away from those positions of confrontation with the state. They have been admitted to the growing band of community organisations whose very existence depends on state handouts. Independence and initiative have been curtailed. Furthermore, they have allowed themselves to dispense with their militant posturing and are now being drawn into open partnerships with the state. What makes this development significant?

The social partnership is important to the state hegemony for a number of reasons. In the first place it targets those working-class areas, urban and rural, which have been most affected by the troubles of the last 25 years, especially those areas which demonstrated their opposition to the state. Local justification for such a move is located in the argument that such partnerships 'empower' local communities. But, rather than enabling either the community or the individual, the social partnerships tend instead, to create a climate of dependency which reinforces the prevailing ideological hegemony.

But there is a deeper and more fundamental question to be asked in response to this section on community action in Northern Ireland. Is there some evidence which points to the existence of an attempt to draw local communities closer to the state in a process of hegemony and, as a consequence, are there examples of developments on the ground which might point to the emergence of a counter-hegemonic bloc?

There are, at least, some indicators that the extension of the welfare state to Northern Ireland, the attempt at reforms by Terence O'Neill, and subsequent reforms on housing and the franchise, as well as the creation of a variety of quasi-governmental agencies such as the Fair Employment Agency, Community Relations Commission and Community Relations Council, are all designed to draw some communities away from a position of confrontation with the state. It could be argued that the very existence of groups such as Dove House and Conway Mill was evidence, from a state perspective, that the embryo of a counter-hegemonic project was in place. The restoration of funding to Dove House, therefore, was a simple but effective means of restoring its hegemony over such a fractious group. Of course, at its most basic, hegemony is rule by consent. But, for it to succeed, it must transcend the corporate limits of the purely economic class and can and must reflect the interests of other subordinate groups too, so that what is created is a hegemony of a fundamental social group over a series of subordinate groups.[29] Therefore, the apparent spread of resources, in the creation of a welfare state designed to assist the working class in making the transition to acceptance of the political, economic and cultural structures of the dominant class, acts as a prelude for the further implementation of reforms.

Just as there are attempts to create the historic bloc which would unite all of the forces in the creation of the hegemony, so also, there are indications of a coalition of forces which suggest the development of a counter-hegemonic force. The emergence of a movement of opposition in the shape of the civil rights movement and the subsequent series of initiatives from the ground, the development of an ethos of cooperation, of fraternity and of egalitarianism, culmi-nating in the concept of community, offered some hope to those struggling for a new alternative political agenda. The indigenous leaders who grew out of this new development acted, initially, as radical intellectuals but were then faced with the more daunting prospect of having to retain a radical agenda against the onset of quasi-governmental agencies anxious to recruit for the extension of the hegemony by using the community structure.

Gramsci places strong emphasis on the need for ideological struggle in response to the process of the transition to socialism. Such a process must inevitably be considered against the ideological background of that demand for change, dependent, to some extent, on the social base of that demand, as well as the objective conditions within which that demand emerges. The objective conditions in which margin-alised communities struggle through a variety of social movements to initiate change are dependent, to a large extent, on the nature of the hegemonic relationship between the ruling, dominant class and members of the working class.

The example of Dove House as a response by people within a mar-ginalised, peripheral community is one example of a social movement challenging, if unconsciously, the basis of that hegemony. Those questions raised in response to the exploration of Gramsci's ideas provided opportunities for a clearer understanding of the nature of a community 'ideology' and its position in relation to the delicate balance of hegemonic relationships within a civil society.

It is in the delicate balance between those relationships that the community movement has sought to make its most important contribution. Conversely, it is also a recognition of the significance of that role, within civil society, that the community movement has become a pivot of increasing attention from the state, and in which its direction is one of its most focused.

7
The United States: Poverty and the Catholic Worker Movement

Radical community action and class in a deprived black ghetto

What was the experience in the United States where several experiments in community action greatly influenced those who saw the processes of community development as having a potential for change, both in Britain and in Northern Ireland?

The question of poverty in the United States has exercised minds within government for most of this century, for example, during his period of office, John F. Kennedy was influenced by the work of sociologist Michael Harrington. In his book *The Other America,* Harrington examined the problem of poverty from two intellectual viewpoints; that which places the problem of poverty within an ethnological framework and the 'culture of poverty' perspective of Oscar Lewis.[1] Lewis defined a more systematic multidimensional aspect of poverty, pointing to a cyclical effect of poverty which indicates that being poor is not just a matter of having less money, lower intelligence, poorer results in education and a lower moral and physical well-being.[2] Harrington pointed to poverty as a social pathology which resulted in those suffering from its worst effects existing as strangers in their own community. In some ways, Harrington was expressing an entirely original view of those living in poverty as representing an altogether different and separate social grouping which were unrepresentative of the norm. In some ways, he was defining what is now more regularly described as the 'socially excluded'. But, instead of referring to the poor as being a part of the working class, he was to refer to them as 'those that progress has left behind': the 'underclass'. But the underlying message in his work is one located in a moral rather than in a sociological or political understanding of the nature of poverty.

Yet another influential work of the time which pointed to the problem as one persuaded by the 'vicious circle' theory was *The Poor Pay More* by David Caplovitz, which highlighted the problem of credit as an example of the spiralling effect of the poor being dependent on hire-purchase and other forms of credit as a means of acquiring goods not normally available to them through other means.[3] Whilst Harrington pointed to the widening corridor of poverty, Caplowitz opened the doors of the slums, the migrant camps and the shanty towns of middle America. In adopting a purely economist position in examining the problem of poverty he tended to focus on the minutiae of the poor consumer, what they buy and how they pay for it. But the problem wasn't a case of identifying its effects as one determined by the low level of work which would examine and indicate the nature of its causes:

> A reformer in American society faces three crucial tasks. He must recruit a coalition of power sufficient for his purpose; he must respect the democratic tradition which expects every citizen, not merely to be represented, but to play an autonomous part in the determination of his own affairs; and his policies must be demonstrably rational.[4]

Perhaps for those reasons many former revolutionaries and radicals, from the Black Panthers to the Socialist Workers Party, eventually turned to the umbrella liberal grouping Americans for Democratic Action. In post-war United States, the standard of living appeared to be accelerating at an incredible pace with those at the bottom of the economic and social ladder benefiting gradually from the Eisenhower Doctrine which claimed that economic growth would, by itself, diffuse prosperity, 'reduce inequalities and resolve social problems'.[5] Terry Lynch of the Washington-located, community-based Downtown Cluster of Organisations saw little alternative to the present system. Inasmuch as he was interested in probing the nature of the problem, his main concern was for the depth of the problem of poverty and the means his group could employ to address it.

To examine the experience of community development in the United States, one must, first of all, have due regard for the background to the struggle against poverty and inequality in America. Four historical events are of particular significance: the great depression, which destroyed the savings of millions of middle and lower-middle class citizens; the Second World War, which ravaged much of Europe, part of Asia and lured the United States into a world-wide conflict; the struggle for black civil rights, and the war in Vietnam. All of these events became watersheds in the fortunes of the American population and contributed to fundamental changes in the lives of its people.

The collapse of the stock market in 1929 caused a shock wave throughout middle America. That section of the middle-income community which had speculated in shares found themselves vulnerable and exposed in circumstances in which the banks and finance houses decided to call in their loans, because of the rapid fall in profit. Most small speculators lost entire investments, threatening their collateral and the basis of their prosperity and security. Frank O'Donovan of the New York Catholic Worker movement described the effects as nothing short of 'disastrous' on the population during that time: 'some people threw themselves out of windows and died because of the effect it had on their families.'[6]

The crash ushered in a general and rapid economic decline. Although the reasons for the collapse are complex, they can be narrowed down to six primary causes: the depressed condition of agriculture; stock market speculation; overproduction of manufactured goods; the failure of purchasing power to keep up to productivity; direct and indirect effects of the First World War, and the self-generating effects of the depression itself.[7] The net consequence of this catastrophe was to result in a domino effect in which the massive American body of consumers reduced the amount of spending and factories were forced to cut back on production. This was to result in a chain reaction, which produced massive redundancies across the entire country.

The optimistic belief of post-war America, that economic growth would manifest itself in a more equitable distribution of wealth, was gradually disappearing. In spite of such optimism, paradoxically, economic recovery appeared to bring about a higher proportion of unemployed. This was most marked amongst those traditionally marginalised areas of communities such as the young, blue-collar workers and non-whites, especially in cities such as Baltimore. The continuing poverty being experienced by blacks, particularly in the rural South, was to result in a tremendous population movement from rural to urban areas. In the years between 1950 and 1960 nearly one-and-a-half million blacks left the South.[8] The consequences of such a movement, of course, exacerbated an already difficult racial problem, with many of those migrants being forced because of their social and economic circumstances to move into already overcrowded inner-city ghettos. The increasingly striking contrast of black inner-city poverty with growing white suburban affluence merely served to consolidate black frustration with American society and to underline the intrinsically unequal nature of that society.

Attempts by government to redress the imbalance by introducing the Civil Rights Law of 1957 were little more than a nod in their direction. But the emergence of the civil rights movement and the Supreme Court decisions to put an end to school segregation and confirm the rights of black voters in the 1960s both marked the changes in American society and the nervous beginnings of community participation in social, political and economic issues.[9] What is of particular interest are the numbers of community activists who moved through the civil rights protests and anti-Vietnam war demonstrations and into community action on social and economic issues. What is also of some interest are the relatively large numbers of activists who started out in their community careers as Catholic priests and nuns.

The comparisons to be drawn between the development of community protest in Northern Ireland with that of the United States suggest that there were some similarities. However, the historical developments of both countries and the treatment of their minorities are not at all linked. The residue of colonial rule and its social and political implications in Ireland are clearly marked and related, at every stage, to the continuing conflict and its consequent economic effects. That cannot be said about the problems affecting the marginalised communities, overwhelmingly non-white, in the United States. Whereas the problems of discrimination in Ireland are in part related to an irrational and paranoid fear expressed by one section of the Northern Ireland community that they would be subsumed by an all-Ireland Republic dominated by a Catholic majority, the same cannot be said of the white majority in the United States. Miller and Rein point to two processes of 'decay' which contributed to the problem facing poor non-whites:

> Destruction of the party foundation of the mayoralty cleaned up many cities but also destroyed the basis of sustained central, popularly-based action. This capacity with all its faults was replaced by the power of professionalised agencies ... The modern city has become well-run but ungoverned because it has become comprised of 'islands of functional power' before which the modern mayor stands denuded of authority.[10]

Blacks were not represented on local authorities and were unable to use the local government system to build a base of power, even within their own areas. Some, frustrated by the failure of radical political groups to address some of these issues turned, instead, to more mainstream politics. For example, Sherry Brown, a former member of the Black Panthers became involved with Americans for Democratic Action (ADA), a mainly liberal coalition of radical working-class activists and a scattering of members of the liberal middle class.[11]

Meanwhile, the administrative agencies responsible for providing services to the ghettos were short of funds and resources. Sanitation services, education and the police deteriorated rapidly. This was to result in the physical state of the ghettos becoming increasingly more uninhabitable, lower standards of education and an increase in alcoholism and drug-related crime. Attempts by groups such as the Mobilisation for Youth to organise a voter registration campaign were opposed by sectional interests.[12] In fact it wasn't until the emergence of the Grey Area Projects of the Ford Foundation that many of the social implications of the ghettoisation of non-whites in American cities began to come together in a concerted, if limited, programme of community action:

> They sought to challenge the conservatism of an impoverished school system; open worthwhile careers to young people disillusioned by neglect; return public and private agencies to a relevant and coherent purpose; and encourage a respect for the rights and dignity of the poor. The projects could not claim, in themselves, to realise so ambitious a programme of reform. But they proposed to demonstrate – in neighbourhoods of five cities, and one state – how the problems might be solved.[13]

There were six Grey Area Projects in 1964: the Oakland Inter Agency Project; Community Progress Incorporated, New Haven; Action for Boston Community Development; Philadelphia Council for

Community Advancement; United Planning Organisation, Washington and the North Carolina Fund. All were initiated by the Ford Foundation, although four received grant aid from the President's Committee.

This attempt to demonstrate *how* problems could be solved, rather than seek to solve the problems themselves marks an important and significant departure. It illustrated, at least, the desire of the projects to be taken more seriously. In addition, the studies of two of the more influential consultants to the Youth Programme, funded by the Ford Foundation, Richard Cloward and Lloyd Ohlin, attempted to demonstrate that juvenile delinquency, rather than being related to individual pathology, should be interpreted instead in terms of educational and economic inequality. In other words, they argued, it was a structural problem requiring a structural solution.

Interestingly, this development echoes the descriptions of leading black psychologist Kenneth B. Clark, that the social and economic stagnation of the poor in black ghettos resulted, not only in disillusionment, but in a cultural stagnation; the 'consequence of powerlessness' which resulted in the poor 'retreating into a protective subculture of poverty characterised by social disengagement and indifference'.[14]

The changes occurred when poor black residents began to assert their right, as citizens, not only to basic civil rights, but to challenge the authorities claiming to speak on their behalf. They began to sit on central planning committees and on local advisory boards. They were beginning to advocate the need for accountability. Any resistance from the authorities or agencies resulted in demonstrations of public protest. The non-white community had already tested their tactics and flexed their muscles in the long haul of the civil rights struggle. They were soon to test that strength again in the opposition to US involvement in South-east Asia.

The Poverty Programme

By the time the Economic Opportunity Act was set in place in June 1965 those instrumental in sponsoring community action through the Ford Foundation and the initial projects were able to claim that they had influenced national policy. Three hundred and forty million dollars was 'appropriated until June 1965 to provide stimulation and incentive for urban and rural communities to mobilise their resources to combat poverty through community action programmes'.[15]

The problem with the Poverty Programme for some activists was that it was being seen as a form of political patronage. Both President Kennedy and Vice-President Johnson were concerned about the future of the black vote in the northern cities. If the black vote was alienated, a Democratic presidential candidate would suffer as a result. And whilst there is little evidence to suggest that the Poverty Programme was initiated with that in mind, there is a view that it may have strongly influenced its direction. This is reinforced by Johnson's speech at a joint session of Congress in 1964 when he attempted to identify the programme with his specific administration. There was some substance to this, of course, as the design of the anti-poverty programme and its direction remained entirely in the hands of the President, officials and the director of the newly created Office of Economic Opportunity (OEO).[16]

But the experiment was, according to Marris and Rein, 'distinguished not for its accomplishments, but for its failures. The war on poverty has degenerated into a nightmare of bureaucratic bungling, overly paid administrators, poorly organised fieldworkers and partisan politics.' Such a critical view was not an isolated one. According to right-wing conservative Republican Senator Strom Thurmond, after the programme had been in operation for a year, 'its history provides a catalog of futility, abuses, political partisanship, wastefulness, slipshod administration and scandal.' Of course, he would have had a vested political interest in seeing the programme disappear.[17]

Coupled with a growing dissatisfaction amongst many of the community-based organisations with the programme and the increasingly bitter confrontations between the groups and the city mayors, the future of the programme was less than secure. With the Vietnam War continuing to dominate the President's attention, and accusations coming from the 'Conference of the Mayors' that Sargent Shriver, the director of the Office of Economic Opportunity, was engaging in 'class struggle', the Poverty Programme was being treated increasingly as a peripheral issue. As a consequence, the budgets were cut in 1966 and Johnson withdrew his personal involvement:

> 1967 inaugurated the middle-age of the OEO. The maverick newcomer had settled down, modestly trimming its ambitions to a stable budget and constraining tolerance, and trading autonomy for respectability. In the event, the right of city government to take over community action agencies was scarcely used; so unassuming had they become.[18]

The initial development which allowed local community associations to organise poor neighbourhoods fell into disuse and gradually became peripheral or 'residual' concerns of the Office of Economic Opportunity. Gradually, the provision of jobs based on local initiative was replaced by larger, more ambitious, but centrally controlled national programmes. The involvement of local community organisations demonstrating the programme's initial commitment to the principle of participation was to take a back seat. As a community-oriented programme, it had now become one based on the needs of government rather than the needs of local communities. The struggle for the control of black working-class communities, however, always remained firmly located in the campaign for civil rights and was to dominate US politics for many more years. But there were other influences within those communities which had developed independent strategies for addressing the problems of poverty.

The Catholic Worker movement

Founded in 1933 during the great depression, the Catholic Worker movement is probably best known for what its members describe as its 'houses of hospitality', located in the many run-down districts of the major cities. There are a few Catholic Worker centres in rural areas but the movement as a whole is located very much within the inner cities such as New York, Chicago, Los Angeles and Baltimore. Its members proudly state that in 1995 there were 134 Catholic Worker communities all, with the exception of three, located in the United States. Its original founder, Dorothy Day, a former radical journalist and her mentor Peter Maurin, a French radical, both now deceased, are still venerated amongst that community. The Catholic Worker is also the name of a news-sheet published by the Catholic Worker community in New York. From 1933 until her death in 1980, Dorothy Day, who joined the Catholic Church in 1927, acted as executive editor. During its history there have been a range of noted Catholic writers for the paper including some of the most radical priests in the United States such as Thomas Merton, Daniel Berrigan and the 'communitarian', Jacques Maritain.[19]

As well as providing hostel accommodation for the homeless and food for the hungry, the Catholic Worker groups are known for activity in support of trade unions, human rights (notably for some the Irish question features prominently in their literature), co-operatives, and the development of what they describe as a 'non-violent culture'. Many of those active in the Catholic Worker movement are pacifist with some also being members of Pax Christi. Substantial numbers were imprisoned in protest against war, racism, and other forms of social injustice. Many of its members have taken strong positions on the issue of conscription during times of war such as Berrigan who played a prominent role in the anti-war movement of the 1960s and early 1970s.[20]

What is especially interesting is that Catholic Worker communities have refused to apply for federal tax-exempt status, because they see it as compromising their position as independent organisations acting in support of the poor, the marginalised and the weak. Such reliance on the state, they feel, would weaken their autonomy and force them into compromising their position with regard to such social issues. Baltimore-based Brendan Walsh and Willa Bickham, and Frank O'Donovan of the New York office all pointed to the significance of their insistence on independence. All felt strongly that the refusal to apply for tax-exempt status was the single most important statement of that independence. When asked about the organisation, all of the members insist that they had no structure. Indeed, it is unlikely that any religious community was ever less structured than the Catholic Worker movement. There is a determination which is reinforced by their insistence that each community is autonomous.

The founder and driving force of the Catholic Worker movement until her death, Dorothy Day, was born in Brooklyn, New York, in 1897. Her family moved into a tenement in Chicago's South Side after surviving the earthquake in San Francisco in 1906. Her father was employed on a Chicago newspaper as a sports reporter and it was during this time that she began to take an interest in social issues, particularly in the problems of the urban poor during the period of the depression. Being something of an independent person, Day dropped out of university after a short time and joined *The Call*, a socialist daily newspaper covering demonstrations, rallies and interviewing workers on strike, revolutionary leaders and trade union organisers. She eventually joined the staff of *The Masses*, a radical magazine which aimed at exposing the 'capitalist nature' of the First World War (1914–18) and opposing American involvement. Her first real experience of the power and repressive nature of the state came when the Post Office rescinded the magazine's mailing licence. Federal officers seized back issues, manuscripts, subscriber lists and correspondence and a number of editors were charged with sedition, including John Reed, now buried in the wall of the Kremlin.

Dorothy Day was no stranger to prison during this period. As one of a group of women who during the First World War had protested at the White House against women being excluded from the franchise she was imprisoned, went on hunger strike and was eventually freed as a result of a presidential order. She refused to joined any political grouping, although clearly she felt more in sympathy with the fledgling socialist and communist parties during the earlier period of her life. So the Catholic Worker movement's origins could be described as being in the socialist and radical traditions of the labour movement of the United States.

Day's introduction to both radical politics as well as the Roman Catholic Church was fraught by personal doubts as well as by her personal experiences. She purchased a cottage on Staten Island from money earned from the sale of film rights to a novel. She lived for a time with an anarchist called Forster Batterham, an English botanist she met in Manhattan. Although Batterham introduced her to a range of new political ideas and concepts, there was little else to keep them together. Day had already moved closer to the Catholic Church whereas Batterham remained resolutely opposed to religion. In addition, the experience of having an abortion created considerable problems for her which probably had a lasting effect and created the conditions in which she would move closer to the position of the church and farther away from the libertarian lifestyle she had adopted until then. She was later to have a child and arranged for the child to be baptised into the Catholic Church.

After the baptism, there was a permanent break with Batterham, who was the baby's father. Shortly afterwards she was herself baptised into the Church and tried to find a way to bring together her new-found religious beliefs as well as her radical social values. She continued to write about the major social issues, except that her writings were now heavily influenced by her religious zeal. In 1932, she reported for *Commonweal* and *America* magazines on the Hunger March in Washington, DC. She reported on the massive demonstrations of protesters parading down the Washington avenues calling for jobs, unemployment benefits, old age pensions, relief for mothers and children, health care and housing. But she claimed that she was kept in the sidelines principally because she was a Catholic and because the march had been organised by the American Communist

Party which, she claimed, was a party 'at war not only with capitalism but with religion'.

It was during this period that she met the French former Christian Brother, Peter Maurin, an immigrant who had left France for Canada in 1908 and later made his way to the United States. He worked his way around the United States doing odd jobs and working as a labourer in a Catholic boys' camp near New York. Maurin was something of a wandering mystic, who had devoted himself to the Franciscan vow of poverty and celibacy. His life was attached to constant prayer and study and he was convinced of the value of the human potential as one which can both embrace the human need for spirituality as well as resolve the human social condition. He found willing disciples, among them George Shuster, editor of *Commonweal* magazine, who eventually introduced him to Dorothy Day.

It was Maurin who convinced Dorothy Day of the need to create ways and means of disseminating their ideas and interpretation of Catholic social teaching by promoting steps to bring about what they described as the 'peaceful transformation of society'. Clearly, Dorothy Day had found in Maurin someone who was able to address both her primary needs. She believed that she had discovered the means to link both the spiritual and the social. They founded the newspaper which became known as the *Catholic Worker* and the Paulist Press printed 2,500 copies of an eight-page tabloid-sized newspaper for $57. Her kitchen was to become the new paper's editorial office and the first edition which appeared on 1 May 1934 was sold for the first time in Times Square, New York for one cent. By the end of the year, 100,000 copies were being printed each month.

There is no doubting the extraordinary nature of the *Catholic Worker* newspaper. In many ways it is a direct expression of the paradox which is the Catholic Worker organisation. It represented the working-class frustration and animosity with the existing social order and argued in support of the labour unions. But unlike most radicals at that time, it adopted a Rousseau-esque view of an ideal future which confronted urbanisation and industrialism. Whilst it adopted a radical as well as a religious position on social and political issues as its editorial policy, there is no doubting its fundamental utopianism.

It was inevitable, especially given the problems associated with the economic crash of the late 1920s, that groups such as the Catholic Worker movement would see a need, not merely to publicise the inadequacies of society, but to do something practical which would alleviate the worst effects of the suffering. This was to inaugurate the principle of the 'house of hospitality' on which the movement was to base much of its activity in years to come. It was the period of the dole queue, of broken businessmen and of hunger. Day wrote: 'grey men, the colour of lifeless trees and bushes and winter soil, who had in them as yet none of the green of hope, the rising sap of faith.' Those who staffed their centres of hospitality received no salary or pension. All were volunteers. All believed in the principle of mercy as a means of addressing social problems. Frank O'Donovan of the New York office confirmed the continuation of this principle: 'if every [Catholic] parish would open their doors to the poor, we would not have the same problems that we do at this time.' Some might suggest that such a missionary approach to the social problems of the inner cities in the United States is both patronising and simplistic. Yet the movement does have a more detailed programme. Whilst its philosophical approach to such problems is based on a Christian understanding, they season their understanding with particles of vaguely leftist-sounding terminology.[21]

In spite of their insistence on the importance of a spiritual approach to social problems, they are not without some sense of the temporal nature of such difficulties. For example, in a reference to its philosophy in the statement of aims and means, the *Catholic Worker* announces that 'in economics, private and state capitalism bring about an unjust distribution of wealth' and that in politics, 'the state functions to control and regulate life.' They refer to the need for a 'distributist communitarianism' which would become 'self sufficient through farming, crafting and appropriate technology'. The Catholic Worker movement in New York proudly announces that it does not have a computer about the place when asked for its e-mail address. The group in Baltimore appear to have a less rigid view on matters of computer technology as they have access to several terminals both in Viva House itself and in the legal service they provide next door in Soweba House.

The Catholic Worker movement was to become a national movement which, by 1936, had opened 33 houses of hospitality across the country. The depression ensured that there would be plenty of willing and grateful clients and that Dorothy Day and her supporters had entered the world of the poverty industry. It became involved in the establishment of farming cooperatives, opening one on Staten Island in 1935, followed shortly afterwards by Mary Farm in Easton, Pennsylvania. Another purchased near Newburgh was described as the Mary Farm Retreat House whilst another was named

the Peter Maurin Farm on Staten Island. Much of this experimentation was abandoned as they realised that their principal vocation
and greatest success lay in the development of the houses of hospitality, mainly located within the large urban sprawls of the cities.

But whilst the movement had its few critics who felt that there may
have been a contradiction between the promotion of communes and
the establishment of soup kitchens as not properly representing the
Christian tradition, it was for the development of a militant pacifism
that the *Catholic Worker* attracted its most virulent opponents. Indeed
it was the Spanish Civil War in 1936 which probably marks the
watershed in pacifist involvement amongst its members after its
formation. Many had been imprisoned during the First World War
because of their opposition to US involvement, but some of those
had been members of socialist organisations such as the IWW at that
time and subject to more widespread acts of oppressive activity from
the Federal authorities. However, the Spanish Civil War became for
many a struggle not only against the tangible manifestation of
spiritual evil but of political evil as well which they saw as
synonymous. What made it even more significant and no less difficult
was that the fascist side, led by Franco, had presented itself as the
defender of the Catholic religion. Most Catholic Bishops and publications supported Franco and the Falangists. In spite of the fact that
some of its members were opposed to fascism, the *Catholic Worker*
refused to support either side in the Second World War. This caused
serious problems for some of the members and as a result the Catholic
Worker lost 70 per cent of its readership.

There is no doubt that this was a period of some concern for Day,
who warned early in the war that they should 'take another look at
recent events in Germany'. She was clearly concerned for the dangers
facing European Jewry and was to become one of the founders of the
Committee of Catholics to Fight Anti-Semitism. The Movement
adopted the same pacifist position during the entire Second World
War in spite of some opposition from members and supporters.
Fifteen houses of hospitality closed in the months following the
United States' entry into the war. But Day's view prevailed. Every
issue of the *Catholic Worker* reaffirmed her understanding of the
Christian life. Many supporters of the movement spent much of the
war years either in prison, or in work camps. Some spent their period
of service as unarmed medical personnel. During the Cold War, they
advocated opposition to the annual defence drill, describing their
civil disobedience as 'an act of penance for America's use of nuclear

weapons on Japanese cities'. It was to herald a long and protracted period of struggle during which Day and her supporters were to spend intermittent periods of time in prison.

They became deeply involved in the civil rights struggle which resulted in the Catholic Worker movement becoming a target of Ku Klux Klan violence. They were fired at on several occasions and Dorothy Day narrowly escaped being hit by gunfire in 1957. She led delegations to Rome to appeal for world peace and to personally thank John XXIII for his encyclical *Pacem in Terris* (1963) which she saw as a confirmation of her position.

Meanwhile the war in Vietnam continued unabated, with the bombing reaching degrees of intensity unheard of since the Second World War. In response, many members of the movement went to prison as the protests continued. They refused to cooperate with conscription; some took part in alternative service and some became involved in acts of civil disobedience. The newspaper editors spent long periods in prison for disobeying the law and 75-year-old Dorothy Day was jailed for the last time in 1973 for taking part in an unlawful picket in support of farm workers. In spite of her protestations against suggestions of canonisation, there is a movement within the United States supporting her election to the calendar of saints. She died in 1980 leaving behind a more substantial movement with more 'soup kitchens' than it ever had before; evidence of the growing strength of the Catholic Worker movement as well as the growing crisis in the United States civil society.

Viva House and the Catholic Worker movement in Baltimore

It is difficult to separate the veneration of Dorothy Day from the day-to-day activities of the supporters of the Catholic Worker movement. The houses of hospitality she helped to establish have her pictures on the walls alongside those of Malcolm X, Martin Luther King and in at least one case, Gerry Adams. Many have identified with the struggle in the Third World and with Ireland, perhaps not surprisingly as many of their members are first and second-generation Irish Americans.

Also, unsurprisingly, many of the people involved in community-based activity in the United States, especially those within the Catholic Worker movement, are either expatriate clergy or former religious who resigned their ministries during the traumatic periods of the Vietnam War or the struggle for civil rights. Willa Bickham and Brendan Walsh were no different. Whilst they came from different parts of the country, Willa from Chicago and Brendan from New York, both clearly were interested in the peace movement with an enduring concern for the problems of the poor in the inner cities. They moved to Baltimore with the specific intention of turning their skills to constructive use. Both saw the Catholic Worker movement as the vehicle for social and spiritual readjustment.[22]

Viva House is part of a two-building terrace in South Mount Street in West Baltimore which was originally squatted in by Brendan and Willa during the days when, they happily admit, they were hippies in the 1960s. The city was important because it represented all that appeared to be precarious about American society. It was a city of over one-and-a-half million people, the majority of them African Americans, situated on the eastern coast of the United States. As a major city it was of special interest because whilst it had experienced long periods of industrial decline, it also had a long and progressive history of trade union and working-class activism. For example, what became nationally known as the great railroad strike of 1877 resulted in widespread confrontation in Baltimore between the workers and the Maryland National Guard in the 'largest single industrial uprising in US history'.[23]

The end of the nineteenth century was a period of major social and economic change in the city. A new reform government in 1898 drafted and introduced a new charter which gave more power to the office of mayor, reorganised the schools under central units, ending the old two-tiered council, as well as limiting the power of the utility functions. The new charter created eight departments, the most radical being the Board of Estimates, which for the first time, placed the central control of the city, especially finance, under one authority.

The charter had the effect of streamlining local services. Prior to this, the Maryland Assembly had the responsibility for passing all local legislation affecting the City. However, after the election of 1922 structural changes took place by initiating a single-tiered Council to replace the earlier two-tiered arrangement. The Annexation Act of 1918 allowed for an extension of the boundaries to take account of the congested suburbs of Baltimore and Anne Arundel Counties.

In 1825, local public spending came to $200,000. One century later, spending had inflated to over $50,000,000. Of course these increases were not without corresponding social and economic changes which included the establishment of a department of public works, massive improvements in health provision, new sewage and drainage systems, the expansion of a public school system, systematic and organised planning of the city, the centralising of the fire and police departments and the provision of a pure water-supply system. However, these developments were accompanied by other problems. During the 1940s ghettos were emerging as the city centre fell into decay, especially as the issue of race became a dominating feature of local government life.

The 1960s saw some major changes in municipal government. The most significant development resulted in a massive federal involvement, particularly in the inner cities, with programmes such as the war on poverty, model cities, and urban renewal. The municipal government became involved in projects such as house-building, harbour development and the creation of neighbourhood associations. Former radical organisations, such as Citizens Planning and a number of neighbourhood associations formed in the 1950s, now work so closely with the administration that the municipal government's own literature admits that they seem now to be 'more a part of the government, than a citizens' group'.

But the area within which the Viva House members see their constituency does little to suggest that the partnership approach has solved any of the serious housing and unemployment problems. The area appears to be run down, with formerly attractive terraced houses boarded and bricked up, giving an appearance of desolation and of urban desertification. Most of them are three storeys built shortly after the American Civil War. What would be identified in Europe as the corner shop is now closed with the windows either smashed or covered and the shop signs fading with time. And as depressing as that is, what is even more saddening is the neatness, the tidiness of the streets, almost as if the authorities had moved in as the occupants moved out, removing any evidence of someone having lived there. What is even more implausible is the contrast between those neighbourhoods, neat, tidy, empty except for the groups of drunks, drug addicts and the seemingly ever-present police cars, and the streets a few blocks away, which have been reoccupied. In one street the windows are covered by wooden boards whilst in the next street they are covered with lace and brightly coloured curtains. These are the areas which Brendan Walsh describes as having been 'gentrified'. Working people live in these houses. The remaining houses are vacant. But where do the alcoholics and the drug addicts live? Where do they eat? They live on the streets and they eat in Viva House.

The nineteenth-century workers' homes in the South Mount area reflect the presence of long-forgotten industry in the city. It has the appearance of having been a busy and prosperous place. The trend to convert workers' homes to flats and rooming houses was accelerated during the Second World War by a large influx of workers from other counties taking advantage of the growth in the armaments industries. Agitation by the Union Square Association in the 1960s prompted the reorganisation of the buildings to single-family dwellings in blocks next to the Square and led to the area being designated a preservation district by the City Council in 1978, allowing speculators and some local investors to take advantage of federal housing legislation. In spite of these serious attempts to raise the standard of the area the city's oldest soup kitchen, Viva House on South Mount Street, is within walking distance of these areas and has been the centre of support for both the poor and tenants adversely affected by restoration and gentrification programs. Clearly there was much which could be described as wrong with the area.

Brendan Walsh describes the area as one in which the local population, many of them driven out of high-rise apartments, had nowhere else to go. Those houses which were open and available were either owned by a local authority which demonstrated little interest in turning them over to the occupants, or by private landlords who were only interested in extracting rent without having to repair the buildings. As a consequence, almost the entire population of the area became, at some point in their lives, recipients of the services provided by Viva House:

> We did a study of the neighbourhood. Back then what we call people who come to the soup kitchen or come to Viva House there would be about 40,000 people. We would see about 1500 different people. Of that group 50% are unemployed between 16 and 64. It pretty much reflects the city about 70/30% black and white. 250 people a week leave the city. 1,000 a month 12,000 a year.[24]

They estimate such a movement as the desertification of approximately one block every week, with some moving to other districts and others moving out of the city altogether. Much of this is corroborated by the decline in church attendance in the district: 'Essentially if you took all of the inner city churches, you couldn't fill the church once for Sunday mass.' There is no doubt that the district is in something of a crisis. Many of the local community groups such as the Martin Luther King community centre, a mere block away from Viva House, are unwilling to complain too loudly about local conditions for fear of losing the federal block funding on which they are dependent. The district is described in David Simon and Edward Burns' prize-winning study of a Baltimore inner-city neighbourhood, *The Corner*, in which the levels of poverty, brutality of law enforcement and inadequacy of the welfare system are graphically described. Indeed, so paranoid have some local community workers become because of the problem of funding for local projects that they have complained bitterly about the book; for example, the local committee of the Martin Luther King community centre believes it provides a negative image of the area. This is all the more surprising as the district is notorious because of the high levels of drug abuse, alcoholism and domestic violence, thus prompting Simon and Burns to write *The Corner*, which described in graphic detail the problems experienced by the inhabitants of the area.[25]

South Mount is an area of contrasting impressions. On the whole most of the streets are structured in the same way: terraced, wide avenues, many with mature trees on either side. Even some of those streets which have become desolate still retain a sense of the Victorian splendour of granite stability. It would have been an area consisting of hard-working people, those on which the steel, railroad and ship-building industries would depend. Even now there is a sense of industry in the walls of these solid-looking, three-storeyed buildings. In spite of the apparent stability of its background, it is also an area in which a considerable amount of prejudice and bigotry existed in the past. Brendan Walsh describes one particular problem affecting a local church:

> The church across the road, the Fourteen Holy Martyrs, was a German ethnic church which catered for a large German population in the district. Because of the increasing number of black children entering the schools the Cardinal told the parish to either integrate the school or close the church. The story is that within a week the priests all left and they closed the church rather than integrate. Now it is a Baptist cathedral.[26]

This relatively minor incident in the history of the city highlights what has become the major social problem of the United States. The question of race is one which dominates the thoughts and everyday working lives of the Viva House members. They are constantly being made aware of the racial imbalance of the city by virtue of the numbers attending their soup kitchen. By and large, the clientele represent the mix of peoples in the immediate vicinity. There are some whites, but they are becoming fewer.

Furthermore, because of the high rates of unemployment, crime is a constant source of concern, not only because of the degenerating effects of living within a crime culture, but also because of the fatigue of having the police on their doorsteps at regular intervals, particularly when the soup kitchen is at its most productive. Willa Bickham describes the area as one completely dominated by the police during periods of high activity, when they invade the district with cars, mounted police and helicopters flying and hovering at unacceptably low levels. Attempts by the police to enter the house are usually resisted by Brendan, Willa and other members of the Catholic Worker movement who strongly oppose the wearing of side-arms in the building.

Viva House caters for huge numbers of people. Indeed it would be difficult to imagine such numbers queuing outside in the street for the pleasure and comfort of sitting in the brightly decorated, relatively small dining room. And yet, queue they do, in increasing numbers. Brendan explains that there are periods in the month when activity is higher than in others: 'People get approximately $300 a month. But that doesn't last very long and so after a couple of weeks when they need to find food, they come to us.' The impression, therefore, is that the latter half of the month is the busiest. But how do they cope with everyone? Walsh estimates the overall annual figure at approximately 40,000 served by Viva House. Of those, 1,500 per month would be regarded as 'different people' and of all of those who attend, approximately fifty per cent would be unemployed.

Clearly the area suffers from a wide range of social problems. Brendan and Willa believe that the unemployment problem is exacerbated by the massive exodus of people from one area of a city. Quite apart from the fact that different districts of the city tend to be characterised by the racial content of its occupants, the area surrounding South Mount Street, being run down through population movement, is overwhelmingly African American. This inevitably results in an even more striking contrast between what is known locally as the 'rust belt' – that area notorious for the decline in industry and subsequent high unemployment – and the 'gentrified' areas beyond it. In addition, the expansion in unemployment figures precipitates other increases in crime, drug abuse and alcoholism. This tends, as a result, to sustain an increase in the police presence and harassment thus providing all of the ingredients for an atmosphere of oppression which results in internal explosions of fury which culminate in rioting, ritual confrontations and, occasionally, shootings and killings.

This dire situation is made even worse by virtue of the fact that all of the major employers, such as Bethlehem Steel, have closed down, to be replaced with nothing more substantial than tourism projects. A common complaint from those seeking work is that they have no real alternative to the low-paid tourism jobs which are currently available. Not only are the jobs of a menial nature, but they are also seasonal with only sufficient paid hours to bring people out of the defined poverty level. This inevitably results in them having little surplus money after they have paid for rent, car, food and other essential services. Even with jobs they are no better off. Poverty exists, therefore, for those in work as well as those without.

Whilst the workers at Viva House recognise the valuable work in which they are engaged, there is a deep and unsettling, if silent, admission that there are structural problems with which their 'soup kitchen' cannot cope. In spite of the substantial support they get from all around them, they realise that what they are facing isn't merely an imbalance of resources but a crisis in the social system. The control of housing by local authorities and the well-organised charitable groups provide the sharpest moments of frustration and anger for those involved in Viva House:

> If the state or the church sees a movement which has its own definite character and is not worried about breaking the law, takes over a building and gives it to a family to use; the state or church or some private organisation comes in, such as Habitat for Humanity, in which former President Carter is involved, and they organise students to rebuild it with the family putting 'sweat equity' into it and then the building is given over to them with a low-interest mortgage. All very legal, all very controlled since almost all of the state and the church is behind it. In the beginning it always starts off with people saying that that house is not being used and we need housing.[27]

Brendan Walsh articulates the frustration of it all. He realises how much people need to be rehoused. He also recognises how they can be sucked into a system which is dominated by an alliance of church and state. He feels instinctively that even the allocation of housing contributes to a system of social control. But whilst Brendan responds to these problems with emotion, his wife Willa articulates a sharper analysis of the situation:

> I am a spiritual person, but I am engaged in a class struggle. Preferential options, liberation theology are all directions that I have chosen to take and this house has definitely been a part of a political struggle. We have had our share of wire-taps and FBI agents investigating us and interviewing our friends – 'who was living here and what was going on?' A number of our friends who work with us have done jail time, continue to do jail time.[28]

It would be fair to say that this is the sharp edge and unrepresentative of much of community work elsewhere. Indeed many in either Ireland or Britain, with the possible exception of a number of Northern Ireland groups such as Derry-based Dove House, would be horrified at the thought of community-based activity such as that carried out in Viva House bringing down the power of the state on one's shoulders. After all, providing for the needy, such as that carried out by the Salvation Army here and everywhere else, is common to most countries. What Brendan and Willa do is little different, it could be argued, from the work carried out every day by those who support the work of Oxfam shops, Children in Need and Help the Aged. And yet, a cursory glance around the walls of the shops and offices which service the poverty industry in Britain and Ireland do not produce pictures of Che Guevara, Malcolm X or even Martin Luther King. In an unspecified way, Viva House represents a quite unique form of the integration of the spiritual and the material.

There are many who marched behind civil rights banners in Ireland and quite a few still alive in Britain who took part in the hunger marches of the 1930s, but there are few who took their commitment to the human rights struggle to the extent of opening and maintaining a service for the hungry for almost thirty years. That is how long Brendan and Willa have been involved in Viva House.

Placing the Catholic Worker movement within an ideological construct would be difficult as their system of organisation, method of work and focus of activity does not fit neatly into any existing patterns. They proudly announce to anyone who comes into contact with them that they do not have a board of directors, pensions plans or sponsors. Furthermore, since the death of Dorothy Day in 1980 there has been no central spokesperson, although many still regard Day, even in death, as their spiritual leader. When pressed on the issue of the editorial policy of the *Catholic Worker*, Frank O'Donovan sought to explain that whilst they do not achieve consensus, they do not believe it to be a practical objective. How then do they decide on what is published? Probably through good old-fashioned strength of will by the most dominating member of the group. Frank is one of two editors on the paper, the *Catholic Worker*, which has a circulation figure of over 80,000, published seven times per year. On these issues, the question is much more easily determined in Viva House where the central group are the family members of Brendan, Willa, Katie and David, who occupy the house and act as caretakers, cooks, managers, service providers, counsellors, legal advisers and dish washers. In short, with the exception of an enthusiastic group of supporters, the family administers and manages the affairs of Viva House including its small publication *Enthusiasm*.

From time to time, the stark manifestations of poverty force conclusions on those in Viva House which are probably not shared universally by all of the members of the movement nationwide. Brendan and Willa feel confident enough to articulate a world-view which is probably not universally shared with the same degree of enthusiasm by their fellow members. Capitalism is at fault, they would strenuously argue, but feel certain that the only way to resolve the problem is to set an example of mercy, charity and compassion. Their insistence on refusing tax-exempt status is no mere symbol of opposition. Indeed, if they applied for it, the breadth of their work would change overnight. They would have sufficient resources to feed the hungry ten times more than they are able to do now. But of course, rightly or wrongly, they would feel the weight of compromise and that would, for them, be one step too far. If what they say is true regarding their commitment to autonomy and independence from the state, then clearly it would be difficult to describe them as being part of an organisation. Without doubt, whatever the difficulties, they work hard at not being a part of an organisation because that would bring commitments which they probably feel they cannot share or support. Being a part of an organisation inevitably results in the creation of structures, of hierarchies, insists on the need for accountability and initiates forms of control which, they would almost certainly agree, would militate against their sense of spirituality. At the end of the day it is that which nourishes their work and sustains their movement:

> We spend as much energy letting people know that they do not cause their squalor or misery. We talk about capitalism, militarism, sexism and racism ... we have been arrested more than fifteen times for resisting that which keeps the poor, poor: the military build-up; the nuclear weapons; the wars in Vietnam, El Salvador, Nicaragua, Northern Ireland; the cutbacks in public housing, welfare and decent jobs.[29]

It gives an appearance of a community work with which people in Britain and Ireland have lost touch. As management groups in community organisations compete for funding from government or from the European Union, the last thing on their minds are the causes of the problems they are attempting to address. In reality the arguments for self-help initiatives are barely a stone's throw away from the accusation that the poor would be poor no longer if they only 'got on their bicycle and went in search of work'. Indeed, it would be difficult to imagine many European community organisations attempting to place the blame for such causes at the door of the state. Drawing such conclusions might just force them to take sides. It might force them to contemplate a future without state funding. Refusing to raise such questions ensures that they can sit on the fence forever – or at least until the rivers of public money begin to run dry.

8
Romania: Charity as Social Control

The decline of the Ceausescu hegemony and the export of charity as a dynamic for social change

Introduction

The people of Romania, the most isolated, downtrodden and pitiable in all the countries of the Warsaw Pact, have taken command of their destiny and brought an end to the tyranny of President Ceausescu. There can be no one who did not rejoice with the Romanian announcer when he told his people on Bucharest radio yesterday: 'We are carrying the first free broadcast on Romanian radio in 40 years. This was a revolution of children and youth. The dictator is overthrown.'[1]

So announced a London *Times* lead opinion two days before Christmas in 1989. All Christendom was called upon to rejoice, not only at the final act of vengeance at the collapse of a despot, but at the fact that it was a popular movement which succeeded in carrying it out. It mattered not that the Ceausescu family had held the reins of government since 1965, or that British governments of all shades had celebrated his rule by inviting him to Buckingham Palace and conferring on him and his wife Elena the Order of the Bath. Elena had been installed as a Fellow of the Royal Society of Chemistry and described as a 'world-ranking scientist and academician'. The stark fact remained that he had been confined at long last to history, executed by a hastily organised firing squad. For many erstwhile supporters it was time to jump ship. Furthermore, and to ensure that the world was under no illusions whatever about his fate and that of his wife, the execution was filmed for all to see.

Revolution, by its very nature is a blunt instrument when applied to political society. It matters little if the direction from which the instrument is hurled is from the political left, or the political right. But rarely before was it so enthusiastically supported by the representatives of the establishment as when *The Times* opened its pages to long and detailed accounts of the history of the Romanian people, of day-by-day accounts of the traumatic events and of the life histories of the participants.

Mark Almond, lecturer in modern history at Oriel College, Oxford, in an article in the same *Times* edition announced that 'the future of Romania looks brighter than for 40 years' especially since 'Ceausescu's regime had ruined the economy and left little behind on which to build.'[2] The great and the good of the media and academia were mustered regularly before the television cameras and microphones and asked to comment on the developments as they occurred. And whilst the hated regime was in the throes of implosion, only a handful appeared to be addressing the problem of reconstruction. And yet that doesn't provide a full picture of what was happening. Whilst there was a hard core of 'revolutionaries' in Romania who were attempting to disentangle the mess left in the wake of the overthrow of Ceausescu, there was much activity in the boardrooms, not just of the multinational corporations anxious to seize an opportunity, but of European and US charitable institutions impatient to provide a service to yet another problem area. Business in the world of charity is brisk and it is expanding by the minute.

But unlike many recipients of First World charity, Romania was untypical in many ways from other countries suffering from political instability and economic stagnation or underdevelopment. To a large extent, it was highly regarded amongst some Western leaders who appreciated Ceausescu's seemingly 'progressive' stance during the Czechoslovakian crisis. Both US Presidents Nixon and Bush paid formal state visits and the Romanian president had received a number of prestigious and significant awards from the heads of state of other European countries. And whilst the fact of Ceausescu's occasional political diversions made his state relatively untypical in the context of the various members of the Warsaw Pact, it nevertheless had a history of development after the Second World War which appeared similar to others, with the exception of Albania, in the Balkans during that period of time.

The first communist government of Dr Petru Groza launched what was described as Romania's 'social liberation'. Elections held in 1946 were won by the progressive and socialist parties. Shortly afterwards, the monarchy was abolished and a 'People's Republic' declared. The Communist and Social Democratic parties united as the Romanian Workers' Party in 1948, the name being changed back to the Romanian Communist Party in 1965. In 1948 nationalisation was introduced and power located firmly at the centre and the planned economy inaugurated.

Romania was unusual during this period for its independent foreign policy. In defiance of the Moscow hegemony whilst continuing to be a member of the Warsaw Pact, Romania refused to participate in the Pact's military manoeuvres, and all Soviet troops were withdrawn from the country in 1958. What is interesting is that whilst Romania remained loyal to the Soviet Union, it also refused to take part in the invasion of Czechoslovakia. What particularly pleased many in the West was that, in spite of considerable Soviet pressure, Ceausescu continued to condemn the assault.

In spite of his foreign interventions, Ceausescu was responsible for initiating a series of major, and to a large extent, useless domestic developments which were noted more for their disruptive nature than for their contribution to the quality of life of the Romanian people. The opening of the Danube Canal in 1984, which was heralded by celebrations and a great fanfare, proved to be of no practical use. The creation of a Metro for Bucharest in 1985 was declared to be a great victory. However the destruction of the Danube Delta as a result of unregulated agricultural development and the belated attempts to rearrange agricultural production by transporting the inhabitants of a majority of the country's villages into hastily constructed concrete blocks of flats, despite the cultural and social upheaval this would have caused, was a catastrophe. Great celebrations were held in March 1989 to record the end of Romania's US$10 billion foreign debt. Meanwhile, the population continued to suffer from prolonged scarcities of almost everything. What was especially exasperating for many citizens was the fact that much of Romania's food was used to help pay the foreign debt, a factor which accelerated the potentially catastrophic shortage of food within the country.

In spite of all this, in November 1987, the Romanian Communist Party congress re-elected Ceausescu as general secretary.

What created the catalyst for the 1989 revolution is generally acknowledged to be the moment when local parish priest Father Laszlo Tokes spoke out against Ceausescu from his small church in Timisoara. This prompted a series of events which culminated in the Reformed Romanian Church expelling him from his post and meetings being held by his parishioners protesting against the decision. This was followed by attempts by the police to curb the street demonstrations and a series of public confrontations.

Eventually, huge crowds which had gathered on Timisoara's main square were confronted by Securitate and army troops.[3] These street confrontations eventually led to what amounted to an insurrection at the Communist Party's headquarters after demonstrators broke in and portraits of the president were burned and destroyed. The Central Committee of the Communist Party insisted on more severe action being taken against the demonstrators and several were killed. Rumours of secret burials and cremation of dead demonstrators swept Timosoara and Bucharest. Eventually the army decided to change sides and came out in support of the protesters.

On 21 December, Ceausescu decided, in an attempt to recover his support, to address a mass rally in front of the Central Committee building in Bucharest. Workers who arrived were turned away after being told that Ceausescu would not be speaking on that day. In the confusion of the events the decision was reversed and the meeting called for later in the day. Eventually as Ceausescu began to speak to the growing crowds from the balcony of the Central Committee headquarters, groups of young people began to jeer. Ceausescu was forced to stop in mid-speech because of the uproar and was led away as the police and army units still loyal to the president attacked the gathering and began making arrests. Soon afterwards they started to fire at the crowds as defensive barricades were erected in the streets.

The following day, Ceausescu again appeared on the same balcony and attempted to address the crowd gathered in the square but people continued to jeer and throw stones at him, forcing him to withdraw. Shortly afterwards the protestors broke through the main doors. But, with the crowd only a short distance away, Ceausescu, his wife Elena and some others escaped by helicopter from the roof. Later that day, the radio and television stations were overrun by the protesters and broadcasts commenced with the new revolutionaries in charge. After capture, Ceausescu and his wife were tried by an anonymous court, condemned and summarily executed by a firing squad. The next day their bodies were exhibited on television new bulletins.

There is some justification for believing that the Ceausescus' swift trial had as much to do with putting a brake on the revolution and saving former Party members than in stopping the expected assaults of the Securitate. When Ceausescu fell, the National Salvation Front was already organised and in place, ready to take control. Indeed, most of its leaders, including President Ion Iliescu and former Prime Minister Petre Roman, were former Communist Party members, suggesting perhaps, that the 'revolution' was not quite as spontaneous as it had been portrayed.

Under the Ceausescu regime, many of the problems faced by those within the Warsaw Pact countries seemed to be more severe. The attempts at a rigidly enforced collectivisation programme created widespread problems of localised poverty as the private plots of land for personal use were, in most cases, so small as to be inadequate for any form of sustained development.

A report published in 1971 by the United Nations on the potential within underdeveloped nations of community development investigated a number of countries including Romania. There is no doubt that the social conditions of ordinary people during the Ceausescu regime were appalling. But there was little of that reflected in the report which was written by a senior academic and Director, Centre de Reserches sur la Jennesse, Bucharest. Consequently, although written some years before the 1989 revolution, the United Nations report viewed the situation in Romania rather differently: 'The state provides assistance to the economic and organisational development of agricultural cooperatives. It allocates credit, makes available technical and material facilities, and is responsible for the renewal of long term contracts for agricultural production.'[4]

The impression offered is of a state machine running smoothly and in which a synergy exists between the state and the peasant producer. However, in truth, the opposite was the case: the regime insisted on the peasants having to surrender all of their private produce to the state in return for credits. Such a situation merely aggravated an already difficult situation, although interestingly, the United Nations report offered a less pessimistic view of conditions during the height of the regime's development programmes:

Romanian communities have tried various forms of organisation and action to solve problems of common concern. In rural communities, special forms of co-operation serve certain common interests within a non-institutionalised framework, such as mutual assistance at harvest time or in the construction of houses, the joint purchase and use of certain agricultural implements, the communal use of pasture-land and common grazing.[5]

The UN also reported that 'old forms of community organisation and action' were being improved upon and that new forms were appearing which were to encourage the extensive participation of the mass of ordinary people in the solution of problems affecting the life and activity of the entire Romanian population. One would be inclined to think that much of this report was either written by an overly-optimistic researcher, or simply produced by an official of a public relations department within the Romanian state rather than by a respected senior academic. Indeed the report stands in stark contrast to that produced by Vice-Chairman of the interim government, Mr Dumitru Mazilu, who was highly critical of the human rights record of the Ceausescu regime and who subsequently spent over a year under house arrest. The fact remains that the state was no longer able to resist the growing demands for fundamental changes. Food was becoming increasingly scarce and with the prospect of having to face yet another bleak winter, the growing mood of pessimism amongst ordinary people emerged as a catalyst for real change. Instead of endorsing the propaganda of the Ceausescu regime, it is surprising that the United Nations did not take cognizance of the serious social and economic consequences arising from the nature of the regime.

The writing appeared to be on the wall when a moratorium was called on the export of domestic food produce to friendly countries, such as the former Soviet Union and some Arab states. There was no doubt that this move would have resolved the immediate problem of food supply for the winter period, but it was never likely to stem the growing protest movement. The agricultural industry in Romania was notoriously inefficient with a large proportion of the annual production being wasted. And yet, in 1972 the United Nations continued to report that all was well amongst the peasantry:

Co-operative farming groups, which the peasants join of their own free will are organised and conducted along democratic lines. The general assembly of co-operating peasants is responsible for all aspects of co-operative production. It is competent to deal with various matters including the utilisation of co-operative land and equipment; investment in physical and social infrastructure; the distribution of income (in cash and in kind) among the co-operative farm members; allocations to the various co-operative funds, such as the reserve and social funds (the latter being used to assist members who can no longer work because of their age); the election of management bodies to oversee the various aspects of co-operative activities.[6]

Once again the United Nations report on 'community development' in Romania appears to be well off the mark. For example, what is not mentioned in this report is the fact that Ceausescu involved the army in both the industrial and the agricultural management structures of Romania – a move which was not widely supported within the army and which may have been a deciding factor in the decision of the army officers to turn their backs on Ceausescu and support the revolution. Mark Almond reported that there was some animosity amongst members of the officer corps at being forced into non-military positions and not being permitted to continue within their chosen career. Clearly such a development would have had humiliating repercussions for their personal and collective sense of status within Romanian society.[7]

The regime constantly insisted that in the period since the end of the Second World War, the participation of the people in the national life and in urban and rural community life had increased steadily. Indeed, it went further and claimed that such participation had led to the formation of organisations by an ever-increasing number of workers, peasants and intellectuals of all ages and from all national groups within the country. Much of what they had to say sounded vaguely familiar. Much of it was dogma with little to do with the reality of the situation on the ground:

> The agricultural co-operative production unit has created the organisational framework required for the economic and social activities of the peasantry, the harmonious merging of the interests of the peasantry with those of the people as a whole, and the organic integration of co-operative agriculture into the process of development of the economy as a whole.[8]

There is no doubt that the conditions in which community development flourishes are different in one national context compared to that of other nations. In Romania, state pronouncements that the whole population 'is taking part in the construction of a socialist society in accordance with a programme drawn up, in co-operation with the masses, by the Romanian Communist Party' were rarely taken seriously and generally treated with scepticism. But, until the cataclysm of 1989, little was said publicly by any of the Western powers, who demonstrated a callous disregard for the regime's human rights record up until that point.

The United Nations report on community development in Romania reported (in 1971) that 'in the past twenty-five years there had been fundamental changes in the economic social and cultural development fabric of the country and in the pattern of mass participation in national and local affairs. Production of industrial and agricultural goods along with services have registered impressive gains.'[9]

If we use 1938 as a base year, the United Nations reported that industrial production in 1968 had risen by 535 per cent and the national income had increased by 519 per cent. Over the same period, per capita income had increased more than fourfold. In 1968, industry accounted for 54.2 per cent of the total product, followed by agriculture 26.2 per cent, construction 9.2 per cent, transport and communications 4.3 per cent and distribution of goods 3.5 per cent. In 1968, the volume of overall industrial production was more than 14 times greater than in 1938 and 917 per cent higher than in 1950, representing an annual growth rate of 13.1 per cent. But there is little evidence to show that these apparently massive increases were having any real effect on the levels of poverty, shortages of foodstuffs, consumer goods and on the general quality of life of ordinary people.

Since the economy under the Communists was centrally planned, the adjustment after the 1989 revolution to a market economy has been slow in terms of real change to the living conditions of the people of Romania, especially those living in the countryside. Agriculture accounts for 31 per cent of the gross national product, a slight increase on the 1968 figures; industry accounts for 55 per cent, also a slight increase and services 14 per cent. Of the workforce of ten-and-a-half million, about 34 per cent are engaged in industry and 28 per cent in agriculture. Romania continues to export minerals, chemicals, machinery and manufactured goods to Germany, the former USSR and Italy.

In spite of the promotion of heavy industry and other infrastructure projects under the Communists – such as the Danube Canal and the Bucharest Metro, the Iron Gate Hydropower Project at Drobeta-

Turnu Severin on the Danube River, the Ploiesti oilfields in Northern Bucharest and the giant iron and steel works at Galati – poverty continued to be characteristic of life in the rural towns and villages. The emphasis on major industrial projects which was a central feature of the Romanian Communist Party's goal of self-reliance inevitably led to shortages of food and consumer goods. After all this was a country which was heavily dependent on local food produce. The change of regime has yet to make a substantial impact on that inescapable fact. Queues continue to grow at shops and petrol stations. But whilst food is still a major problem, there are also shortages of medicine, clothes and even bedding.

The problem of Aids as an example of social neglect

What made the problem of Romania so difficult to understand, in spite of the more obvious examples of the political abuse of power, was the hideous exposure to the widespread epidemic of Aids, especially amongst young children. Dr Jean Gabriel Babon of the Paris-based Medecins du Monde launched an appeal immediately after it was confirmed that the problem was endemic as a result of blood tests which had been carried out by a French team. What they had discovered was that one in five children, out of a total of 837 tests based on a study of several hospitals across the country, were HIV-positive. Indeed, so damaging was the report of the French that it was immediately suppressed by the Ceausescu administration. It was only after the December revolution that the problem came to light and the issue was addressed.

What was the extent of the problem? In the first place the problem was hidden from view by Ceausescu because he refused to admit, either that the problem existed, or that it was accurate. His view reported in several newspapers at the time was that it was a disease which was confined to the capitalist countries of the West and to Africa. Most of the problem existed in the overcrowded orphanages. The director of one, in Bucharest, blamed a combination of lack of resources, constant power cuts, shortage of drugs and the pervasive influences of the Securitate, Romania's secret police at the time. He was reported as saying that he was warned by the authorities not to say anything about the problem, on pain of death. But, chronic as the problem undoubtedly was, the state of the hospitals themselves illustrated the abject failure of the regime to provide the most basic services. The hospitals were disgustingly filthy, bed linen was replaced sporadically, the children were ill fed, often unclothed, sleeping in their own urine, clearly distressed and constantly crying.

The high incidence of Aids amongst the children created an immediate crisis amongst those agencies concerned to have them adopted. Yet another French Aids expert and president of Medecins du Monde, Dr Jacques Lebas, claimed that the epidemic was worse than anything experienced before and that it was much worse by far than the problem of Aids in Africa. Much of the blame for the extent of the problem was the failure of the regime to provide untainted blood supplies and the multiple use of needles. What was even more disturbing about this difficulty was the discovery that instead of the problem having a vertical effect, that is, passing from children to parents and vice versa, the epidemic had a lateral consequence. In other words it was passing from child to child; the inevitable consequence of the multiple use of unclean syringes.

It was to attempt to alleviate some of these problems that organisations were established to meet those needs and it was at Fagaras in the centre of Romania that they decided to establish a base.

Fagaras

The town of Fagaras lies just between the cities of Sibui and Brasov with the Transylvanian Alps to the south and the Carpathian mountain range to the east. It is a town with little to offer the tourist in terms of places to see or the investor in terms of developed skills or of existing industry. Indeed, for many who visit Fagaras the most striking thing about the town apart from the thoroughly drab nature of its architecture, is how little commercial activity takes place. Shops are few in number; the standard feature of most Western towns of comparable size, the supermarket, is non-existent. It is almost impossible to visit a restaurant. A bar or the Romanian equivalent of the public house is shared with a small grocery. It does have numerous combinations of unattractive, multi-storey apartment blocks which present a picture of a place in which people eat, sleep and vanish during working hours. Humourless and dull, the town has become a place in which many of its inhabitants spend their waking hours in other places, either in Brasov to the east or in Sibui to the west. There are some chemical manufacturing plants and smaller developments but in reality it has become a dormitory development in which community life, as it is understood in the West, is virtually non-existent. Before that, it would have been a healthy and vibrant market town for the peasants in the surrounding countryside or for the villages dotted around its exterior.

Fagaras offers little in the way of relief for the visitor or tourist, in spite of the massive drive towards tourism in the country as a means of inviting foreign income. One recent visitor to the town described it as a small town but with a population which seems to exceed its physical size. His description of the local hotel as one which brings to mind a Victorian school dormitory in which little thought or concern is given to decoration, with broken light switches, no cooked meals, tea or coffee, and washing facilities which are only available at certain times of the day. He didn't witness any commercial activity other than a few ill-stocked shops, stalls within a large area that passes for a supermarket, and melon sellers on the street who remain with their tiny stall until all stock is exhausted, sometimes having to sleep alongside their wares. Impoverishment appears to exist everywhere.

Before the revolution of 1989, the provisions of the Constitution on administrative organisation, allowed for administrative territorial units such as the department, the town, the municipality and the commune. On the face of it, there appeared to be a logical and well-structured administration. In truth it was little more than a self-serving bureaucracy with its own internal dynamic and momentum which bore little relation to reality or to the real needs of ordinary Romanians. However, the United Nations report on community development in the country reported glowingly that:

> the principles underlying the present territorial administrative organisation of Romania include the following: a) closer coordination between the central administration of the state and lower administrative units; b) the provision of specialised assistance and practical support to the departments, towns, municipalities and communes; c) the simplification and rationalisation of local administrative organs; d) the consistent application of national policies to ensure the full equality before the law of all citizens without distinction as to national origin.[10]

Since the collapse of the Ceausescu regime, much of this has changed. There appears to be little left of the old state and its organs although it would be difficult to imagine the state continuing in any form if it did not retain at least some of the more efficient sections of its burgeoning bureaucracy. The fact that the politicians of this era are, by and large, politicians of the old era in new clothes suggests strongly that the only thing which has changed is the title of the ruling party and a vague, if yet unclear, genuflection to some form of democracy. Poverty and suspicion remain and whereas it is generally, if privately, acknowledged that when the old Romanian Communist Party was in control everyone had something, now only a few share everything and most have nothing.

The Romanian Relief Fund

The messages of despair which emanated from Romania during the period surrounding the transition of power, particularly that explosive period when freedom for the Romanian people hovered delicately between success and defeat, were heard amongst groups of people in Ireland and elsewhere. For years, many of them had focused their interest on support for traditional Third World projects in Africa and Latin America. Many were professional community workers whereas others were perceived as well-meaning amateurs. However, it would be quite wrong to accuse many of them as 'professional' carers, or even as 'amateur' charity workers. Indeed, some of them at one time would have been actively engaged in radical politics in Ireland, as indeed others would have been in other countries.

But the problems of the Romanian population struck a chord for many as an example of a people, within the European family of nations, to whom practical help could be offered. In other words, regardless of the physical hurdles of the Irish Sea and the English Channel, one could drive to Romania. Even though it might take several days to get there, once on the continent there was nothing to stop a fleet of vans and lorries transporting clothes, medicine, food and other items to a people who would benefit from them. It appeared for some a more practical and tangible way of responding to need. Furthermore, the relief workers could get to grips with these massive social problems. They could see the effects of their work, they could talk to the recipients and sense their appreciation. It was, after all, better than collecting pennies for anonymous black babies in Africa. In response to that need the Romanian Relief Fund was established a short time after the calls for assistance went out over Romanian radio and television.

Two organisations responded to that call and continue to work closely together. The Methodist Mission in Derry and the Rosemount Resource Centre, also in Derry, are examples of community action which have engaged in providing community services within the Derry area to people experiencing different levels of poverty and disadvantage.

There is nothing especially unusual about either of the two groups involved in this exercise. The Rosemount Resource Centre is a neighbourhood community development project which caters for the needs of people who live in the immediate area, whether they be on issues such as housing welfare rights support, child care provision, supporting the elderly or a local women's group. It has been involved in a small number of other initiatives such as the formation of an information technology training centre and a partnership with projects on the cross-border, Republic of Ireland side of Donegal. There were times when it became involved in local protest activity against British Army harassment of young people as well as the erection of a massive observation tower in the middle of the neighbourhood. Much of that activity has disappeared, not only because of the political developments which have taken place in recent years, but also because there was a fear that too much publicity was likely to draw down the displeasure of the civil servants responsible for managing core funding for these projects.

The Methodist Mission emerged as a result of the attempt to deal both with the problems of alcoholism, particularly amongst men in the town, as well as the related problem of homelessness. Based in the Crawford Square area of the town, some members of the Mission met with some hostility from residents, led strangely enough by a former well-known civil rights activist and an erstwhile member of the Rosemount Resource Centre team after it supported the establishment of a mental health support unit in the area. The Mission caters for approximately twenty men, some of whom have been residents for some years and others who stay for shorter periods. They are offered accommodation, meals and, where requested, counselling and support. It has a regular staff, some of them former residents, who provide security at night, cook meals and assist in the maintenance of the building, a large terraced dwelling. By and large, the group have never been involved in any other activity, other than the Romanian Relief Fund.

There is a long history of involvement in religious missionary and foreign aid work in the provincial towns and cities of Ireland such as Derry. Indeed, the churches everywhere in Ireland, urban and rural, are heavily engaged in organising collections for a range of activities in Africa and Latin America. Most of it is directed towards missionary-focused activities in which a number of Irish-based religious organisations are involved. Some are much more organised, employing collectors and local or regional organisers, such as the national Roman Catholic charity known as Trocaire (compassion). But it is probably in more recent years that a secular movement has emerged in Derry, particularly around the issue of Romanian relief. That is not to say that there is no church involvement. After all, the Methodist Mission, whilst being staffed and supported by non-religious personnel, is essentially a church-based initiative. However, most of the people involved in the Romanian Fund are involved for humanitarian rather than religious reasons and almost all come from strongly working-class backgrounds. Aside from the Mission manager, all of the other workers in the programme are volunteers, many of them unemployed.

The manager of the mission, Sean Boyle, is extremely conscious both of his role and his motivation as well as his own background. He is aware of the problem of being accused of taking advantage of a situation in Romania and of exploiting it for his own purposes or for that of his employers. He insists that it is nothing to do with either the export of Western religious values, or, for that matter, the export of charity. He is conscious of the need to ensure that whilst he is transporting aid to the poorest and most vulnerable sections of the Romanian people, it is important to understand Romanian sensitivities about this matter:

> For example, we had one of our vans burned and because we were about to travel within a few days we were obliged to borrow one from another organisation engaged in similar work. Painted on the side were the words 'Humanitarian aid for Romania'. That caused us a number of problems. Indeed the words went down like a lead balloon in the areas we visited. The Romanians didn't like the idea of a van travelling through Europe with those words painted on the side. We were told this in no uncertain terms when we arrived.[11]

Clearly the Derry-based organisation was sensitive to the Romanian dilemma. The directors of the orphanages were grateful for the materials and technical expertise which the group were bringing to these remote areas of the country. But Sean knew the meaning of such irritation. He was raised within a large working-class family in an area of the city renowned at the time for its high levels of poverty and deprivation.

There were sensitive issues to take account of in Fagaras other than the official concern for the perceptions of neighbouring countries through which the convoys had to pass. The manager of the Rosemount Resource Centre, a large community-based group, was aware of the problems being created as a result of the aid provision. Because they provided support to a grouping of around eight orphanages in the district surrounding Fagaras, it was becoming clear to the Irish group that many of the orphans were experiencing some resentment amongst the locals because, in some cases, they were now better clothed than the inhabitants.

The orphanages form the basis for the aid delivered by a convoy of vans from the northwestern city of Derry in Ireland to the area surrounding the city of Brasov and its smaller neighbouring town of Fagaras. Although Tommy McCourt is interested in focusing his own attentions on the Fagaras town itself and the surrounding districts, the coordinator of the operation, Sean Boyle, explains that his organisation attempts to provide support the length and breadth of the country, even though he recognises the immensity of the undertaking:

> We have centred our operations in Brasov and Fagaras is one of the towns within our area of activity. But we deliver aid the length and breadth of Romania. Most of the building projects are in the Brasov area. We have built up a fairly good relationship with what is called the Children's Protection Agency, a state agency. In the past everyone had a title, everyone was a Director. Now there is only one overall director of the agency. He has control over all of the orphanages. Some of the work we carry out is physical work such as construction, although some of our work is simply delivering aid. We refurbish buildings, provide toilets, running water, bathrooms and so on ... We also supply cleaning materials.[12]

The orphanages continue as a direct legacy of the old Ceausescu regime. Ten years after the fall of the dictator, the orphanages remain as a testimony both to the inefficiency as well as to the cynical nature of the old Stalinist state. But they are important not merely because they are, by themselves, a clear example of social need in these remote and forgotten areas, but because they are a vitally important part of the local village and in some cases, town infrastructure. Tommy McCourt explains their significance:

Our main involvement is with the orphanages. It is important to note that they appear to be the only evidence of any real community-based activity in these areas. There is a large orphanage problem in Romania, some locals try to explain it away as a gypsy problem, but in some cases it appears to be the only economic activity in the village. The villagers hang about the place, using it as a coffee house, a place to gather and meet with others, even in the midst of all of these children wandering about, some crying, others confined to their cots. It is almost as if the children were simply an appendage, as if they weren't even there.[13]

He went on to explain the nature of the orphanage. In some cases, they are the only centres of economic activity. Some members of the community are employed in them. The orphans are available as cheap labour to local farmers. In one case, a young man from an orphanage who was offered a place in a college was severely beaten as a message to others that such ambition was frowned on by the villagers and farmers. As far as they were concerned, the orphanage, to all intents and purposes, was their property and a valuable source of farm labour. This is a far cry from the organised system of management and public accountability suggested by the author of the UN report in 1971 when he said:

> Another way in which the community participates in the management of public affairs is through civic central groups. These groups are composed of persons from the various occupational, professional and age groups who are elected by trade unions, civic and mass organisations. They are responsible for overseeing the managerial activities and working conditions in industrial enterprises, territorial health units, health resorts and rest homes. It is expected that the competent authorities will act on their findings and recommendations.[14]

If even a part of that were true, there would be at least some evidence remaining of a civilised, orderly society in which poverty would be addressed in some systematic way. If the state could not do it, would other structures emerge? Tommy McCourt explains:

> The place was very impoverished. I didn't see any industrial activity at all. People just seemed to be walking about, although there was a market. It seems still to be largely a peasant economy. There

doesn't seem to be any other form of commercial activity, it is very much an individual effort by people trying to eke out a living for themselves. There are beggars everywhere although the Romanians all claim that the beggars are gypsies. Along the sides of the road people are trying to sell small craft goods, wood or leather. They try to flag down passing traffic. During Ceausescu's time the local manufacturing industries were connected to the local schools. There was a formal relationship between the schools and industry in which one would support the economic and training needs of the other. But since the collapse of the regime all of that structure has gone.[15]

Just as the Ceausescu structures disappeared overnight, so apparently did the will or initiative of the local people disappear as a means of addressing social disadvantage. When asked if there is any community attempt to deal with the problems of under-development in these areas, particularly in the light of the suggestion of the UN report that some community-based structures existed before 1989, both McCourt and Boyle could only point to the orphanages. Tommy suggested that anything which hints of Ceausescuism is immediately frowned upon. He refers to a discussion on the positive advantages of forming tenants' associations in the grey apartment blocks: this was dismissed by locals as verging on the profane. 'They sound just like the old communist bloc committees', would be their response; clearly a reference to the party-organised structures. Any reference to people organising themselves is seen as an attempt to create political alternative organisations, to recreate a past with hints of socialism. References to community activity is challenged by references to communism. They are not ready for it. And yet there are many reasons for change. In the ten years since the passing of the old regime, the benefits of the free market have yet to be felt in towns and villages in areas like Fagaras. Already there are signs of the new democratic edifice beginning to crumble. People are beginning to question their condition. Sean Boyle listens to the complaints:

Some are getting very rich. Although some industries have moved into cities such as Brasov that movement is not felt in towns such as Fagaras. There is some evidence of a growth of affluence in those cities for example, some shops have a heavy western influence. There is a university in Brasov and a civil service centre, but there are also the large old industrial plants. Heavy steel plants which are just rusting away. There is very little manufacturing. Large numbers of people in rural areas are depending on craft goods, a few small bakeries and small shops. Little else. No public buses. People do say that during the Ceausescu regime everyone had a little, whereas now a few have a lot and the rest have nothing.[16]

In spite of the fact that the poor are likely to continue to be poor within these areas, there is little evidence that any of them are moving in a direction which might begin a process of reconstruction. Clearly, for whatever reason, the communities in these remote areas are unlikely or unwilling to look at the potential for change through the creation of self-help projects. Whether that reticence is driven by a reluctance to face unknown challenges or because of a more sinister fear of being branded communists remains to be seen. There is no doubt that they lack the confidence to deal with these issues themselves and at the same time any suggestion of state involvement appears to some of them at least, to smack of old-style Ceausescuism. There is also a problem in that they percive the larger political parties to be the same as before. Many do not see any difference, except that now they feel as if they have less than before. Tommy McCourt discussed these issues with locals:

> The people believe that the politicians involved then are still involved. They see them as shrewd operators. What may have been the old community apparatus in one town has simply become the new party apparatus. This has resulted in a lot of cynicism amongst the population and something which is exacerbated by the fact that most multinational companies are paying small local wages. There is a certain amount of pessimism amongst people on the ground. When I asked them if they thought that Romania might enter the European Union at some stage, at least one person said that the elite in the country would prefer it to move in a direction similar to that of the Latin American countries in which they would continue to be the elite and the rest of us would remain permanently in servitude.[17]

If things are so bad there what can a few small community initiatives achieve several thousand miles from their base in the North-west of Ireland? The Romanian Fund consists of a number of local community workers with long organisational experience, and a team of house painters, electricians, plasterers, plumbers and nurses available to assist in some of the building and construction projects which have been in progress over a number of years.

There has been a consistency of commitment by this group which appears for some to be unique in the world of aid and charity. Dr Lana Body, a specialist in an Aids and tuberculosis clinic was reported in 1996 as saying that whilst she receives support from agencies in France, Germany and England, she prefers to work with 'the Northern Irish ones who always keep their promises whether for medicine or clothes or blankets'.[18]

In spite of the fact that one of the constituent members of the Romanian Fund in Derry is a church-based organisation, Sean Boyle insists that they have no religious agenda in transporting aid:

> There was a sort of evangelical approach by some of our members at the start. A small number were involved in the Christian Fellowship, but we are basically a secular group with peoples of various religions involved. We do not transport bibles, nor would we want to although there are some groups there who see that as their priority. Some of the groups we work with have a religious background, particularly some groups from Germany. But there is a suspicion of some who attempt to proselytise. We are not white missionaries who come to give handouts although some groups do that, but as a charity we try to avoid it being seen as that.[19]

There is no doubt that they hope to see some form of development taking place which would eventually become an organic one. Both McCourt and Boyle are involved in attempting to focus their attentions on providing for a specific need which they identify as something which their skills could address. In the changing atmosphere since the state attempted to take control of the chaotic situation in the children's orphanages, some adjustments were made which resulted in other problems beginning to emerge. The attempt to rationalise the structures of the orphanages by removing those who passed the age 18 barrier only resulted in the problem being passed elsewhere. Those who were forced to leave simply found themselves wandering the streets with nowhere to live and no job to go to. The Derry group are now working on a plan to find both the means to construct a purpose-built hostel with training facilities which could be used as a stepping-stone for those emerging from the orphanages.

Perhaps the involvement of this group is having a small but significant effect, not only in terms of the relatively substantial aid programme in which they are involved through the systematic transporting of materials, but in chipping away at the core of resistance which has been built up over the years since the collapse of the old regime. As small as it may be, the local group who are attempting, in a very small way, to find accommodation for the orphan homeless shows that, at least for them, the success of charity begins at home. McCourt illustrated the severity of the problem facing groups in some of these areas:

> When they reach the age of 18 the kids are basically shown the door. Some turn to prostitution because they have no jobs or places to go to. There are some attempts being made to provide for them. Six young men who were forced to leave the orphanage because of the change in policy were forced to sleep in the street. There would have been some volunteering by those who staffed the orphanages to assist in finding accommodation, but it was a very unsatisfactory situation. The problem remains that much of the volunteering is mainly foreign based, there are still very few local people becoming involved.[20]

This begs the question why those Irish volunteers become involved. Do they do it out of a real and genuine concern for the needs of people living in desperate states of poverty? Or is it a form of philanthropy driven by the spiritual needs of the providers? It is always difficult to be precise about this aspect of charitable work, particularly when one is confronted by community activists who take time to engage in collecting and organising loads of equipment and other materials and then physically transport them over several days of tortuous driving the four thousand miles round trip to and from Romania, across Europe. It could easily be argued that it really does not matter because the questions are irrelevant as long as someone in need benefits from the work being carried out by these groups. But whilst there may be some truth in this, it does allow us to raise the question, if not of motivation, then of effect. What effect can this work have, other than that of minimal relief?

It is hard to imagine a society bereft of social structures. It is almost as if civil society never existed in Romania during the period following the war against Germany in 1946. When the question of structures is raised, those involved in attempting to either provide relief at its most basic, or those who see the opportunity for wider questions such as local participation in self-help to be addressed, state unequivocally that no such structures exist. In the area of home-based craft, manufacture which directly draws together both the community-focused cottage industry and a local culture administration must have existed, at the very least, to coordinate and distribute crafts for the tourism industry. This was how it was envisaged by the authors of the UN report:

> The presidents of the Union of Writers, the Union of Artists and the Union of Composers and the representatives of the central council of the General Union of Trade Unions, of the National Union of Agricultural Co-operatives and the central committee of the Union of Communist Youth are members of the executive bureau of the Committee and have the right to speak and vote. This structure is also maintained at the local level to ensure participation at all levels in the development of cultural activity.[21]

Has all of this disappeared? Whether of value or not, such a structure must be of special significance in drawing together vital components of an industry which, to all intents and purposes, no longer exists. And yet a recollection of its existence cannot be so far into distant memory that it cannot be brought once again to the surface. It seems that if those structures which can be used to both coordinate and rationalise local craft production can be revived, regardless of their past, they should be resuscitated as quickly and as painlessly as possible. So what has happened to the trade unions, former cooperatives, the communist youth and women's groups, the social and cultural organisations, as well as the creative artists' unions, scientific, technical and sports associations? The UN report recorded what it described as 185,000 'civic committees' in existence in 1971.[22] Have they simply disappeared into history after the revolution with no further function or was the report simply an absurd invention? If even a part of that was true and actually represented some form of community-based formation, can they not, even ten years afterwards, form the basis for new local initiatives? Or has there been the post-Ceausescu equivalent of the cultural revolution as well, in which everything remotely connected with the old regime has been purged, including the memory of it? Should the charitable organisations involved in providing relief ask those pertinent questions? Of course one might suggest that such recommendations from organisations such as the Derry-based Romanian Relief Fund would be received with considerable suspicion by the local authorities and make their position untenable. A reluctance therefore by the Irish relief organisers to engage in such a dialogue would be understandable in the circumstances.

It suggests that the present project to maintain a contact, however tenuous, is the most important for those involved in the Relief Fund. If so, it does raise questions about motivation. Are they involved in a dam-plugging exercise as distinct from them becoming involved in some kind of community-based fire-fighting operation? There is a distinct difference between the two in the world of community development. In the former it could be said, if true, that they were stemming the flow of frustration amongst the poorer sections of the Romanian population by plugging small holes of potential discontent. On the other hand, perhaps what they are really doing is to engage in dampening the fires of extreme poverty, giving people the opportunity to breathe once again in an atmosphere free from the dangers of the flames and the smoke of anger and desperation. It is difficult to be certain. These are not men and women who are immersed in a naive view of life. Indeed many of them have been brought up in the cauldron of Irish politics in which motivation is seen as being at the core of a person's involvement in public life. It could be argued that they are stepping into a role which should be the responsibility of the state. They freely admit that they supplement the frugal amounts given to work in the orphanages by the Romanian government. In one newspaper report, they accepted that the state offered a paltry £10,000 against a project designed to upgrade living conditions for girls in an orphanage in Hamerod, close to Fagaras, which was going to cost £150,000.[23] The balance was going to be raised in areas such as the North-west of Ireland. The Romanian government will gladly, perhaps even greedily, allow this to take place in spite of its sensitivity about the use of the words 'humanitarian aid' to be displayed on van and lorries.

The main problem of course is that there appears to be no evidence of an indigenous community-based initiative in the areas around Fagaras which will offer the local inhabitants a sense of their own power and capability. Even one organised to rationalise pig farming and designed to provide some basic income for local people is organised by an American who insists that at some point in the future he will pass control of the project on to the local community. Whether or not that will really happen remains to be seen.

Does the export of charity reinforce dependency and act as a controlling mechanism within the community development process? It is always easy in hindsight and with the comfortable benefit of being able to observe such conditions from a distance, whether geographically or philosophically, to be critical of activities which allow for even a limited form of relief to be passed on from one sympathetic community to another. It matters not for some people with what could be described as an internationalist perspective to take advantage of and reach for opportunities which alleviate suffering in other parts of the world. They would argue that it is done from that understanding of the situation rather than from a religious or moralist perspective. In either case it is commendable, but does it either advance the physical condition of the recipients, or even assist them in creating the infrastructures which would allow for such a development to take place? Time will tell, but, unless there is a clearer appreciation of those issues, little advance is likely to be made and the activists will be forced to continue with their convoys into the distant unforeseeable future.

Conclusion

The introduction to this book suggested in its opening paragraph that the association between the community and the state is both 'unsteady' and 'occasionally fractious' and tends on occasions to reach critical moments in that relationship. That suggestion, naturally, raised a number of questions which formed the core of the book. Is there a relationship between the state and community action? But, whilst this work initially concentrated on the issue of social control, it developed wider terms of reference informed by the study of Gramsci's concepts of hegemony and civil society.

The book's structure was designed to present a world-view of the circumstances in which the community sector plays a role in the affairs of the entire community. To that end the centrality and importance of the theories and ideas of Antonio Gramsci cannot be overemphasised.

Much could be made of the fact that there are certain areas of community action which have not been included in the study. It is one which is becoming informed by an increasingly wider audience. Those engaged in community work range, for example, from the voluntary worker focusing on the problems of the local neighbourhood, to the social policy expert interested in the wider European influences of such activity. It has both a domestic as well as an international dimension. It can be measured in both micro and macro terms.

It was stated at the outset that this was not a study which is based on the values of a few communities through their involvement in community action except in so far as those values have a bearing on the creation or development of a counter-hegemonic project. However, because it is the contention of this work that there are certain counter-hegemonic projects operating at different levels and with differing agendas within the wider community and because there are certain cultural reasons for that development, the book is located within that field of activity. It is a study of groups based within largely working-class areas which have a radical perspective of development. It was not an examination of community values, unless those values affect or influence the development of the counter-hegemonic project.

The outline of the work described the evolution of community action and how it has been informed and influenced by US and British experiences in the Poverty Programmes and the Community Development Projects. An examination of the origins of the community movement and its ideological base provide us with a theoretical context against which community action does not sit as a separate and alien ideology or method of development outside our own experiences. On the contrary, the very nature of its evolutionary progress has ensured both a domestic as well as an international dimension which has allowed for the inclusion of egalitarian and democratic principles in its perspective of society. Indeed, it is this very reference to society, and in particular the state and civil society, which forms the theoretical focus of the study. Therefore the section on the case studies, whilst contributing to the whole of the work, become most significant when informed by the ideological direction of the participants, in the light of their views on community development *in relation to* the state and society. But perhaps more specifically it exposes the existence of several separate, if related, sets of relationships.

In this regard, therefore, the theories of Gramsci become central. At a general level, it was his contribution to understanding of the state, of hegemony and civil society which allowed for a probing of the nature of the society in which we live and an examination of its potential either for progress or for regression. But at a specific level it was his focus on the role of the intellectual which allowed for a critique of the community worker as an agent of the hegemony or alternatively as an organic intellectual acting to undermine it.

The civil society of Gramsci is one in which, in a capitalist context, power is determined by the ideological hegemony of the dominant or ruling class which is then diffused throughout that society. Is there one civil society or two within the nation state? Is there a Catholic, as well as a Protestant civil society, or an African-American and Caucasian one, or as in the case of Romania, a rural versus an urban one? Grattan was certain in his work on Northern Ireland that a unionist hegemony predominated and that power was exercised through a diffusion of unionist values via the Protestant working class. What was not clear, however, was whether such values operated in the same way throughout the Catholic community and in such a way as to ensure the acceptability of the dominance of the unionist ruling class, by Catholics.

This question, therefore, is determined by how we understand civil society from the point of view of the various religio-ethnic/class communities within it. The complexity of the question is made even more difficult by the nature of the separate societies in which we live. Has the nationalist community within Northern Ireland, for example, existed in a society in which they willingly accepted the values and morals of the dominant ruling class? The answer to that question is clear. But, have they knowingly or unknowingly, willingly or unwillingly accepted the hegemony of that class? Clearly, the answer is that, until very recently, one section of the community did accept it whilst the other, clearly, did not. The nationalist community has consistently voted for political parties, or taken part in abstentionism, demonstrating opposition both to the partition of the country and to the dominance of the Unionist Party. Such opposition has been expressed in a variety of ways, reflecting, at different times, a regard for cultural values which could not be identified as sympathetic to Unionism. Nor could their loyalties be clearly defined as being directed either to the ruling class in a state of which they were not a part. Whilst reflecting the values of the ruling class within the Republic of Ireland, that state, which is universally regarded as presenting a 'nationalist' face, is adjudged by the nationalist minority in the North, as intrinsically incomplete. In other words, the national revolution, begun in this century in 1916, is still unfinished.

In essence, this is the central political issue for many nationalists involved in community action in the northern part of Ireland irrespective of their social and economic agenda. The demand for civil rights was a mere prelude, for some political activists in the nationalist community, to the central issue of national reunification. For those who struggled, the prospect of a reformed six-county state was not merely unlikely, it was also undesirable. In community development terms, the political vetting issue in which Dove House amongst others was to feel the cold wind of the state bureaucracy, became the dividing line between those who wanted to continue on the radical path and those who found ways and means of excusing their continuing participation. What it does reinforce is that the nationalist community in Northern Ireland do not see themselves as fully-fledged and uncritical citizens of the state in which they now live. The 'unprecedented concentration of hegemony', described by Gramsci, in this instance has not had the beneficial effect intended by the ruling class in Northern Ireland. So what implications does this have for the future hegemony in Northern Ireland and, as a consequence, its civil society?

Plainly, if we were to accept Grattan's contention that a Unionist hegemony is dominant, then the possibility of creating a counter-hegemony based solely on the nationalist community would be both unlikely, and possibly, counter-productive because of the problems inherent in a divided society. If we were to argue that a historic bloc comes to fruition when the hegemony of one ruling class is replaced by the hegemony of another, then the prospect of such an occurrence in a divided society where allegiances exist on the basis of sectarian, rather than class, allegiance is extremely doubtful.

This brings us to the principal issue. Does the community movement, with its guiding principles of opposition to racism, anti-sectarianism and support for cross-community strategies of development, offer the opportunity for the creation of a counter-hegemonic bloc? Community action plays a significant role within economically deprived and politically ravaged communities, both as facilitator in the struggle for change and as informant in the process of acculturation. It does not operate in quite the same way within the Protestant community because of the degree to which that community has adopted the hegemonic values of the unionist ruling class, as well as their traditional reluctance to seek avenues of opposition to what they perceive to be their state. Furthermore, community action is both supported and influenced by government intervention through a range of economic initiatives. So, does the involvement of government in this process act to stimulate this development, or does it, in believing it to have revolutionary potential, act instead to hinder its progress? Does the community movement contain within its structures the potential for creating the basis for profound social change, for crossing the community relations barrier and for creating a counter-hegemonic force, which can initiate the process of social change? Given the scenario described in the preceding paragraph, such a prospect would depend on the translation of those common-sense values which exist within two distinct communities, into ideas which bridge that divide. But there are also examples of conservative ideologies, particularly that associated with the communitarian movement, which have co-opted the notion of community as a means of minimising its radical potential and drawing it closer to the prevailing hegemony.

In each of the case examples, the questions of hegemony, civil society and the role of the intellectual are paramount. When translated into questions related to the concrete conditions of Northern Ireland, the United States and Romania, they become matters exploring the relationship of the community activist to the state, the nature of that relationship in terms of progress and/or regression and the central role of the community development worker as both 'intellectual' and/or as 'radical intellectual' in determining the extent to which each project is either integrated with, or kept in isolation from, the structures of the state.

It set out to examine the processes of community development in relation to a specific state-led programme of activity and the effect that had on certain organisations and their members. It must be said that the study of any project must be seen as a part of a historical process. In other words, each element of the method cannot be seen in isolation but must be considered in context. Any attempt to understand the significance of community development must be seen within a general view of society as a whole. The emergence of a programme of community development amongst a section of any community is an indicator of the social and political awareness of those engaged in that process.

The adoption of those concepts informed by the Italian Marxist, Antonio Gramsci, was inevitable once the attempt to search for a set of ideological tools had begun. The view of those who advocated a social control model became a futile attempt to find a framework in which the development of community participatory activities could be placed. The notion of a harmonious civil society within which a range of hegemonic relationships exist presented the work with a near-ideal state in which the fluctuating and mercurial philosophy of the community activist could be placed. The idea of the intellectual moving in one direction and then in another satis-factorily explained the nature of the activity in which they were engaged. They are leaders within their own communities and whilst this was adequately reflected in the examples in the United States, especially, as well as in Northern Ireland, it does little to inform us and help us to understand their difficulty in creating the counter-hegemonic project.

But, if we are to adopt Gramsci's position of the community worker, either as 'intellectual' in the classical sense or as 'radical' or 'organic intellectual' in the revolutionary sense, and place him/her within an enabling role as a radical 'agent of change', then their motivations are important because of their positions in relation to the predominant hegemony. Furthermore, their respective positions in relation to that hegemony determine, also, the nature of the relationship between community organisations and the state.

Whether seen as a traditional intellectual reinforcing the state's ideological position, or acting as a radical intellectual in challenging the state, the community activist is significant in so far as he or she is involved in, or acting on behalf of, a community-based organisation. They can have a meaningful local impact on the world-view of the members of their communities. The activists in Viva House and in the earlier life of the Dove House project are a testament to the impact of such radical action. But it is not crucial that he/she is a member of such an organisation as there are many categories of such community workers, both official and unofficial, professional and semi-professional. Such intellectual workers operate within their own specific, often personal political, agenda and often without reference to a local neighbourhood structure. As such, they can and do influence and inform the development of ideas within the community development field. However, in some circumstances they are not accountable to anyone or to any community except themselves, acting only as individual lobbyists.

Is there sufficient potential within the community movement for radical social change in spite of the fact that it could be seen as an agent of the dominant hegemony? This is extremely important because it suggests, on the one hand that a counter-hegemony can be built on the basis of existing opposition within civil society, and on the other, that the community movement utilising government initiatives and state funding can be converted into an agent of that counter-hegemony.

The use of the vetting procedures implemented by the government in Northern Ireland were designed specifically to guarantee against the 'misuse' of public funds for, according to Hurd, 'directly or indirectly improving the standing or furthering the aims of a paramilitary organisation'. But would they also be used against organisations if the use of such funds by those organisations were directed, instead, towards the creation and development of what could be described as counter-hegemonic ideas, such as promoting the Irish language and campaigning actively on a range of social, economic and political inequalities? This question is important because it lays open the possibility that there are organisations which do not clearly fit into Hurd's category of subversives, but who do operate an agenda which militates against the long-term political interests of the state.

Such organisations are, obviously, less easy to identify. But do they exist? The contention is that they do, but in a fragmented and unco-ordinated way, making the prospect of the creation of a historic bloc both unlikely and improbable in present circumstances. The many failed attempts to create real community networks with a coherent, independent programme are proof of this. But the initiative in Baltimore in which the local group around Viva House were able to exist independently from the state because of a steadfast refusal to become embroiled in the 'tax exemption' business is an interesting example of local independence. It is interesting also because of their insistence on that independence being tied to a radical understand-ing of the class nature of American society. The problem, however, is that they must inevitably remain tied to their determination to place all of their eggs in the basket of spirituality and Catholicism. In spite of their sterling work in the area of human rights, whether by providing basic sustenance for the poor or by advocating more open government and an end to repression, they will always be limited by their inability to tie themselves to the building of a wider movement which will ultimately challenge the existing dominant hegemony. And whereas the communitarian supporters of Etzioni attempt to engage the body politic in a discourse on obscure nineteenth-century notions of subsidiarity and the need for 'respon-sibility instead of "rights", groups such as Viva House are engaged in the practice of linking both.

A more crucial question to be answered is whether the community movement operates as an agent of the hegemony of the ruling class? That it sets out to solve the political needs of the ruling administra-tion is without doubt. There is ample evidence for this. It is often hailed as a showpiece of initiative, demonstrating the partnership of community and government's commitment to the needs of local economic development as well as to the social needs of communi-ties. It represents a substantial investment by government. In short, it is suggested that it is a valuable strategical instrument available to central government. If this is so, then the community movement is, without doubt, a valuable agent of the hegemony of the ruling class, whether consciously or unconsciously. This is confirmed by the views of many of the workers and volunteers in each of the organisations. Even though there were some prepared to work within that regime, the evidence indicates strongly that many believed it to be a futile exercise. Many feel that they were merely plugging the dam.

But, evidence does point to the *potential* amongst those participants, especially those with a greater commitment to community action, to act as radical intellectuals within the context of their own neighbourhoods and acting to undermine the class interests of the state. But what is important here isn't whether the activities or aims of the organisation are designed, subjectively, to undermine the interests of the state or actually achieve that goal, but whether, objectively, they are *perceived* by the state as having that purpose. Hence the view of Hurd, in his statement to the House of Commons, that public funds might 'indirectly' improve the standing of paramilitary organisations. This was also the opinion of other community activists and confirmed by Rolston. However, they are compromised at all times, if they aspire to a radical purpose; if they, at the same time, accept state support.

On the other hand, however, some of those participants were of the opinion that community development was of such a vacuous nature that it held little real potential for change. If we were to take as one indicator of social change the possibility of creating democratically accountable institutions which minimise a community's sense of alienation and dependency then, according to some of the participants, that hope constantly evades them. Community organisations create 'buffers' between the community and the state, offering the state a breathing-space. It is a dilemma and a difficult one to resolve.

But then, how could it be otherwise? After all, many community initiatives emerge as a result of government-inspired interventions, implemented as community-based programmes, using European Union and United States funding. One could argue that such interventions transform the community-based organisation from one influenced totally by local, neighbourhood considerations and accountable to local communities, to one influenced by the interests of the state and accountable to its stringent financial controls. The focus, therefore, has shifted quite fundamentally.

This view is reinforced, if not corroborated, by the separation of professional from voluntary worker. A number of participants suggested that the differentials were not only significant, but also deliberate. Indeed, one believed that the policy of creating such differentials results in a fundamental transformation of interests amongst the professional workers from *committed activist* for the local community to *confirmed apologist* for the state, or more succinctly, from radical intellectual to traditional intellectual. After all, there is a distinct recognition by many of the participants that if the government hadn't intervened and provided funding for the organisations, in the words of one of them, they would be 'snookered'. In other words, they have become dependent on the state. For some, that satisfactorily describes the nature of the relationship of the state to community action.

The view persists that once the state becomes involved in the provision of resources of any kind, the traditional independence of the community sector is immediately compromised. However, it was also argued that there were some positive aspects to such intervention. For some, it is seen as securing the future of the community-based organisation. For others, it is seen as reinforcing the dependency of the local population. Others might suggest that whilst they were easing the burden of marginalised working-class communities, they were not addressing the problem of the structural inequalities of a modern, Western, capitalist society.

But what of the experience of those engaged in the relief work in Romania? How can they advance a radical perspective of community action? It must be said that whereas those involved in providing relief to Romania did not see themselves engaged in transporting a set of radical alternatives to the Romanian situation, it must be considered in the light of the separate radical practice of at least one of them in Ireland. The export of charity irrespective of the underlying motivation cannot but help those within Romania whose needs are basic and specific. Clearly, the showcase for the 1989 revolution lies in the major cities of Bucharest and Brasov, rather than in the remote and relatively powerless rural hinterland of Fagaras. In those circumstances, the transport of aid, even after ten years of political and economic transformation, appears to be something of a developmental anachronism. During that period of time, some indigenous infrastructure should have emerged which could build on the success and experience of those coming from Ireland, Germany, France and elsewhere. What would be worrying, if it were not for the dedication of the relief workers, is the apparent reluctance of the Romanians to take advantage of those organisational skills which are available. The prospect of a reaction to any form of community-based activity does not augur well for the future development of an independent and progressive sector in Romania in which the export of charity has become a poor substitute for organic leadership or for an indigenous form of community action.

The emergence of a series of distinct and separate models of action between those organisations involved in such work offers the possibility of some understanding about the nature of community action. These models, whilst not exhaustive, help to define the nature of each of their respective relationships to the state and form the basis for an understanding of a state/community development paradigm.

The ideas and concepts of Antonio Gramsci have been the subject of intense interest and speculation for many years and many contributions have been made to reach an understanding of the potential of his contribution to social change. The issues raised by the original examination of Gramsci's theories force one to conclude that many engaged in community action operate within their perceptions of a civil society and do so in the full knowledge that they subscribe to the hegemonic values of the state. To a very large extent, those who do so act to administer and manage one small section of the hegemony. They become, as a consequence, an extra-bureaucratic arm of the state and, by implication, an extension of the hegemony.

In those circumstances, the radicalism of many within community action and the community groups is channelled into the bureaucracy of the 'community' organisation and, as a consequence, the social, political and economic programme of the state. In those circumstances, many operate in a manner which makes them more conscious of the needs of the state bureaucracy than of the needs of their local communities. Dearlove warned: 'What is most noticeable when considering the control and regulation of community action is the apparent absence of, and indeed the lack of necessity for, any overt control.'

Presumably he is referring to that point in which the corporate interests of the ruling class, according to Antonio Gramsci, 'become the interests of other subordinate groups too'. Surely that must be the pinnacle of the development of the ideological hegemony or that position in which the control of the state is no longer seen as manifest and transparent. It is a warning with which the community activist should be constantly reminded when considering the potential of working within the area of influence of the state, with the objective of using it to engage in creating a counter-hegemonic project for its social and political transformation.

Notes

Chapter 1: The State and Hegemony

1. F. Field, 'Political and Moral', in D. Atkinson, (ed.), *Cities of Pride: Rebuilding Community, Refocusing Government*, Cassell, London, 1985, p. 24.
2. J. Hall (ed.), *Civil Society: Theory, History, Comparison*, Polity Press, Cambridge, 1995, p. 1.
3. Ibid., p. 6.
4. M. Loney, *Community against Government*, Heinemann Educational Books, London, 1983, pp. 129–45.
5. L. Salamini, *The Sociology of Political Praxis*, Routledge and Kegan Paul, London, 1981, p. 3.
6. C. Boggs, *Gramsci's Marxism*, Pluto Press, London, 1976, p. 3.
7. Salamini, *The Sociology of Political Praxis*, p. 3.
8. Ibid., p. 5.
9. Ibid., p. 5.
10. A. Gramsci, *Selections from Prison Notebooks*, Lawrence and Wishart, London, 1976, p. 357.
11. Boggs, *Gramsci's Marxism*, p. 114.
12. V.I. Lenin, *The State and Revolution*, Progress Publishers, Moscow, 1969, p. 9.
13. A.S. Sassoon, *Approaches to Gramsci*, Writers and Readers, London, 1982, p. 110.
14. F. Engels, *Marx and Engels Selected Works*, Progress Publishers, Moscow, 1970, p. 577.
15. J. Joll, *Gramsci*, Fontana, 1977, p. 81.
16. Gramsci, *Selections from Prison Notebooks*, p. 235.
17. Ibid., p. 237.
18. Ibid., p. 238.
19. S. Hall, *Drifting into a Law and Order Society*, Cohen Trust, London, 1980.
20. Gramsci, *Selections from Prison Notebooks*, p. 243.
21. Ibid., pp. 181–82.
22. Ibid., p. 184.
23. Ibid., p. 36.
24. Salamini, *The Sociology of Political Praxis*, p. 28.
25. Ibid., p. 28.
26. Boggs, *Gramsci's Marxism*, p. 23.
27. Ibid., p. 23.
28. Ibid., p. 129.
29. Ibid., p. 36.
30. Ibid., p. 37.
31. Gramsci, *Selections from Prison Notebooks*, p. 377.

32. Ibid., p. 377.
33. A. Grattan, 'The Majority's Minority', Unpublished PhD thesis, University of Ulster, 1988, p. 117.
34. Salamini, *The Sociology of Political Praxis*, p. 145.
35. Ibid., p. 137.
36. Ibid., p. 140.
37. A. Gramsci, cited in R. Simon, *Gramsci's Political Thought: an Introduction*, Lawrence and Wishart, London, 1982, pp.58–63.
38. Gramsci, *Selections from Prison Notebooks*, p. 12.
39. Ibid., p. 419.
40. Ibid., p. 323.
41. Salamini, *The Sociology of Political Praxis*, p. 89.
42. Ibid., p. 89.
43. Gramsci, *Selections from Prison Notebooks*, p. 377.
44. Ibid., p. 377.
45. Ibid., p. 327.
46. Ibid., p. 331.
47. Ibid., p. 418.
48. Ibid., p. 158.
49. Ibid., p. 12.
50. Ibid., p. 9.
51. Ibid., p. 13.
52. Ibid., p. 9.
53. Ibid., p. 332.
54. Salamini, *The Sociology of Political Praxis*, p. 27.
55. Ibid., p. 27.
56. British Union of Fascists: a relatively minor attempt to develop a British strain of European fascism. They were at first influenced by the rise of Mussolini but afterwards became more interested in the German variety. Their uniforms were banned in 1936 as a result of the Public Order Act and they gradually went into a decline and disappeared at the beginning of the Second World War. See, for example, O. Mosley, *My Life*, Nelson, London, 1968.
57. Iron Guard: Romanian fascist organisation which became a major political force between 1930–41. Founded in 1927 by Corneliu Zelea Codreanu, it was originally called the Legion of the Archangel Michael.
58. Blueshirts: Irish fascist organisation led by Eoin O'Duffy a former Garda (police) Commissioner in the period following the civil war. The Blueshirts are better known for their opposition to the IRA and for their involvement in the origins of Fine Gael. See, for example, M. Manning, *The Blueshirts*, Gill and Macmillan, Dublin, 1970.
59. Taoiseach John A. Costello (1891–1976), Former Prime Minister of the Irish Free State. He is best known for his declaration in Canada that Ireland should become a republic. See: for example, B. Farrell, *Chairman or Chief? The role of Taoiseach in Irish Government*, Pluto Press, Dublin, 1971.
60. J.J. Lee, *Ireland 1912–85: Politics and Society*, Cambridge University Press, Cambridge, 1990, p. 184.
61. Fine Gael and Fianna Fail: literally, 'Family of the Gaels' and 'Warriors of Ireland'. Both political parties have their origins in the broad republican

family, of which the original Sinn Fein was the parent grouping, which split over the issue of partition in Ireland.

62. James Connolly (1868–1916) was one of the leaders of the Easter Rising (1916) who led the socialist 'Citizen Army'. He was executed by the British for his part in the rising.

63. Eamon De Valera (1882–1975) was a former Taoiseach (leader) of the Republic of Ireland Government and Uachtarain (President) between 1959 and 1973. He was sentenced to death for his part in the Easter Rising (1916) and the sentence commuted to life imprisonment. He was released shortly afterwards.

64. Republican Congress, 1934: the 'Congress' was an attempt to develop a broad socialist base for the disparate socialist and republican groupings which emerged out of the Irish civil war (1921). Two of the founders were George Gilmour and Peader O'Donnell. See, for example, M. McInerney, *Peadar O'Donnell, Irish Social Rebel*, O'Brien Press, Dublin, 1974.

65. Salamini, *The Sociology of Political Praxis*, p. 67.

66. Gramsci, *Selections from Prison Notebooks*, p. 52.

67. Salamini, *The Sociology of Political Praxis*, p. 69.

68. J.V. Femia, *Gramsci's Political Thought*, Clarendon Press, Oxford, 1987, p. 7.

69. Salamini, *The Sociology of Political Praxis*, p. 369.

70. Ibid., p. 45.

71. A. Gramsci, cited in J.V. Femia, *Gramsci's Political Thought*, Clarendon Press, Oxford, 1987, p. 332.

72. Ibid., p. 17.

73. Salamini, *The Sociology of Political Praxis*, p. 370.

Chapter 2: Coercion, Community and Civil Society

1. M. Loney, *Community against Government: The British Community Development Project 1968–78*, Heinemann Educational Books, London, 1983, p. 152.

2. See, for example, M.Haralambos and M. Holborn, *Sociology: Themes and Perspectives*, 3rd edn, Collins Educational, London, 1994, pp. 580–645.

3. A. Briggs, *The Age of Improvement*, Longman, London, 1959, p. 260.

4. G. Crabbe, 'The Village', in A. Clayre, (ed.), *Nature and Industrialisation*, Open University Press, London, 1977, p. 16.

5. J.A. Mayer, 'Notes towards a Working Definition of Social Control in Historical Analysis', in S. Cohen (ed.), *Social Control and the State*, Basil Blackwell, Oxford, 1985, p. 17.

6. T. McCauley, cited in Clayre (ed.), *Nature and Industrialisation*, p. 234.

7. R. Crotty, *Ireland in Crisis: a Study in Capitalist Colonial Underdevelopment*, Brandon, Dingle, 1986, p. 25.

8. Briggs, *The Age of Improvement*, p. 302.

9. *The Times*, 10 April 1848.

10. See, for example, Northern Ireland Council for Voluntary Action (NICVA), *The Political Vetting of Community Work in Northern Ireland*, Belfast, 1990.

11. J.A. Mayer, 'Notes towards a Working Definition...', in Cohen (ed.), *Social Control and the State*.
12. S. Spitzer, 'Security and Control in Capitalist Societies', in J. Lowman (ed.), *Transcarceration: Essays in the Sociology of Social Control*, Gower, Aldershot, 1979.
13. Douglas Hurd, the Rt Hon. Former Secretary of State for Northern Ireland and Foreign Secretary in the Thatcher administration.
14. J. Midgley, *Community Participation, Social Development and the State*, Methuen, London, 1986, p. 18.
15. A. Scull and S. Cohen, 'Social control in history and sociology', in Cohen (ed.), *Social Control and the State*.
16. Briggs, *The Age of Improvement*, p. 9.
17. J. Dearlove, 'The Control of Change and the Regulation of Community Action', in D. Jones and M. Mayo (eds), *Community Work One*, Routledge and Kegan Paul, London, 1975, p. 23.
18. R. Hofstadter, *The Age of Reform*, Vintage, New York, 1955, p. 14.
19. Crotty, *Ireland in Crisis*, p. 23.
20. F. Kitson, *Low Intensity Operation*, Faber, London, 1971, p. 8.
21. R. Miliband, *The State in Capitalist Society*, Heinemann, London, 1975, p. 44.
22. J. Dearlove, 'The Control of Change...', in Jones and Mayo (eds), *Community Work One*, p. 23.
23. See, for example, NICVA, *The Political Vetting of Community Work in Northern Ireland*.
24. J.A. Mayer, 'Notes towards a Working Definition...', in Cohen, (ed.), *Social Control and the State*, p. 17.
25. J. Anderton, cited in J. Dearlove and P. Saunders, *Introduction to British Politics*, Polity Press, Cambridge, 1991.
26. I. Meszaros, *The Necessity for Social Control*, Isaac Deutscher Memorial Lecture, Merlin Press, London, 1971, p. 33.
27. Ibid., p. 33.
28. F. Engels, *Selected Works, Marx & Engels*, Progress Publishers, Moscow, 1970, p. 576.
29. Spitzer, 'Security and Control in Capitalist Societies', in Lowman (ed.), *Transcarceration* p. 48.
30. Ibid., p. 49.
31. Ibid., p. 51.
32. Engels, *Selected Works, Marx & Engels*, p. 576.
33. K. Marx, *Selected Works, Marx & Engels*, Progress Publishers, Moscow, 1970, p. 37.
34. J. Dearlove, 'The Control of Change...', in Jones and Mayo (eds), *Community Work One*, p. 23.
35. F. Piven and R. Cloward, *Regulating the Poor*, Tavistock, London, 1972, p. 44.
36. Spitzer, 'Security and Control in Capitalist Societies', in Lowman (ed.), *Transcarceration...*', p. 55.
37. Ibid., p. 55.
38. W. Hutton, 'Why Declining North depends on South', *Irish News*, Belfast, 4 February 1994.

39. F. Gaffikin and M. Morrisey, *Northern Ireland, the Thatcher Years*, Zed Books, London, 1990, p. 35.

40. J.A. Mayer, 'Notes towards a Working Definition...', in Cohen (ed.), *Social Control and the State*, p. 25.

41. Ibid., p. 26.

42. C. Boggs, *Gramsci's Marxism*, Pluto Press, London, 1976, p. 38.

43. M. Repo, 'Organising the Poor against the Working Class', in J. Cowley (ed.), *Community or Class Struggle*, Stage One, London, 1971, p. 74; B. Rolston, 'Community Politics', in L. O'Dowd, B. Rolston and M. Tomlinson (eds), *Northern Ireland: Between Civil Rights and Civil War*, CSE Books, London, 1980.

44. J. Fish, *Black Power, White Control: the Struggle of the Woodlawn Organisation in Chicago*, Princeton University Press, Princeton, 1973, p. 178.

45. S. Cohen, *Visions of Social Control, Crime, Punishment and Classifiication*, Polity Press, Cambridge, 1983, p. 41.

46. Boggs, *Gramsci's Marxism*, p. 23.

47. Marx and Engels, *Selected Works, Marx & Engels*, p. 571.

48. Engels, *Selected Works, Marx & Engels*, p. 461.

49. G. Lichtheim, *Marxism: a Historical and Critical Study*, Routledge and Kegan Paul, London, 1961, p. 374.

50. A. Gramsci, cited in L. Lawner (ed.), *Letters from Prison*, Quartet, London, 1971, p. 136.

51. Lichtheim, *Marxism...*', p. 374.

52. Ibid., p. 373.

53. Boggs, *Gramsci's Marxism*, p. 23.

54. Fenians (*c.*1858): a nineteenth-century republican organisation in Ireland whose aim was the overthrow of the British administration. It is unusual as an Irish revolutionary organisation for having recruited an army in the United States to fight against the British in Canada.

55. Chartism (*c.* 1838): group of political reformers in Britain which reacted to the failure of the Bill of 1832 to extend the franchise to the working class. It derived its name from the 'charter' which set out their demands. One of the principal leaders was Feargus O'Connor who was accused of being a Fenian.

56. Marx, *Selected Works, Marx & Engels*, p. 37.

57. V.I. Lenin, *The State and Revolution*, Progress Publishers, Moscow, 1969, p. 14.

58. G. Kruss, 'Adult Education and Transformation: The Case of African Indigenous Churches in South Africa', Unpublished PhD thesis, University of Ulster, 1992, p. 75.

59. A. Gramsci cited in J.V. Femia, *Gramsci's Political Thought*, Clarendon Press, Oxford, 1987, p.109.

Chapter 3: Community as Counter-Hegemony

1. S. Baine, 'The Political Economy', in D. Jones and M. Mayo (eds), *Community Work One*, Routledge and Kegan Paul, London, 1974, p. 42.

2. 'Entrism': the (mainly) Trotskyist tactic of entering larger mass-based working class political parties. It caused considerable problems for the leadership of Neil Kinnock who engaged in unprecedented attempts to have large numbers of the Militant tendency expelled.

3. M. Loney, *Community against Government: The British Community Development Project 1968–78*, Heinemann Educational Books, London, 1983, p. 148.

4. J. Dearlove, 'The Control of Change and the Regulation of Community Action', in D. Jones and M. Mayo (eds), *Community Work One*, Routledge and Kegan Paul, London, 1975, p. 23.

5. H. Specht, *Community Development in the United Kingdom: An Assessment and Recommendations for Change*, Association of Community Workers, London, p. 4.

6. Community Development Review Group (CDRG): an umbrella organisation for a number of leading community workers in Northern Ireland. It was responsible for a number of important studies and publications in the late 1970s and early 1980s. Most of their members are now leading administrators in a number of semi-state agencies.

7. P. Logue and S. Keenan, *Community Work in Northern Ireland* (pamphlet), Workers Educational Association, Derry, 1980, p. 1.

8. L. Corina, 'Community work and local authority decision-making: potential and problems', *Community Development Journal*, vol.11, no.3, 1976.

9. M. Loney, *Community against Government*, p. 161.

10. Ibid., p. 160.

11. M. Repo, 'Organising the Poor against the Working Class', in J. Cowley (ed.), *Community or Class Struggle*, Stage One, London, 1971, p. 74.

12. Muintir na Tire: (tr. 'People of the countryside') a rural organisation formed in 1931. It emerged from the cooperative tradition in Ireland founded by Plunkett.

13. N. Polsby, *Community Power and Political Theory*, 2nd edn, New Haven, London, 1980, p. 41.

14. See, for example, Community Development Review Group (CDRG), *Community Development in Northern Ireland*, Belfast, 1991.

15. See, for example, Association of Metropolitan Authorities (AMA), *Community Development: the Local Authority Role*, AMA, London, 1989.

16. Ibid., p. 5.

17. P. Commins, 'Community Development: principles, determinants and practice', in *Report, Interskola 86 Conference*, Linking and Informal education to Community development in Sparsely Populated Areas, Galway, 1986.

18. M. Mayo, 'Community development – a radical alternative?', in R. Bailey and M. Brake (eds), *Radical Social Work*, Arnold, London. 1975, p. 141.

19. D. Smith, 'Equality and inequality in Northern Ireland', in *Perceptions and Views*, Policy Studies Institute, London, 1987, p. 20.

20. M. Broady and R. Hedley, *Working Partnerships: Community Development and Local Authorities*, National Coalition for Neighbourhoods, Bedford Square Press, London, Ch. 3.

21. Community Development Review Group (CDRG): an organisation estab-lished by a number of prominent community activists in Northern Ireland in the mid-1980s. It published a number of reports, including a collection of papers delivered at a conference in the University of Ulster, Magee College. See, for example, E. Deane (ed.), *Lost Horizons: New Horizons*, WEA, Derry, 1989.

22. P. McLenaghan and P. Shanahan, *Final Evaluation Report*, EU-supported Transfrontier Community Economic Development Innovatory Training Project, 1987–90, Community Development Studies Unit, University of Ulster, Magee College, Derry, 1990.

23. C. McConnell, 'Providing Community Development in Europe', in *Report, Council of Europe, Research and Policy paper*, no.15.

24. Smith, 'Equality and inequality in Northern Ireland', p. 20.

25. Dearlove, 'The Control of Change...', in Jones and Mayo (eds), *Community Work One*, p. 33.

26. A. Long, *Participation and the Community*, Pergamon, Oxford, 1976.

27. C. Curry, *Report: Enterprise in Communities*, Springfield Action Team, Belfast, 1988, p. 15.

28. F. Gaffikin and M. Morrissey, 'Community Enterprise in Northern Ireland: Privatising Poverty', in Deane (ed.), *Lost Horizons: New Horizons*, Ch.5.

29. Ibid.

30. Ibid.

Chapter 4: The Co-option of Radicalism

1. M. Reid, 'Rurality to Region in France', Unpublished thesis, Masters in Rural Development (MRD), University College, Galway, 1990, p. 10.

2. G.D.H. Cole, cited in A. Wright, 'Tawneyism revisited: Equality, welfare and socialism', in B. Pimlott (ed.), *Fabian Essays in Socialist Thought*, Heinemann Educational Books, London, 1984, p. 91.

3. Wright, 'Tawneyism revisited...', in Pimlott (ed.), *Fabian Essays in Socialist Thought*, p. 91.

4. See, for example, R. Crossman (ed.), *New Fabian Essays*, J.M. Dent, London, 1952.

5. R. Jenkins, cited in Wright, 'Tawneyism revisited...', in Pimlott (ed.), *Fabian Essays in Socialist Thought*, p. 91.

6. P. Marris and M. Rein, *Dilemmas of Social Reform*, Routledge and Kegan Paul, London, 1972.

7. O.P. Chitero, *Community Development: Its Conceptions and Practice with Emphasis on Africa*, Gideon S. Were Press, Nairobi, 1994, p. 40.

8. E.R. Chadwick, cited in E. Kwo, 'Community education and community development: the British colonial experience', *Community Development Journal*, vol.19, no.4, 1984.

9. D. Brokensha and P. Hodge, *Community Development: an Interpretation*, Chandler Publishing, San Francisco, 1969, p. 28.

10. Colonial Office Memorandum, 'Education policy in British tropical Africa', cited in Kwo, 'Community education and community development...'.

11. Ibid.

12. A. Crossland, *The Future of Socialism*, Jonathan Cape, London, 1956, p. 326.

13. R. Abel-Smith and P. Townsend, cited in Wright, 'Tawneyism revisited...', in Pimlott (ed.), *Fabian Essays in Socialist Thought*, p. 92.

14. R. Titmus, cited in Wright, 'Tawneyism revisited...', in Pimlott (ed.), *Fabian Essays in Socialist Thought*, Ch.7.

15. M. Loney, *Community against Government: The British Community Development Project 1968–78*, Heinemann Educational Books, London, 1983, p. 152.

16. J. Greve, 'The British Community Development Project: some interim comments', *Community Development Journal*, vol.8 no.3, 1973.

17. Community Development Projects (CDP), *Gilding the Ghetto: the State and the Poverty Experiments*, CDP Inter-project Editorial Team, London, 1977, p. 2.

18. Ibid., Preface.

19. CDP, *Inter-project Report*, CDP, London, 1974.

20. D. Corkey and G. Craig, 'Community work or class politics?', in P. Curno (ed.), *Political Issues in Community Work*, Routledge and Kegan Paul, London 1978, p. 50.

21. R. Bryant and P. Oakley, 'Community development and the role of the change-agent', *Community Development Journal*, vol.19, no.4, 1984.

22. F. Gaffikin and M. Morrisey, 'Community Enterprise in Northern Ireland: Privatising Poverty', in E. Deane (ed.), *Lost Horizons: New Horizons*, WEA, Derry, 1989, Ch.5.

23. CDP, *Gilding the Ghetto*....

24. Loney, *Community against Government*..., p. 41.

25. Dr Maurice Hayes, a former Catholic senior civil servant. He was appointed chairman of the Community Relations Commission and resigned following a dispute with the then Minister, Ivan Cooper. He has also served as Ombudsman for Northern Ireland and as a member of the RUC police review commission. See, for example, Hayes, M., *Black puddings with slim: a Downpatrick boyhood*, Blackstaff, Belfast, 1996.

26. National Grange: a national voluntary agency in the United States at the beginning of the 1900s.

27. M. Adamson and S. Borgos, *This Mighty Dream*, Routledge and Kegan Paul, Boston, 1984, p. 55.

28. Ibid., p. 56.

29. See, for example, S. Alinskey, *Reveille for Radicals*, Vintage Paperbacks, New York, 1969.

30. Marris and Rein, *Dilemmas of Social Reform*, p. 15.

31. See, for example, W. Biddle and L. Biddle, *The Community Development Process*, Holt, Reinhart and Wilson, New York, 1965.

32. R. Moynihan, cited in Marris and Rein, *Dilemmas of Social Reform*, p. 74.

33. M. Harrington, *The Other America: Poverty in the United States*, Penguin Special, Harmondsworth, 1966, p. 4.

34. Cited in Loney, *Community against Government*..., p. 148.

35. L. Corina, 'Oldham CDP: Community work and local authority decision-making: potential and problems', *Community Development Journal*, vol.11, no.3, 1976.

Chapter 5: Community, Catholicism and Communitarianism

1. D. Atkinson (ed.), *Cities of Pride: Rebuilding Community, Refocusing Government*, Cassell, London, 1985, p. 1.
2. F. Field, 'Political and Moral', in Atkinson, (ed.), *Cities of Pride...*, p. 24.
3. B. Rodgers, *The Battle Against Poverty, Vol.2: Towards a Welfare State*, Routledge and Kegan Paul, London, 1969, p. 33.
4. See, for example, A. Etzioni, *The Spirit of Community: the Reinvention of America*, Simon and Schuster, New York, 1993.
5. *The Economist*, 18 March 1995, p. 20.
6. Ibid.
7. Revd. S.Trumbone, http://www.gmt.it/pages/communitarianism/referenc.html#TOP
8. A. Etzioni, 'Responsibility', in Atkinson, (ed.), *Cities of Pride...*, p. 33.
9. J. Demaine, 'Beyond Communitarianism: Citizenship, politics and education', in J. Demaine and H. Entwhistle (eds), *Beyond Communitarianism*, London 1996, p. 26.
10. O. Mosley, *Tomorrow We Live*, Abbey Supplies Ltd., London, 1936.
11. Etzioni, 'Responsibility', in Atkinson, (ed.), *Cities of Pride...*, p. 33.
12. C. Handy, 'Types of Community', in Atkinson (ed.), *Cities of Pride...*, p. 32.
13. Etzioni, 'Responsibility', in Atkinson (ed.), *Cities of Pride...*, p. 33.
14. A. Gramsci, *Selections from Prison Notebooks*, Lawrence and Wishart, London, 1976, p. 203.
15. Etzioni, 'Responsibility', in Atkinson (ed.), *Cities of Pride...*, p. 33.
16. Ibid., p. 34.
17. Field, 'Political and Moral', in Atkinson (ed.), *Cities of Pride...*, p. 27.
18. P. Spicker, 'The principle of subsidiarity and the social policy of the European Community', *Journal of European Social Policy*, vol.1, 1991, p. 3.
19. O. Mosley, *Tomorrow We Live*, Abbey Supplies Ltd., London, 1938, p. 57.
20. Field, 'Political and Moral', in Atkinson (ed.), *Cities of Pride...*, p. 27.
21. Pius XII, cited in Spicker, 'The principle of subsidiarity...', p. 4.
22. Spicker, 'The principle of subsidiarity...', p. 24.
23. D. Clarke, 'The Conservative faith', in P. Buck (ed.), *How Conservatives Think*, Penguin, Harmondsworth, 1975.
24. O. Mosley, ' The People's State – a Classless System', in *Tomorrow We Live*, Abbey Supplies Ltd., London, 1938, p. 57.
25. K. Grasso, *Catholicism, Liberalism and Communitarianism: The Catholic Intellectual Tradition*, Rowan and Littlefield, Maryland, 1995, p. 16.
26. Ibid., p. 5.
27. Gramsci, *Selections from Prison Notebooks*, p. 12.
28. C. Wolfe, cited in Grasso, *Catholicism, Liberalism and Communitarianism...*, p. 91.
29. F. Engels, 'Origin of the family, private property and the state', in *Marx and Engels, Collected Works*, Progress Publishers, Moscow, 1970, p. 474.
30. Gramsci, *Selections from Prison Notebooks*, p. 300.
31. C. Boggs *Gramsci's Marxism*, Pluto Press, London, 1976, p. 3.

32. Demaine, 'Beyond Communitarianism...', in Demaine and Entwhistle (eds.), *Beyond Communitarianism*, p. 16.
33. T.H. Marshall, cited in Demaine, 'Beyond Communitarianism...', p. 19 in Demaine and Entwhistle (eds), *Beyond Communitarianism*, p. 16.
34. M. Ignatieff, *The Needs of Strangers*, Chatto and Windus, London, 1984, p. 120.

Chapter 6: Northern Ireland: the Evolution of a Counter-Hegemony

1. J. Bardon, *A History of Ulster*, The Blackstaff Press, Belfast, 1991, p. 625.
2. See E. McCann, *War and an Irish Town*, Pluto Press, London, 1993.
3. Interview with Ivan Cooper, former Minister for Community Relations in the 'power-sharing' Assembly led by Brian Faulkner. He was a founding member of the SDLP.
4. Interview with Niall Fitzduff, current Director of the Rural Community Network in Cookstown and formerly a member of the development staff of the Community Relations Commission.
5. I. Cooper, interview.
6. H. Griffiths, 'The aims and objectives of community development', *Community Development Journal*, vol.19, 1974.
7. I. Cooper, interview.
8. I. Cooper, interview.
9. Interview with Eamonn Deane, currently Director of the Holywell Trust, a community-based training and development initiative in Derry, N. Ireland. He had been active in the formation of the Bogside Community Association in the early 1970s.
10. J. Oliver, cited in B. Rolston, 'Community Politics' in L. O'Dowd, B. Rolston and M. Tomlinson (eds), *Northern Ireland: Between Civil Rights and Civil War*, CSE Books, London, 1980.
11. Report, Community Worker Research Project, *Evaluation Report*, Belfast, 1982.
12. New University of Ulster: established after the recommendations of the Lockwood Commission. It was established in controversial circumstances because of the campaign to have it situated in the larger city of Derry. It was replaced by a reorganisation which resulted in the addition of two campuses in Jordanstown and in Derry. It is now known as the University of Ulster.
13. R. Woods, 'The State and Community Work in Northern Ireland, 1968–82', Unpublished thesis, University of Ulster, Jordanstown, 1989, p. 184.
14. Ibid., p. 185.
15. Sinn Fein: (tr. Ourselves Alone) the oldest political party in Ireland, founded in 1902 by Arthur Griffith. There have been several splits from Sinn Fein since its foundation which might test the view that there is a historical continuity between the Griffith organisation and the present of which Gerry Adams is the President.
16. CDRG, *Community Development in Northern Ireland*, Belfast, 1991, p. 1.

17. Ace Vetting: for a full account of the issue of political vetting of the Action for Community Employment (ACE) schemes see, for example, Northern Ireland Council for Voluntary Action (NICVA), *The Political Vetting of Community Work in Northern Ireland*, Belfast, 1990.

18. M. Murray and J. Greer, 'State – community relationships in rural development', *Community Development Journal*, vol. 29, no.1, 1994.

19. P. Lowe, 'The role of rural development in community regional policies' in M. Cuddy (ed.), *Revitalising the Economy: How can it be done?*, Centre for Development Studies, Galway, 1990, p. 45.

20. J. Hume, 'Regional Policy and the feasibility of integrated programmes in northern peripheral regions', in M. Cuddy (ed.), *The Future of Regional Policy in the European Community: Implications for Ireland*, Social Science Research Centre, Galway, 1987, p. 64.

21. The Bogside: A district in Derry in Northern Ireland. It took its name from the fact that it sat on the remains of a swamp. The area now known as the Bogside was originally one single, very narrow little street. A chart dated 1799 names the street as 'Long Bogside'. It is a mainly working-class community, strongly nationalist with a history of high unemployment, and sectarian discrimination. It has been in the news for the past thirty years because of its position as an area noted for its militant republicanism and opposition to the British presence.

22. See, for example, P.E.S. Ua Conchubhair (ed.), *Essays on Social Class and Irish Culture*, University of Ulster, Derry, 1989.

23. Conradh na Gaeilge: (tr. Gaelic League) founded in 1893 by Douglas Hyde, a Protestant who became the Republic's first President. It exists, primarily, to encourage support for the revival of the Irish language.

24. Gregory Campbell: a member of the Northern Ireland Assembly, Derry City Councillor and leading member of the Democratic Unionist Party (DUP).

25. Martin McGuinness: Member of Parliament for Mid-Ulster and member of the Northern Ireland Assembly. He is also Vice President of Sinn Fein.

26. See, for example, O. Lewis, *Five Families: Mexican Case Study in the Culture of Poverty*, Souvenir Press, London, 1976.

27. See, for example, Gerry Adams, *The Politics of Irish Freedom*, Brandon, Dingle, 1987.

28. See, for example, E.B. Tylor, *Primitive Culture: Research into the Development of Mythology, Philosophy, Religion, Art and Customs*, Vol. 1, Harper, London, 1958.

29. Gramsci, *Selections from Prison Notebooks*, pp. 12–13.

Chapter 7: The United States: Poverty and the Catholic Worker Movement

1. M. Harrington, *The Other America*, Penguin, Harmondsworth, 1971, p. 87.

2. See, for example, O. Lewis, *Five Families: Mexican Case Study in the Culture of Poverty*, Souvenir Press, London, 1976.

3. D. Caplovitz, *The Poor Pay More: Consumer Practices of Low Income Families*, Free Press of Glencoe, Illinois, 1963, cited in P. Marris and M. Rein, *Dilemmas of Social Reform*, Routledge and Kegan Paul, London, 1972, p. 15.
4. Marris and Rein, *Dilemmas of Social Reform*, p. 7.
5. Ibid.
6. Interview with F. O'Donovan, joint editor of the *Catholic Worker* (New York), also leading member of the Catholic Worker movement in Mary House in New York.
7. H. Bragdon and C. McCutcheon, *History of a Free People*, Macmillan, New York, 1964, p. 57.
8. Marris and Rein, *Dilemmas of Social Reform*, p. 12.
9. M. Loney, *Community against Government: The British Community Development Project 1968–78*, Heinemann Educational Books, London, 1983, Ch.1.
10. M. Miller and M. Rein, 'Community action in the United States' *Community Development Journal*, no.4, 1975.
11. Interview with Sherry Brown, Chairperson of the Washington (DC) chapter of Americans for Democratic Action. Also a former member of the Black Panthers.
12. Marris and Rein, *Dilemmas of Social Reform*, p. 13.
13. Ibid., p. 15.
14. Miller and Rein, 'Community action in the United States'.
15. Marris and Rein, *Dilemmas of Social Reform*, p. 14.
16. See, for example, M. Loney, *Community against Government...*, p. 27.
17. Marris and Rein, *Dilemmas of Social Reform*, p. 210.
18. Ibid., p. 250.
19. See, for example, M. Watkins and R. McInerney, 'Jacques Maritain and the rapprochement of liberalism and communitarianism', in Grasso, K. (ed.), *Catholicism, Liberalism and Communitarianism: The Catholic Intellectual Tradition,* Rowan and Littlefield, Maryland, 1995.
20. For a complete analysis of the American anti-war movement during the 1960s, see T. Anderson, *The Movement and the Sixties: Protest in America from Greenboro to Wounded Knee*, Oxford University Press, New York, 1996.
21. *Catholic Worker*, New York, vol. LXVI, no.2, March–April 1999.
22. L. Zeidman, 'Willa Bickham and Brendan Walsh: Stirring things up', in E. Fee, L. Shopes and L. Zeidman (eds), *The Baltimore Book, New Views of Local History*, Temple University Press, Philadelphia, 1991, p. 151.
23. Ibid., p. 152.
24. Interview with Brendan Walsh, member of the Baltimore-based Viva House, one of the 'soup kitchens' in the network of 'hospitality houses' of the Catholic Worker movement.
25. D. Simon and E. Burns, *The Corner: A Year in the Life of an Inner-city Neighbourhood*, Broadway Books, New York, 1998.
26. B. Walsh, interview.
27. B. Walsh, interview.

28. Interview with Willa Bickham, member of the Baltimore-based Viva House, one of the 'soup kitchens' in the network of 'hospitality houses' of the Catholic Worker movement.
29. W. Bickham, interview.

Chapter 8: Romania: Charity as Social Control

1. *The Times*, London, 23 December 1989.
2. M. Almond, 'After the revolution, reconstruction', *The Times*, 27 December 1989.
3. Securitate: The secret police units during the period of the Ceausescu regime. They were to be disbanded immediately after the revolution of 1989.
4. O. Badina, 'Community Development in Romania' in *Report, Popular Participation in Development: Emerging Trends in Community Development*, United Nations, New York, 1971, p. 194.
5. Ibid., p. 194.
6. Ibid., p. 200.
7. Almond, 'After the revolution, reconstruction'.
8. O. Badina, *Report*, 1971, p. 198.
9. Ibid., pp.194–95.
10. Ibid., p. 195.
11. Interview with Sean Boyle, manager of the 'City Mission', a Methodist Church hostel for homeless men, based in Derry. He is also the leading organiser for the Romanian Relief Fund.
12. S. Boyle, interview.
13. Interview with Tommy McCourt, manager of the Rosemount Resource Centre. He is involved in a number of other local initiatives, including the provision of computer training. He has been to Romania on a number of occasions and is interested in providing training for ex-residents of the orphanages, particularly in Fagaras.
14. Badina, *Report*, p. 198.
15. T. McCourt, interview.
16. S. Boyle, interview.
17. T. McCourt, interview.
18. *Derry Journal*, Derry, 16 October 1990.
19. S. Boyle, interview.
20. T. McCourt, interview.
21. Badina, *Report*, 1971, p. 202.
22. Ibid., p. 204.
23. *Derry Journal*, Derry, 23 November 1990.

Bibliography

Adams, G., *The Politics of Irish Freedom*, Brandon, Dingle, 1987.

Adamson, M. and Borgos, S., *This Mighty Dream*, Routledge and Kegan Paul, Boston, 1984.

Alinskey, S., *Reveille for Radicals*, Vintage Paperbacks, New York. 1969.

Anderson, T., *The Movement and the Sixties: Protest in America from Greenboro to Wounded Knee*, Oxford University Press, New York, 1996.

Association of Metropolitan Authorities (AMA), *Community Development: the Local Authority Role*, AMA, London, 1989.

Atkinson, D. (ed.), *Cities of Pride: Rebuilding Community, Refocusing Government*, Cassell, London, 1985.

Badina, O.,'Community Development in Romania' in *Report, Popular Participation in Development: Emerging Trends in Community Development*, United Nations, 1971.

Baine, S., 'The Political Economy', in D. Jones and M. Mayo (eds), *Community Work One*, Routledge and Kegan Paul, London, 1974.

Bardon, J., *A History of Ulster*, The Blackstaff Press, Belfast, 1991.

Biddle, W. and Biddle, L., *The Community Development Process*, Holt, Reinhart and Wilson, New York, 1965.

Boggs, C., *Gramsci's Marxism*, Pluto Press, London, 1976.

Bragdon, H. and McCutcheon, C., *History of a Free People*, Macmillan, New York, 1964.

Briggs, A., *The Age of Improvement*, Longman, London, 1959.

Broady, M. and Hedley, R., *Working Partnerships: Community Development and Local Authorities*, National Coalition for Neighbourhoods, Bedford Square Press, London, 1989.

Brokensha, D. and Hodge, P., *Community Development: an Interpretation*, Chandler Publishing, San Francisco, 1969.

Bryant, R. and Oakley, P., 'Community development and the role of the change-agent', *Community Development Journal*, vol.19, no. 4, 1984.

Caplowitz, D., *The Poor Pay More: Consumer Practices of Low Income Families*, Free Press of Glencoe, Illinois, 1963.

Chitero, O.P., *Community Development: Its Conceptions and Practice with Emphasis on Africa*, Gideon S. Were Press, Nairobi, 1994.

Clarke, D., 'The Conservative faith', in Buck, P. (ed.), *How Conservatives Think*, Penguin, Harmondsworth, 1975.

Clayre, A. (ed.), *Nature and Industrialisation*, Open University Press, London, 1977.

Cohen, S., *Visions of Social Control, Crime, Punishment and Classification*, Polity Press, Cambridge, 1983.

Commins, P., 'Community Development: principles, determinants and practice', in *Report, Interskola 86 Conference, Linking and Informal Education to Community Development in Sparsely Populated Areas*, Galway, 1986.

CDRG, *Community Development in Northern Ireland*, CDRG, Belfast, 1991.

Community Development Projects (CDP), *Gilding the Ghetto: the State and the Poverty Experiments*, CDP Inter-project editorial Team, London, 1977.

Community Worker Research Project, *Evaluation Report*, Belfast, 1982.

Conchubhair, P.E.S. Ua (ed.), *Essays on Social Class and Irish Culture*, University of Ulster, Derry, 1989.

Corina L., 'Oldham CDP: Community work and local authority decision-making: potential and problems', *Community Development Journal*, vol. 11, no. 3, 1976.

Corkey, D. and Craig, G., 'Community work or class politics?', in Curno, P. (ed.), *Political Issues in Community Work*, Routledge and Kegan Paul, London, 1978.

Crabbe, G., 'The Village' in Clayre, A. (ed.), *Nature and Industrialisation*, Open University Press, London, 1977.

Crossland, A., *The Future of Socialism*, Jonathan Cape, London, 1956.

Crossman, R. (ed.), *New Fabian Essays*, J.M. Dent, London, 1952.

Crotty, R., *Ireland in Crisis: a Study in Capitalist Colonial Underdevelopment*, Brandon, Dingle, 1986.

Curry, C., *Report: Enterprise in Communities*, Springfield Action Team, Belfast, 1988.

Dearlove, J., 'The Control of Change and the Regulation of Community Action', in, Jones, D. and Mayo, M. (eds), *Community Work One*, Routledge and Kegan Paul, London, 1975.

Dearlove, J. and Saunders, P., *Introduction to British Politics*, Polity Press, Cambridge, 1991.

Demaine, J., 'Beyond Communitarianism: Citizenship, politics and education', in Demaine, J. and Entwhistle, H. (eds), *Beyond Communitarianism*, London 1996.

Elshtain, J., 'Catholic Social Thought, the City and Liberal America' in Grasso, K. (ed.), *Catholicism, Liberalism and Communitarianism: The Catholic Intellectual Tradition,* Rowan and Littlefield, Maryland, 1995.

Engels, F., 'Origin of the family, private property and the state', in *Marx and Engels, Collected Works*, Progress Publishers, Moscow, 1970.

Engels, F., *Marx and Engels, Selected Works*, Progress Publishers, Moscow, 1970.

Etzioni, A., *The Spirit of Community: the Reinvention of America*, Simon and Schuster, New York, 1993.

Farrell, B., *Chairman or Chief? The role of Taoiseach in Irish Government*, Pluto Press, Dublin, 1971.

Fee, E., Shopes, L. and Zeidman L. (eds), *The Baltimore Book: New Views of Local History*, Temple University Press, Philadelphia, 1991.

Femia, J.V., *Gramsci's Political Thought*, Clarendon Press, Oxford, 1987.

Field, F.,'Political and Moral', in Atkinson, D. (ed.), *Cities of Pride: Rebuilding Community, Refocusing Government*, Cassell, London, 1985.

Fish, J., *Black Power, White Control: the Struggle of the Woodlawn Organisation in Chicago*, Princeton University Press, Princeton, 1973.

Gaffikin, F. and Morrissey, M., *Northern Ireland, the Thatcher Years*, Zed Books, London, 1990.

Gaffikin, F. and Morrisey, M.,'Community Enterprise in Northern Ireland: Privatising Poverty', in Deane, E. (ed.), *Lost Horizons: New Horizons*, WEA, Derry, 1989.

Gettelman, M., 'Charity and Social Class in the United States, 1874–1900' *American Journal of Sociology*, no. 22, April/July 1963.

Gramsci, A., *Selections from Prison Notebooks*, Lawrence and Wishart, London, 1976.

Grasso, K. (ed.), *Catholicism, Liberalism and Communitarianism: The Catholic Intellectual Tradition*, Rowan and Littlefield, Maryland, 1995.

Grattan, A., 'The Majority's Minority', Unpublished PhD thesis, University of Ulster, 1988.

Greve, J., 'The British Community Development Project: some interim comments', *Community Development Journal*, vol. 8, no. 3, 1973.

Griffiths, H., 'The aims and objectives of community development', *Community Development Journal*, vol. 9, 1974.

Hall, J. (ed.), *Civil Society: Theory, History, Comparison*, Polity Press, Cambridge, 1995.

Hall, S., *Drifting into a Law and Order Society*, Cohen Trust, London, 1980.

Haralambos, M. and Holborn, M., *Sociology: Themes and Perspectives*, 3rd edn, Collins Educational, London, 1994.

Harrington, M., *The Other America: Poverty in the United States*, Penguin Special, Harmondsworth, 1966.

Hofstadter, R., *The Age of Reform*, Vintage, New York, 1955.

Hume, J., 'Regional policy and the feasibility of integrated programmes in northern peripheral regions', in Cuddy, M. (ed.), *The Future of Regional Policy in the European Community: Implications for Ireland*, Social Science Research Centre, Galway, 1987.

Joll, J., *Gramsci*, Fontana, Glasgow, 1977.

Ignatieff, M., *The Needs of Strangers*, Chatto and Windus, London, 1984.

Kitson, F., *Low Intensity Operation*, Faber, London, 1971.

Kruss, G., 'Adult Education and Transformation: The Case of African Indigenous Churches in South Africa', Unpublished PhD thesis, University of Ulster, 1992.

Kusmer, K., 'The Function of Charity in the Progressive Era: Chicago as a Case Study', *Journal of American History*, December 1960.

Kwo, E., 'Community education and community development: the British colonial experience', *Community Development Journal*, vol. 19, no. 4, 1984.

Lawner, L. (ed.), *Letters from Prison*, Quartet, London, 1971.

Lee, J.J., *Ireland 1912–85: Politics and Society*, Cambridge University Press, Cambridge, 1990.

Lenin, V.I., *The State and Revolution*, Progress Publishers, Moscow, 1969.

Lewis, O., *Five Families: Mexican Case Study in the Culture of Poverty*, Souvenir Press, London, 1976.

Lichtheim, G., *Marxism: an Historical and Critical Study*, Routledge and Kegan Paul, London, 1961.

Logue, P. and Keenan, S., *Community Work in Northern Ireland* (pamphlet), Workers Educational Association, Derry, 1980.

Loney, M., *Community against Government: The British Community Development Project 1968–78*, Heinemann Educational Books, London, 1983.

Long, A., *Participation and the Community*, Pergamon, Oxford, 1976.

Lowe, P., 'The role of rural development in community regional policies', in Cuddy, M. (ed.), *Revitalising the Economy: How can it be done?*, Centre for Development Studies, Galway, 1990.

Marris, P. and Rein, M., *Dilemmas of Social Reform*, Routledge and Kegan Paul, London, 1972.

Mayo, M., 'Community development – a radical alternative?', in Bailey, R. and Brake, M. (eds), *Radical Social Work*, Arnold, London. 1975.

Marx, K., *Selected Works, Marx and Engels*, Progress Publishers, Moscow, 1970.

Mayer, J.A., 'Notes towards a Working Definition of Social Control in Historical Analysis', in Cohen S. (ed.), *Social Control and the State*, Basil Blackwell, Oxford, 1985.

Meszaros, I., *The Necessity for Social Control*, Isaac Deutscher Memorial Lecture, Merlin Press, London, 1971.

Midgley, J., *Community Participation, Social Development and the State*, Methuen, London, 1986.

Miliband, R., *The State in Capitalist Society*, Heinemann, London, 1975.

Miller M. and Rein, M., 'Community action in the United States', *Community Development Journal*, no. 4. 1975.

Mosley, O., *Tomorrow We Live*, Abbey Supplies Ltd., London, 1936.

Murray, M. and Greer, J., 'State – community relationships in rural development', *Community Development Journal*, vol. 29, no. 1, 1994.

McCann, E., *War and an Irish Town*, Pluto Press, London, 1993.

McConnell, C., 'Providing Community development in Europe', in *Report, Council of Europe, Research and Policy Paper*.

McInerney, M., *Peadar O'Donnell, Irish social rebel*, O'Brien Press, Dublin, 1974.

McLenaghan, P. and Shanahan, P., *Final Evaluation Report*, EU-supported Transfrontier Community Economic Development Innovatory Training Project, 1987–90, Community Development Studies Unit, University of Ulster, Magee College, Derry, 1990.

Northern Ireland Council for Voluntary Action (NICVA), *The Political Vetting of Community Work in Northern Ireland*, Belfast, 1990.

Piven, F. and Cloward, R., *Regulating the Poor*, Tavistock, London, 1972.

Polsby, N., *Community Power and Political Theory*, 2nd edn, New Haven, London, 1980.

Reid, M., 'Rurality to Region in France', Unpublished thesis, Masters in Rural Development (MRD), University College, Galway, 1990.

Repo, M., 'Organising the Poor against the Working Class', in Cowley, J. (ed.), *Community or Class Struggle*, Stage One, London, 1971.

Rodgers, B., *The Battle Against Poverty, Vol. 2: Towards a Welfare State*, Routledge and Kegan Paul, London, 1969.

Rolston, B., 'Community Politics' in O'Dowd, L., Rolston B., and Tomlinson M. (eds), *Northern Ireland: Between Civil Rights and Civil War*, CSE Books, London, 1980.

Salamini, L., *The Sociology of Political Praxis*, Routledge and Kegan Paul, London, 1981.

Sassoon, A.S., *Approaches to Gramsci*, Writers and Readers, London, 1982.

Scull, A.and Cohen, S., 'Social control in history and sociology', in Cohen, S. (ed.), *Social Control and the State*, Basil Blackwell, Oxford, 1985.

Simon, D. and Burns, E., *The Corner: A Year in the Life of an Inner-city Neighbourhood*, Broadway Books, New York, 1998.

Simon, R., *Gramsci's Political Thought: an Introduction*, Lawrence and Wishart, London, 1982.

Smith, D., 'Equality and inequality in Northern Ireland', in *Perceptions and Views*, Policy Studies Institute, London, 1987.

Specht, H., *Community Development in the UK: An Assessment and Recommendation for Change*. Association of Community Workers, London, 1975.

Spicker, P., 'The principle of subsidiarity and the social policy of the European Community', *Journal of European Social Policy*, vol. 1, 1991.

Spitzer, S., 'Security and Control in Capitalist Societies', in Lowman, J. (ed.), *Transcarceration: Essays in the Sociology of Social Control*, Gower, Aldershot, 1979.

Tylor, E.B., *Primitive Culture: Research into the Development of Mythology, Philosophy, Religion, Art and Customs*, Vol. 1, Harper, London, 1958.

Watkins, M. and McInerney, R., 'Jacques Maritain and the rapprochement of liberalism and communitarianism', in Grasso, K. (ed.), *Catholicism, Liberalism and Communitarianism: The Catholic Intellectual Tradition*, Rowan and Littlefield, Maryland, 1995.

Woods, R., 'The State and Community Work in Northern Ireland, 1968–82', Unpublished thesis, University of Ulster, Jordanstown, 1989.

Wolfe, C., 'Subsidiarity: The "Other" Ground of Limited Government', in Grasso, K. (ed.), *Catholicism, Liberalism and Communitarianism: The Catholic Intellectual Tradition,* Rowan and Littlefield, Maryland, 1995.

Wright, A.,'Tawneyism revisited: Equality, welfare and socialism', in Pimlott, B. (ed.), *Fabian Essays in Socialist Thought*, Heinemann Educational Books, London, 1984.

Newspapers

M. Almond 'After the revolution, reconstruction', *The Times*, 27 December 1989.

Catholic Worker, New York, vol. LXVI, no.2, March–April 1999.

Derry Journal, Derry, 23 November 1990.

The Economist, 18 March 1995.

W. Hutton, 'Why Declining North depends on South', *Irish News*, Belfast, 4 February 1994.

The Times, 10 April 1848.

Index

perspective 18, and vulgar materialism 20, and factory councils 21, on structure and superstructure 26, and anti-economism 36, on historicism 37, and ideological hegemony 43
Grasso, K., 129, 130
Grattan, A., 217, 218
Greer, J., 156
Greve, J., 99
Grey Area Projects, 6, 96, 112, 173
Grido del Popolo, Il, 16
Griffiths, H., 142, 145, 146, 150
Groza, P., 194
Guevara, Che, 189
Gulbenkian Foundation, 96

Habitat for Humanity (US), 188
Hall, J., 14
Hall, S., 23
Handy, C., 121
Harman, H., 115
Harrington, M., 111, 169
Hayes, M., 105, 141, 142, 143, 145
Hedley, R., 83
Hegel, G., 15, 62
Hegemony, 1, 2, 5, 9, 19, 21, 23, 25, 43, 47, 129, 135, 143, 166, 215, 216, 218, 219, 221, 224, and counter-hegemony 5, and political hegemony 17
Help the Aged, 189
Hillfields project, 113
Hofstadter, R., 51
Home Office (UK), 6, 106
Housing action, 68
Hume, J., 146, 156
Hungary, 67
Hunger marches, 189
Hurd, D., 48, 49, 50, 220, 221, 222

Ideology, 29
Ideological hegemony, 51, 52, 68, 105, 216, 224
Ignatieff, M., 134
Iliescu, I., 196
Imperialism, 18
India, 94
Industrial Workers of the World (IWW), 4, 181
Industrialisation, 44
Intellectual, organic, 33, 65, 220
Intellectual, radical, 219, 220, 222, 223
Intellectual, traditional, 32, 220, 223

Inter-Project report, 101
Ireland, Republic of, 7, 25, 26, 35, 43, 204, 217, 223, and fascism 35, and community development 57, and Gaelicisation 125
Irish language, 158, 159, 164, 221
Irish music, 164
Irish question, the, 46
Irish Republican Army (IRA), 36
Iron Guard (Romania), 35
Italy, 35

Jenkins, R., 93
John XXIII, 182
Johnson, L.B., 6, 75, 106, 110, 175

Kautsky, K., 16, 18, 34, 36
Keenan, S., 70, 71
Kennedy, J.F., 6, 93, 106, 109, 169, 175
Kenyan Land Army (Mau Mau), 52
Kinnock, N., 5
King, Martin. L., 182, 189
Kitson, F., 5, 51
Kremlin, the, 178
Kruss, G., 65
Ku Klux Klan, 182

Labour Party (UK), 5, 68, 92, 95, 129, 143, 165, and Clause Four, 5
Labor Unions (US), 70
Labour Party (Ireland), 35
Labriola, A., 16
Lebas, J., 201
Lee, J., 35, 120
Leech, E., 115
Lenin, V.I., 3, 16, 17, 18, 19, 22, 61
Leo XIII, 124, 126, 127
Leopold I. (Belgium), 126
Lewis, O., 162, 169
Liberal Democrats (UK), 129
Liberal Party (UK), 125
Liberalism, 117, 125, 131
Libertas Praestantissimum, 127
Local Enterprise Development Unit, 88
Locke, J., 42
Lockwood Committee, 139
Logue, P., 70–1
Loney, M., 46, 67, 75, 80, 103
L'Ordine Nuovo, 16
Los Angeles (US), 175
Loughry College (NI), 155
Lowe, P., 156
Loyalism (NI), 143
Loyalist working-class, 161